AF506233

Religion, Material Culture
and Archaeology

Bloomsbury Advances in Religious Studies

Series Editors:

James Cox

This groundbreaking series offers original reflections on theory and method in the study of religions, and demonstrates new approaches to the way religious traditions are studied and presented.

Studies published under its auspices look to clarify the role and place of Religious Studies in the academy, but not in a purely theoretical manner. Each study will demonstrate its theoretical aspects by applying them to the actual study of religions, often in the form of frontier research.

Other titles available in the series:

Appropriation of Native American Spirituality, Suzanne Owen

Becoming Buddhist, Glenys Eddy

Community and Worldview among Paraiyars of South India, Anderson H. M. Jeremiah

Conceptions of the Afterlife in Early Civilizations, Gregory Shushan

Contemporary Western Ethnography and the Definition of Religion, Martin D. Stringer

Cultural Blending in Korean Death Rites, Chang-Won Park

Globalization of Hesychasm and the Jesus Prayer, Christopher D. L. Johnson

Innateness of Myth, Ritske Rensma

Levinas, Messianism and Parody, Terence Holden

New Paradigm of Spirituality and Religion, MaryCatherine Burgess

Redefining Shamanisms, David Gordon Wilson

Reform, Identity and Narratives of Belonging, Arkotong Longkumer

Religion and the Discourse on Modernity, Paul-François Tremlett

Religion as a Conversation Starter, Ina Merdjanova

Spirit Possession and Trance, Patrice Brodeur

Spiritual Tourism, Alex Norman

Theology and Religious Studies in Higher Education, Edited by D. L. Bird and Simon G. Smith

Religion, Material Culture and Archaeology

Julian Droogan

Bloomsbury Advances in Religious Studies

B L O O M S B U R Y

LONDON · NEW DELHI · NEW YORK · SYDNEY

Bloomsbury Academic

An imprint of Bloomsbury Publishing Plc

50 Bedford Square	175 Fifth Avenue
London	New York
WC1B 3DP	NY 10010
UK	USA

www.bloomsbury.com

First published 2013

British Library Cataloguing-in-Publication Data
A catalogue record for this book is available from the British Library.

ISBN: HB: 978-1-4411-9577-7

Library of Congress Cataloging-in-Publication Data
Droogan, Julian.
Religion, material culture, and archaeology / Julian Droogan.
p. cm. – (Bloomsbury advances in religious studies)
Includes bibliographical references and index.;
ISBN 978-1-4411-9577-7 – ISBN 978-1-4411-8431-3 (ebook (pdf))   1. Material culture–Religious aspects.   2. Religion and culture.   3. Archaeology and religion.   4. Religious life.   I. Title.

BL65.C8D76 2012
200.9–dc23
2012019253

Typeset by Newgen Imaging Systems Pvt Ltd, Chennai, India
Printed and bound in Great Britain

Contents

Preface

First as an archaeologist with an interest in non-modern epistemologies and religion, and later as a scholar of religion with a background in archaeology, I have long found the relationship between the material past and the stories, rituals and religious practices that so often cling to archaeological sites in the landscape fascinating and profound.

While conducting fieldwork in rural India it was commonplace to see temples, mosques or later religious shrines built upon, or even out of, the remains of much earlier religious buildings. Ruined monuments that were thousands of years old could be found being used by local groups as places of ritual possession where an individual was believed to be touched by a god, caves containing prehistoric art were sites of religious devotion, monoliths that were once part of ancient funerary assemblages were moved around the landscape, their great stone mass appropriated as a table for the local village councils to deliberate around. Sometimes, if an extensive urban site lay buried nearby, the shattered fragments of Hindu/Buddhist/Jain sculptures and architecture could be found piled up in the village fields, daubed with red vermillion, marked with votive offerings and thus giving over as a shrine to a local deity. Religion, as it was lived within the local landscape, appeared to be inseparable from its material contexts, and these material contexts consisted mostly of objects from the archaeological past. Material culture, including objects, artefacts, sites and whole environments, was playing an active role in the religious lives of the local communities. People appeared to be creating the religious present through an ongoing dialog with the material past, and this material was considered powerful, active and potent.

This close observable relationship between archaeology, material culture and religious practice and narrative, however, raised substantial problems. I have often felt bemused when observing the relative lack of interest awarded by the majority of archaeologists to the serious engagement with the concept 'religion' in the pasts that they reconstruct. This appears to mirror the rather appendage-like way material culture has been considered – when considered at all – by those engaged in the academic study of religion. Many archaeologists will tell you that the search for religion has no place in serious, grounded archaeology, that it is too difficult and open to wild speculation; while the material elements of religion have long appeared secondary or even invisible in the writings on that intangible and rarefied realm 'religion'. In both fields, however, these long-held attitudes are slowly changing, and the possibility for a fruitful and mutual cross-disciplinary exchange between archaeology and studies in religions is now emerging. This book stems from my attempt to chart the contours of this mutual scholarly exclusion, explore its history and causes, and suggest some ways in which this divide can be bridged. It is also an attempt to begin to understand some of the ways in which material culture from the archaeological past co-creates the religious present; how material objects can become active and seemingly autonomous social agents that play important roles in religious life.

My main aim is to explore and explain the problem of religion in archaeological theory and method over the past century, to use this as the basis to assess the viability of a contemporary 'materiality of religion', and to begin to chart some of its potential characteristics in a preliminary fashion. My purpose is not to look for religion in the material past or to synthesize any new archaeology of religion. Other scholars, mostly archaeologists with a great deal of hard-earned field experience and in-depth knowledge of particular cultures and periods, have attempted this with varying levels of success. Their contributions will be looked at and discussed in the pages that follow. Rather, it is the relationship between archaeological theory and religion that is examined here, and through doing this the fascinating but difficult interface between religiosity and material culture is charted.

Archaeology, it may be claimed, is perhaps an unlikely area of focus in a book on advances in religious studies. It has been chosen as the primary field of enquiry, however, only in part because of a desirability to explore the problematic history of the relationship between the discipline of archaeology and the field of studies in religion. More importantly, archaeology has been chosen because it allows one to understand relationships between religion and materiality that draw on the long timeframes that are uniquely available from the archaeological study of material culture. Furthermore, the active role that so many sites and structures from the archaeological past often play in religious traditions in the present is one important area where an understanding of the materiality of religion adds substantially to the methodological tools available to the multidisciplinary field of studies in religion.

The first part of the book is structured as a critique of the polarity between religion and material culture that is apparent within both the academic field of studies in religion and the discipline of archaeology. In order to achieve some conceptual clarity an attempt is made to define the notoriously difficult term 'religion'.

Following this, a detailed examination of the attitudes shown towards the relationship between material culture and religion by successive schools of archaeological theory throughout the past century is presented. I have examined a series of what I see as crucial issues, such as the role of Durkheimian and Marxist perspectives in considerations of the materiality of religion, especially of religious expression as a means for communicating that most invidious of terms 'ideology'. Related assumptions about the primarily reflective, communicative or symbolic nature of material culture are examined also: assumptions that have at times prevented an understanding of the material dimensions of religion as functioning as potent and active social agents. Problems with the nature of the sacred and profane dichotomy when applied to the material past are then considered, as are archaeological attempts to engage with supposedly religious landscapes through phenomenologies of the sacred and the profane. Throughout, I have attempted to show how assumptions about the nature of both religion and material culture have prevented the possible emergence of an autonomous archaeology of religion until very recent times. Conversely, it is shown also how similar assumptions have largely prevented those within the diffuse and multidisciplinary field of studies in religion from a critical engagement with the materiality of religion as an area of primary study in and of itself, rather than as an appendage of more traditional approaches to religion that rely on a psychological, historical or confessional paradigms.

After charting the problematic history of the relations between archaeology and studies in religion, the materiality of religious life is explored further in the final chapters. In particular, contemporary archaeological concerns with the reflexive nature of material culture and its role in the perpetuation of social life are described as being useful tools that could be adopted by those working in studies in religion. Here, I argue that the material components of religion – artefacts, ritual sites, whole landscapes including natural features – often have the ability to act as primary locales for the perpetuation of religious life. Specifically, the archaeological concern with landscape is explored and the role of locales of religious action in the perpetuation of religious continuity and change are examined. It is argued that in many cases it is the primary material nature of such sites that embodies religious meaning and mediates elements of religious continuity and change in social life – often over extended periods of generational time.

In the last section, the critical examination of archaeological approaches to the materiality of religion is furthered through the consideration of some non-archaeological ways of examining the social roles that material culture plays in religious life. Concepts of agency, abduction and socio-technological networks are adopted from the work of the late anthropologist Alfred Gell and critical theorist Bruno Latour. These theoretical tools are used to elaborate further on the role of religious materialities in the structuration of religious life. Through doing this, a way of approaching the materiality of religion is suggested, one that is particularly useful to understanding how objects and sites that are part of the archaeological record play an important part in the formation and perpetuation or religious meanings in the present.

Acknowledgements

To Anna, without whose love and support I could never have completed this book.

My deepest appreciation goes to all the people who provided invaluable assistance, advice and support to this project, from the perspectives of archaeology, studies in religion or, occasionally, both. It can be frustrating being asked to advise and assist in a cross-disciplinary project, and I thank all those who rose to the challenge with such enthusiasm and encouragement. I claim, however, all errors and omissions as my own.

I would also like to sincerely thank the University of Sydney and Macquarie University for offering me the opportunity to pursue and complete this research, likewise the University of Leiden for its warm hospitality and generous assistance.

1

Introduction: The Spiritual versus the Material?

One of the major aims of this book is to argue that human religiosity is rarely separate from the material environment through which it is expressed, and that to conceive of material culture and religious culture as opposing or mutually exclusive spheres of human experience and activity is to limit our understandings of both fields.

This statement may appear intuitively obvious and simple to illustrate. At a popular level the religions of the world are often characterized by their striking material identities. Elaborate, often exotic, costumes, ritual paraphernalia, art, iconography, monuments, temples, shrines and whole religious landscapes are some of the primary expressions of a religious tradition. Often, for those experiencing a religion from the outside, these are the most obvious, immediate, enchanting, colourful and exciting features, representing difference but also points of access into the unknown. In the age of globalized tourism this connection between exotic materiality, foreignness and the experience of the religious is an especially prevalent and important aspect in the manufacturing of many tourist experiences.

Equally important and perhaps universal is the tendency for religious narratives, stories and institutions to derive much of their authority and legitimacy from tradition and the past. While a religion's sacred traditions concerning the past may be preserved and codified as oral or textual history, there is always a discourse with the material past that takes place in tandem. In such cases, material culture often appears to be perceived as a source of religious power and authority. The use of the term 'power' can be understood here to refer to a perception of material things as autonomous agents, objects or places that project meaningful influence into the world, apparently independent of any human input. The term 'authority' suggests that this agency is legitimized through references to a referent or cosmology that transcends the individual or social group, perhaps hallowed by its associations with the past. Material things and places can come to embody religious authority and act as powerful expressions that appear to exert influence and act autonomously through time. In such cases, material culture acts as a lens that focuses the power of the supermundane, the agency of that which is beyond the human, into the everyday world. Its very materiality, perhaps even perceived permanence, gives structure and solidity to values, powers and forces that may be thought derived from beyond the material sphere. Sometimes the seeming immutability of a material thing gives the values and powers it confers the appearance of being eternal and unchanging fixtures of a non-human order.

The landscapes of India and China are layered with material reminders of numerous religious worlds. Buddhist stupas and sites of remembered history such as Bodhgaya point to the many-levelled religious landscapes of India. In China, whole mountains may be embellished with statues, temples, inscriptions, pilgrim's paths and much more. A similar situation also extends to the so-called historical religions, Judaism, Christianity and Islam, which claim to derive much of their authority from revealed texts detailing their people's ongoing conversation with a transcendent God. But even for these religions of the book, material culture is still of primary importance as a source of authority and power. The Hajj to the Kaaba, built on the site of a pre-Islamic sanctuary, unifies all Islam both globally and with its pre-Islamic roots, causing enormous numbers of people to move and act in concert across both space and time. The Christian cult of relics has a long and complex history, as does the cult of icons. Even Judaism, so long expressed in Diaspora through textual, oral and action-based modes of self-identity, is intimately connected to the power and authority that appears to emanate from the sites of ancient Palestine; the Western Wall being just one example. Of course, all three historic religions are entangled in the many-layered sacred landscapes, monuments and material relics of the Holy Land. These are only some of the barest and most basic examples of the central place that materiality occupies in some of the better-known world religions.

One could continue almost indefinitely on the ways in which material culture appears to be central to religious life. A moment's thought and the relationships appear so obvious as to hardly bear further elaboration. Yet, one of the aims of this examination is to show that in the scholarly and academic study of religion these two spheres – the 'material' and the 'spiritual' – have often been presented as having radically differing, even opposing, natures. When they have been considered together it has usually been by implication rather than as part of a conscious attempt to examine their associations. In most cases, a progressive scheme, a teleology even, has been applied to their relationship. Currents of thought influenced by a Marxist perspective, in particular, have generally treated religion as a secondary belief or emotion arising out of the harsh material conditions of existence. In such contexts, religion may be reduced away as an unfortunate epiphenomenon arising out of the incongruities of human subjective existence in the hard and objective material world. Other philosophic and religious traditions have expressed an assumption that 'true' religiosity is an existential or experiential state that is fundamentally separate from the world of material things, not really related to items of material culture, and concerned with transcendence over the material world rather than immanence within it. In such a context, the material aspects of religious life may be characterized as representing primitive, ignorant or savage religiosity, rather than true 'spirituality', 'transcendence' or 'purity'. In either case, there is a highly problematic relationship between religion and materiality expressed in many of the influential religious, philosophic and academic traditions of modernity. This larger problem serves as the context for the arguments outlined in the following pages.

In the title of this introductory chapter the perceived opposition between materiality and religion is referred to, in somewhat colourful and evocative theological language, as a polarization between the 'spiritual' and the 'material'. This evocative use of the language of Christian theology serves a purpose however, as it alludes to the deep and long-lasting character of the quasi-Gnostic split between the transcendent religious and the immanent material in a number of Western discourses. This perceived split is explored in more detail from the perspectives of both studies in religion and archaeology in the next chapter, so it is enough here to point out that this dichotomy is deeply entrenched in the thinking processes of modernity, reflected in much of the academic study of religion as well as within Christian discourse, and capable of taking on a number of forms.

As well as structuring consideration of the make-up of specific religions, and of religion in general, this split between the intangible spiritual and the prosaic material has also sometimes characterized how moderns perceive their relationship *to* religion. For instance, Timothy Dant in his overview on the sociology of material culture writes of an explicitly historical dichotomy between religious belief in the past and material embodiment in the present. He sees in the traditional past a common set of religious beliefs that gave a society its coherent identity and individuals a sense of common purpose. For the inhabitants of late modernity, however, it is our shared experience of embodiment, our practical experiences of the material world we live in on a daily basis that give us a sense of inhabiting a shared universe of common meaning (Dant, 2005). It is also common to hear this polarity expressed in the neo-Romantic language of antiscientism and antimodernity: 'modern science strips meaning from the world by reducing it to pure immanence or materiality and matter is the antithesis of spirit and meaning' (Bennett, 2001, p. 63). Religion and materiality literally constitute different realities, and oppose one another in terms of form, meaning and value, and never the twain shall meet.

It is also possible to equate this split between religion and materiality with that between mind and body, or even subject and object, and to acknowledge it as one of the defining characteristics of post-Cartesian modernity. Thus, implications of this Cartesian split have been well analysed within studies in religions, but the depth to which this dichotomy has coloured understandings about religion and materiality is less commonly expressed. In the academic world, for instance, the discipline of archaeology has in the main ignored religion, and the discipline of studies in religion has largely ignored archaeology, predominantly because there has been little specific theorization of the materiality of religion. Until recently, the relationships between material culture and religious perception, experience, action, communication, continuity and change have either been largely ignored, or have been theorized from a perspective that is unsympathetic to religion as an autonomous category of human individual and social life. In the main, this has had the unfortunate effect of either erasing religion from the archaeological record, or reducing it down to a secondary consideration that is derivative of greater social realities.

An explicit conflict between the categories of the 'material' and the 'religious' is apparent within the methodological presuppositions of both the discipline of archaeology and the field of studies in religion. One, mostly unstated, assumption from within the discipline of archaeology is that visible material culture is somehow opposed to the hidden religious belief. It will be explained below how this distinction between the material and the spiritual is mirrored in the distinction between the 'profane' and the 'sacred', and in the notion of 'functional' versus 'non-functional'. The material culture that makes up the archaeological record is a result of 'action' and 'practice' and is thus visible, while religion is supposed to be the provenance of 'thought' or 'belief' and is hidden or symbolic. On a number of levels the two are presented as inimical, and seemingly opposed. But these polarities give a distorted impression of the nature of religion and prevent any true engagement with religiosity in a material context. This book aims to examine the nature of these problems and to suggest some contributions to the way in which they can be overcome.

Perhaps the main assertion of this book is that through examining the relationship between the discipline of archaeology and field of studies in religion a framework for understanding the nature of religion as a materially embedded phenomenon can begin to be mapped. The multidisciplinary field of studies in religion has been adopted as a focus for inquiry as it contains within its rather diffuse boundaries the majority of attempts to engage academically with the multifaceted subject of religion. It is also the academic perspective from which this book is written, and the audience that will most probably find its contents of most interest. The discipline of archaeology has been adopted as a focus as it has traditionally been the field of enquiry into human life that has had the most concern with material culture and with materiality in general. The nature of archaeology as a practice has always been to reconstruct information about the human past through the collection and examination of its material residues. This primary focus on materiality has been its defining characteristic, separating it from other disciplines such as anthropology, which may work with oral discourse, or history, which draws on the written word. More and more this material focus – long seen by many as a limitation and hindrance to attempts to speak confidently about the past with any level of sociological depth – is being used by archaeologists as the basis of a range of unique methodological insights. Increasingly, the nature of archaeology as a theoretical discipline has been to explore ways in which material culture can be seen to have related to the wider aspects of human culture in general, and to be able to chart some of these relationships through examinations of that material residue. This engagement with materiality is becoming the defining feature of archaeology as a body of theory, again separating it from the majority of the wider humanities and social sciences.

Yet, as this exploration hopes to make clear, there has never been a close relationship between archaeology and studies in religion. Archaeology has for the most part, but by no means completely, put human religiosity to one side in its considerations of material culture, while studies in religion have, until very recently, largely avoided any primary examination of materiality in favour of the more insubstantial aspects of religious life. In this way, archaeological assumptions about the relationship between religion and the material record are an illuminating insight into the problem of the perceived polarity between religion and materiality, which is the context of this work. At the same time, an understanding of how exactly material culture has been thought to relate to human religious life, and a critical examination of such assumptions drawn mainly from the discipline of archaeology, allows those who are interested in the material aspects of religious life to begin to think about ways in which religion is materially embodied. This applies to religion in the material present, in the archaeological past, and some of the interesting dialectics that exist between the two, such as the contemporary incorporation of archaeological artefacts and sites into religious belief, story and practice.

It is important at the outset to state some of the things that this book does not attempt to do. It does not attempt to synthesize any archaeology of religion, or a methodological approach to uncovering religion from, say, the prehistoric material past. Any law-like theory generated to uncover the distinctly religious from the material past in a foolproof or universalistic manner is bound to fail, to be overly particularistic in its definition of what religion is, and, by applying the hard category of 'religious' rather than 'non-religious' on to the material record, to replicate its own categorizations in the distant past. The current methodological mood in most schools of archaeology is to promote a deeply contextual and reflexive approach to the materiality of the past to avoid any universalistic and ahistoric generalizations, and for good reason (this is explored further in Chapter 3). It will be seen that for archaeologists who have begun to think about the wider implications of religion in the archaeological record, the problem has often been one of all or nothing (see Shults, 2010, p. 74); either religion is embedded in virtually every aspect of past material life and is thus unrecoverable except through a deep contextual understanding of the culture at hand, or religion can be uncovered as a distinct phenomenon, as, for instance, the sacred/ritual as opposed to the profane/domestic, in which case it becomes an aberrant and strange category of unexplained objects on the fringes of the functional and explicable.

An example is the site of Catalhoyuk, in Turkey, where starting in 1961, the original discoverer and excavator James Mellaart uncovered what he revealed to be an early Neolithic farming town 13 hectares in extent with levels going back to 7200 BCE. Mellaart freely interpreted portable art and wall reliefs as evidence for a Neolithic fertility cult centred on the tensions between a Mother Goddess and primordial Bull God, and as a result posited the existence at the site of a prehistoric matriarchal social organization (Mellaart, 1997). Over the past two decades, however, Ian Hodder, the most influential writer in the postprocessual movement in archaeological theory, has re-excavated much of Catalhoyuk and attempted to use multivocal interpretative processes to recreate differing impression of the site, many of which are highly antagonistic to any interpretation of Mother Goddess worship (2006; 2010a). Instead, Hodder has used a particularly fine-grained, multidisciplinary and analytically precise research methodology to examine, among other things, patterns of movement, use and decoration within Catalhoyuk's houses over generational time. This has led to informed theorization about the cosmological significance of house structure, the symbolic expression of ritual time and space within homes, tensions between notions of domestic and wild expressed in house layout and art, and a religious worldview based around notions of spiritual and hunting prowess, initiation, the veneration of ancestors and periodic feasting (see Hodder, 2010b).

It must be fully recognized at the outset that significant and substantial practical problems abound for any attempted archaeology of religion, but this does not prevent an examination of the relationship between archaeology *and* religion from being both an interesting and useful exercise.

What this book does attempt to do is to examine archaeological approaches to materiality and to religion in an attempt to begin to understand how any materiality of religion would look. 'Materiality of religion' refers to an understanding of some of the ways in which religious life, actions and experiences are intimately connected with the material aspects of the world. Archaeology is a useful field for such an examination because, as noted above, it is primarily concerned with human materiality. But more importantly it deals with human interactions with the material world over very long spaces of time, often over centuries or millennia, and thus holds the potential for a long-term perspective on religiosity and its relationship with other spheres of human life (see Mithen, 2003; Van Huyssteen, 2010). Archaeology is also capable of encompassing all of human (pre)history, stretching over almost every land portion of the globe. If there is any way to begin to gain a larger perspective on the relationships between religion and materiality, it is through the mass of accumulated archaeological data, and archaeological insights on how materiality effects and participates in social life over the long term. In this way this exploration takes a macroscopic and generalized view of the relationships between religion and material culture, rather than a specific and highly contextualized one. It is hoped that the enormity of the apparent dichotomy between religion and materiality in modern thinking, and the relative lack of examinations of their problematic relationship justifies such a broad and theoretical perspective.

Although this book is structured as a critical examination of archaeological approaches to religion and, to a lesser extent, studies in religion's approaches to materiality, it is not the aim to be unduly harsh and dismissive of either field. Although all effort has been made to critically historicize and explain the numerous perceived failings (especially of the discipline of archaeology in regard to religion), this has been in order to uncover the exact relationships posited between material culture and religion and to see where such ideas have failed. It is certainly not my intention to imply that any singular theorized archaeology of religion is a viable or desirable goal, or that archaeological considerations of issues of religion should have been easily attempted and ubiquitous throughout the literature. The next chapter identifies and examines great failings in both disciplines' approaches, or lack of, towards the materiality of religion, and this double failing is the strikingly problematic context within which this exploration of materiality and religion operates and was conceived. It is argued that archaeology cannot afford to ignore considerations of religion in the material record, and the whole aim of this body of work is to begin to rectify the lack of considerations of the material world found within the discipline of studies in religion. Yet, it is not the aim of this author to perform such a critique, or attempted rectification of an unhappy situation, in a spirit of arrogance or dismissal, but instead to do so in a spirit of multidisciplinary collaboration and as but one piece of a much wider attempt to build methodological and theoretical bridges.

Through examining the relationships between archaeology and the materiality of religion in an attempt to begin to understand how materiality interacts with religiosity, it is hoped that this book achieves a number of things. First, it is hoped that it helps clarify and define an exceedingly problematic area of academic speculation, that of the interface between materiality and religion. It has already been noted that this problem served as the context of this research, and that the hope is to begin to bridge the perceived divide between the two. Through this examination, the nature and character of the divide have been clarified and the problem has been mapped. In this respect, this work is part of a larger body of similar academic considerations of the interaction between materiality and religion.

For instance, since 2005 the journal *Material Religion* has played an important role in fostering the embryonic academic study of the materiality of religion. As noted in the editorial statement of its premier volume (Plate et al., 2005, pp. 4–9), the journal is an explicit response to the conventional assumption that religion is solely concerned with speech and reason. Instead, the examination of material religion includes all the objects that constitute a lived religion, their uses and their roles. Not only is material religion an examination of how material things reflect or are shaped by lived religion, or how religious people understand religious 'things', such as iconography, relics, art, and the like, but it is an acknowledgement of 'what the images or objects or spaces themselves do, how they engage believers, what powers they possess' (Plate et al., 2005, p. 7). This attempt to explore the perceived polarity between material culture and religion through the medium of archaeology, to look at some of the religious potencies and agencies the material residues of the archaeological past possess, is an attempt to add one more perspective to this growing body of exciting work.

Second, it is hoped that this book provides a critical exposition of the numerous attitudes towards religion that have been expressed in the various methodological positions taken by archaeologists over the past century or so. Few have written specifically or at any length the history of archaeological attitudes to the relationship between material culture and religion, and of those who have their work has either become out of date (Demarest, 1987) or is from the perspective of archaeology (Maberg, 1977). In either case it is brief. There are, however, some notable exceptions.

One recent exception, for example, is the work by Timothy Insoll, *Archaeology, Ritual, Religion* (2004), which explicitly addressed religion in archaeological theory and practice, but again from the perspective or archaeology rather than studies in religion. Insoll's main thesis is that religion structures most elements of daily life in non-modern societies, and so cannot easily be separated from other spheres of human activity as reflected in the archaeological record. The result is that any archaeology of religion will be a holistic endeavour predicated on very fine-grained and highly contextual understanding of a particular culture (1999; 2004a, pp. 17–18). Insoll's work is explored further in the succeeding chapters.

Another, more interdisciplinary, author who is an exception to the general rule is Miguel Astor-Aguilera, who has written extensively and with great insight on the relationship between archaeology and religion, and has done so from a perspective that could be broadly termed material culture studies. In his *The Maya World of Communicating Objects* (2010), in particular, Aguilera, unpicks many of the received disjunctions between archaeology and studies in religions and also considers the active and dynamic role that material objects from the archaeological record play in indigenous cosmologies: cosmologies that do not necessarily conform to Western assumptions about religion or rest upon received binaries, such as the 'sacred' and the 'profane', or 'supernatural' and 'natural' (2009, pp. 159–60).

The third major exception to the general lack of archaeological considerations of religion (where the term 'religion' is specifically used) is the work at Catalhoyuk by Ian Hodder and his team, introduced above. Hodder's research at Catalhoyuk shows an ongoing interest in the role that religious and spiritual life play in structuring everyday life and encouraging an ever-deepening human entanglement with the material world. In particular, his *Religion in the Emergence of Civilization*, presents an interdisciplinary study of the 'role of spirituality and religious ritual in the emergence of complex societies' (2010, p. 1). This experiment in interdisciplinary collaboration included archaeologists, natural scientists, anthropologists and theologians, although unfortunately the study of religion as a distinct field was not included. The aim of the experiment was to ascertain what role religion played in the development of complex agriculture, domestication and urban living. Hodder's work, examined again in a later chapter, is part of a wider series of reinterpretations of the Neolithic in Anatolia and the wider Near East that suggest that religious life and the creation of ritual centres may have been directly associated with the gradual domestication of plants and animals and the creation of sedentary life (Hodder, 2006, p. 236; 2010a; 2010b; Mithen, 2003).

It is hoped that this overview of archaeological attitudes towards the religious will help those within the studies in religion community to better understand how their discipline has looked from the perspective of archaeology, and perhaps offer some archaeologists a self-critical perspective on their discipline's history of thinking about religion in the material past.

Also, this piece of work identifies a number of ways in which religion is embodied within material culture, especially material culture from the archaeological past. This refers primarily to how objects from the archaeological past can be perceived as being religiously potent and active by communities in the present, rather than how any present-day researcher can identify the long-dead prehistoric religious associations out of the archaeological record. In the final chapter, notions of agency, socio-material networks and intersubjective relationships between people and things are taken from disciplines outside of archaeology and coupled with an understanding of the phenomenological landscape utilized by postprocessual archaeologists. Such a synthesis of approaches allows for a rich and multilayered understanding of the materiality of religious landscapes, monuments and locales of long-serving religious continuity and change. It also takes note of and explores some of the apparently active and primary religious potencies that are expressed by certain objects and locales that are themselves part of the visible archaeological record.

Before moving any further and exploring the interaction between archaeology, materiality and religion it is necessary to have some clear concept about what is meant by these three terms.

Archaeology

Archaeology is the examination of the human past through the means of its material residues. As noted above, it has always been this focus on materiality and its discarded nature that has distinguished archaeology from other related disciplines such as anthropology and history. Archaeology is sometimes considered (especially in North America) as one branch of the overarching academic project of anthropology, and this close relationship is particularly clear in the case of ethnoarchaeology; the attempt to divine formulas useful to the archaeological interpretation of material culture from the anthropological observation of contemporary human groups. The issue of how exactly one defines the discarded nature of the material examined is difficult. Archaeology certainly differs from anthropology, which often concerns itself with material things in its examinations of a culture, and also from art history, which almost always does so. In either case it is possible that the material objects under examination may have been discarded at some point during their existence. Anthropologists, however, will generally interpret any material aspects of a culture in the context of that living social reality, while art historians can use definitions of 'art' to attempt to distinguish their examinations of discarded or lost material things from that of archaeologists.

The dividing line between archaeology and the emerging interdisciplinary field of 'material culture studies', however, is more difficult, perhaps even impossible, to draw. This can be illustrated by the number of archaeologists who have written influential work on the material aspects of human life outside of archaeological contexts, two prominent examples being Christopher Tilley (1999) and Michael Schiffer (1999). This book can also be considered as contributing to this broadening of archaeological method and theory concerning the social implications and roles of material culture outside of once traditional boundaries.

The equally difficult boundaries in time between archaeology and earlier antiquarianism are briefly addressed in Chapter 2, as are the sometimes-hazy lines between archaeology and forms of speculative and even quasi-religious pseudoarchaeology. The especially fascinating question of pseudoarchaeology, its often close relationship with new religious movements, is explored in Chapter 2 as it relates directly to the interface between religion and archaeology. It must also be recognized that the field of archaeology is divided up into a number of thematic subdisciplines, such as historic archaeology, classical archaeology, ethnoarchaeology, and so on. Although the theoretical positions regarding religion charted in Chapter 3 can be applied to almost all of these subdisciplines, it should be noted that the forms of archaeology most commonly cited in this work are prehistoric, and landscape archaeology. Cognitive archaeology is another subdiscipline that features prominently in this book and can be considered, for the purposes of this section, predominantly a form of prehistoric archaeology. This is largely because these subdisciplines have both at times been concerned with religiosity in some way, and also because both have been on the forefront of theoretical developments in material culture studies.

Material Culture

There is no set definition for material culture in the wide literature touching on material culture theory. Apart from the purely ideal, the mental and, dare it be said, the transcendent, very little is not materially embodied in some fashion. Text on a page is material, as are our bodies, our brains and the chemical bases of our thoughts. Even sound waves, which make up the basis of verbal communication, are material. However, for the concept of material culture to have any validity it must be defined more specifically than this. Attempts have ranged from 'all data directly relating to visible or tangible things such as tools, clothes, or shelter which a person or persons have made' (Kieschnick, 2003, p. 19) – and where 'data' includes both the ideas and the practices associated with the objects – to 'phenomena produced, replicated, or otherwise brought wholly or partly into their present form through human means' (Schiffer, 1999, p. 12; see also Deetz, 1977, pp. 24–5).

A distinction must be made between the study of material culture on the one hand, and the process of materialization on the other. The later term denotes all forms of embodied practice and technology, including dance, performance, pilgrimage, the human body, music, art, costume, and so on. Material culture, however, rarely focuses on human embodiment but instead on externalized material contexts (see Arweck and Keenan, 2006). Material culture may be durable and remain as autonomous objects to be identified in the archaeological record; materialization is usually action-centred and thus constrained by considerations of temporally. These actions and performances, however, may leave durable traces.

The dividing line between material culture and materiality is problematic also, for the former term implies human modification or at least instrumental use, while the latter does not. In this book, the terms material culture and materiality are both used in a broad manner. They refer to manufactured elements of culture that are materially embodied, such as artefacts, architecture, monuments, and so on, as well as to objects which are materialized but that are not usually seen as being manufactured, such as natural features, places and, indeed, whole landscapes. It is argued that although such natural places exist prior to, and independent of, human interference they can nevertheless be considered as being cultural in at least two important regards.

First, while being perceived, no object remains isolated from taking an active part in the culture or society of those who perceive it. As argued further on, the act of human perception causes most material things to become social subjects in some form. In this way, natural places often occupy prominent positions within enculturated landscapes and as a result they may be constructed as highly meaningful places in the minds of those who dwell around them. They may also exert agency and interact with people as mediums for action and actors in the structuration of social life.

Second, and more dramatically, once natural places have acquired a particularly significant role in the daily practices of local human communities they often become the focus of prolonged human activity that may result, in time, in their modification, embellishment and perhaps even entire artificial recreation. In short, natural places often have an active role as places of significance in the cultural landscapes of communities, and as a result they have a tendency through time to attract palimpsests of material culture around themselves, as well as the various oral discourses such as religious story, legend and myth.

Religion

Religion is without doubt the most difficult of the three terms to define. Most definitions of religion, from Tylor's belief in spiritual beings, Marx's emotive sigh of distress in the face of an unfair world, to Clifford Geertz's emphasis on the role of symbols in transforming people's moods and motivations and bringing them into some form of alignment with a general order of existence (Geertz, 1960; 1966) have highlighted an element of belief, emotion, mood, perception or some form of interiority at their core. It will be shown in the following chapters that archaeologists have also made some form of interiority, usually with reference to a transcendent order, the locus for their, often inexplicit and unacknowledged, definitions of religion. Critiques of an overreliance on interiority and the mood of the individual believer in definitions of religion, to the exclusion of embodied practice, action, materiality and community expectation, have served to make it difficult to rely on any of these former definitions today (Asad, 1993). For Asad, any definition of religion as some form of individual interiority reveals both a Protestant as well as a post-Enlightenment bias towards the types of religion that emerged in Western Europe in the face of gradual and progressive secularization of large domains of private and social life. Their contingency on Western modes of experience suggests that they should not be exported to other contexts. This is of paramount importance for any archaeological engagement with religion, as archaeologists deal not only with distance in space, but are uniquely faced with the problem of significant and sometimes vast distances in time as well. Furthermore, definitions of religion that privilege the individual and their interiority (for instance, 'belief') over the social, the externalized and the engaged will reinforce the perceived separation between religion and the material world.

So for the purposes of this book, a definition of religion which encompasses discourse and interiority as well as practice and engagement with the external world (including the material world) has been adopted. The following is a provisional working definition that is taken, in part, from Lincoln (2003, pp. 5–8):

> Religion can be thought of as a discourse whose concerns transcend the human and contingent and that claims for itself a similarly transcendent status, that includes a set of practices whose goal is to produce a proper world, as defined by a religious discourse, and that can be engaged in by either an individual, a community or formalized into an institution.

This working definition has the benefits of including individual, group, communal, private, interior and external practices and beliefs. It also holds open the potential for elements of materiality to play important and active roles in religious life. The concept of discourse is not restricted to words and text, but may be used to refer to relations between people and material things as well. Definitions of religion that rely on any transcendence beyond the limits of the material universe have been avoided. The reference in the above definition to religion 'transcending' the human and contingent can point instead to any objectified social relationship, collective norm or ideal; these may be 'transcendent' in the sense that they are consensually imagined realities that transcend the individual and the contingent. It will be argued in Chapter 5 that much religion consists of relational forms of reciprocity between perfectly mundane and everyday subjects. Furthermore, the focus on practices aimed at producing a proper world acknowledges the central importance of often prediscursive practical and day-to-day interactions with a cosmological or religious landscape as a central aspect of religious life in many traditional cultures.

* * *

The book consists of four major chapters leading from the most general to the more specific, and a fifth discussion chapter recapitulating the argument from a broader perspective. Chapters 2, 3 and 4 all progressively narrow the boundaries of the research and focuses on an ever-tighter examination of the relationship between religion and materiality. The final fifth chapter serves to re-examine each of the preceding chapters in light of an expanded understanding of materiality and religion drawn from the previous critiques. In this way, it serves to open the argument from the more narrow back through to the universal and consider some of the religious qualities which material culture projects, both in the archaeological past and in the present.

Chapter 2: Religion, material culture and archaeology

This chapter provides an overview of the problematic nature of the relationship between the academic field of studies in religion and the discipline of archaeology. In this way, it acts as an introduction to the themes covered in the remainder of the work. Both studies in religion and archaeology are introduced, as well as the perceived polarity between material things and religious life that has been maintained by each.

First, the conflicting perspectives on materiality and religion within the discipline of archaeology and the multidisciplinary field of studies in religion are examined and put into their historical context.

Second, the lack of considerations of the material elements of religious life in work from studies in religion is explored. It is noted that for the most part studies in religion has avoided both materiality generally, and drawing on archaeological sources in particular. It is explained that there has been a pronounced ambivalent approach towards materiality, observable in the attitudes held by nineteenth-century anthropologists such as Edward Tylor, and that this ambivalence has remained influential since.

Third, this chapter provides an introduction to some of the problems that archaeology has in recovering religion from the material record. Practical problems with uncovering disembodied and abstracted 'religion' from within the archaeological past are explored, specifically the tendency for generic material categories, such as funerary monuments or graves, to be associated automatically with religion, to the exclusion of most other forms of material culture. The resulting bias in which the archaeological record is divided into 'normal' functional artefacts and 'abnormal' non-functional religious artefacts and objects is then introduced. An attempt is also made to couple these practical issues surrounding the identification of religion in the material past with accompanying theoretical issues, especially the condition of modernity under which archaeologists work and the prejudices of secularism.

Overall, it is shown that there is a problematic conceptual mode relating to the categories of religion and materiality common to both studies in religion and archaeology. It is argued, however, that this problem is not sufficient cause to leave religion out of archaeological interpretations of the past, or material culture out of academic studies of religion.

Chapter 3: Archaeologies of religion

This chapter examines the history of archaeological attitudes and assumptions regarding the materiality of religion over the course of the twentieth century. Various schools of archaeological interpretation, such as the cultural–historical, anthropological, processual, environmental, cognitive and early postprocessual, are examined sequentially. The relationships between archaeology, religion, ritual and material culture are examined together, with the place held by religion in social life, and its interaction with materiality, considered especially.

The overall failure to address religion in the archaeological record is attributed to theoretical assumptions drawn from Durkheimian functionalism and Marxist ideology that have coloured how both religion and material culture have been thought to act within society, and the roles and functions they have been thought to play. These theoretical hindrances are examined in the context of the successive understanding of material culture that they have facilitated. In such a way, the problematic concepts of material culture and religion, identified in the last chapter are examined further and in more detail.

It is argued that an emphasis on functionalism in regard to religion, where religion is seen as symptom of larger social reality, and Marxism, where religion is understood as an intrinsically false manifestation of other social processes, most usually ideology, have both effectively prevented archaeologists from examining religion in its own terms. It is explained how, in this context, material culture has been theorized as either reflecting ossified belief-systems, or used as a medium of relatively inert ideological communication and contestation. This has prevented the archaeological record from being examined as a locale of other forms of autonomous religious action and experience. It has also reduced the role of material culture in human social life to that of communication, to the reflective transfer of discursive information.

In the end, it is argued that neither cognitive, processual, nor postprocessual archaeologies of religion have escaped a functionalist or a Marxist position when addressing religion in the material record.

Chapter 4: Sacred and profane landscapes

This chapter looks at how a phenomenological approach to the archaeology of landscape can open the way towards an understanding of some of the relationships between religion and material culture. Examinations of the reflexive relationship between society and landscape in prehistory have caused landscape archaeologists to inevitably, and somewhat inadvertently, enter into speculation on religion in the past. It is explained how the phenomenological method has been utilized by landscape archaeologists and it is argued that this use of phenomenology to 'enter into' past worlds has led them to invariably engage with past religious cosmologies and worldviews.

It is posited that the dominant interpretative bias that has entered into the phenomenology of landscape has been the application of the sacred and profane dichotomy on to the material of the past. This division of the world into two essentialist spheres is seen as being conceptually false and methodologically misleading. This dichotomy, however, forms the basis for the differentiation between the ritual and the domestic in much archaeological categorization. Implicit in the sacred and profane dichotomy is the concept of some form of essential sacred 'power' that is either inherent in the material landscape or experienced universally by all human subjects. Modes of landscape archaeology and ways of understanding ritual that do not rely on an application of the sacred and the profane to the prehistoric landscape are also considered.

It is argued that to move away from the dichotomization of the past into the polarities such as 'sacred' and the 'profane' or the 'ritual' and the 'domestic' is desirable. However, archaeological attempts to do so, and instead see religion as a phenomenon that saturates all human action and that is embedded in all aspects of past life, have rarely been able to synthesize ways of identifying religion in the material past. What such examinations of past landscapes have been able to do, however, is to open up ways of looking at the material world as religiously active and potent, rather than as neutral or simply reflective.

Finally, Anthony Giddens' theory of structuration and Pierre Bourdieu's habitus are examined in the context of the material landscape and it is suggested that landscape archaeologists have created a way of looking at the material world that is amenable to it being both cosmologically infused and religiously engaged. Material things can be religious subjects as well as objects. This leads to the possibilities of a substantive way of approaching the materiality of religion, which is the subject of Chapter 5.

Chapter 5: Archaeology and the materiality of religion

In the final section of the book the previous chapters are revisited in reverse order and the conclusions reached in each are coupled with further approaches to the materiality of religion that have not originated from within the discipline of archaeology.

In this way, the ideas of structuration and habitus utilized in the landscape archaeology critiqued in Chapter 4 are coupled with a more active and dynamic understanding of material agency, taken from the work of the art historian Alfred Gell. The problematic understanding of material culture, primarily as a form of symbolic communication, explored in the context of Marxist and Durkheimian 'symbolist' understandings of materiality in Chapter 3, is resolved through the adoption of the ideas of index and abduction, also taken from Gell. The exploration in Chapter 2 of the perceived dichotomy between religion and materiality, and its origins in the thought patterns of modernity, is furthered through a consideration of Bruno Latour's notion of non-modern hybridized networks of human and non-human agents forming the basis of social life.

In this way, a discussion of the relationships between material culture and religion that goes beyond the purely archaeological, although still using archaeological evidence, is initiated. Elements of the materiality of religion that have already been covered are further examined and speculated upon in light of the wider theoretical considerations. For instance, notions of animism as one of the primary forms of religious engagement with the material world, the role of material culture in the structuration of society, the existence of an indwelt 'power' seeming to independently arise out from parts of the material world, and the nature of such sites of long-standing religious 'power' remaining in the face of continuous cultural and religious change are all re-examined.

In this way this final section provides an elaboration and discussion on some of the possible ways in which materiality and religion interact. The section ends with a summing up of some further forms of material and religious interaction, some of which have already been identified by other fields, and some of which are novel and would make promising areas of further study.

2

Religion, Material Culture and Archaeology

This chapter provides an overview of the problematic relationship between studies in religion and archaeology. In so doing, it acts as an introduction to the themes covered in the remainder of the book. The aim is to introduce both the field of studies in religion and the discipline of archaeology, as well as the perceived polarity between material things and religious life that has been maintained by each. This general conceptual schism provides the context for a deeper examination of the ways in which materiality and religion have been thought about within specific archaeological methods in Chapters 3 and 4.

In the first part of this chapter some conflicting perspectives on materiality and religion held within archaeology and studies in religion are discussed. It is suggested that the roots of this conflict can be traced to particular ideas about the nature of material culture and its relationship with religion. These contextual subjects are not addressed in their own section sequentially, but rather throughout the body of the chapter as a whole. For instance, through an historical examination of the origins and early development of archaeology and the academic study of religion in the nineteenth century, it is argued that there have long been perceived oppositions and discordances between the categories of religion and material culture. In both archaeology and studies in religion, material culture has often been assumed to be contradictory, even diametrically opposed, to religious life. Hence, this chapter identifies and clarifies two sets of polarities. First, an academic discordance between archaeology and studies in religion that provides the context for this examination. The second is a more fundamental polarity between the phenomena 'religion' and 'materiality', observable in both academic fields and contributing to their overall discordance.

This chapter also explores the general lack of considerations of the material elements of religious life found within the academic field of studies in religion. It is noted that for the most part, studies in religion has avoided both materiality generally, and drawing on archaeological sources in particular. Through an examination of the early textual origins of the field, it is explained that there has been from the beginning an ambivalent approach towards materiality, observable in the attitudes held by nineteenth-century anthropologists such as Edward Tylor. For instance, material culture was at one time used as a tool in diagnosing the levels of 'cultural evolution' of particular peoples, while at the same time, any progression in a people's religious life was generally held to necessitate emancipation from this materiality of religion. Further developments that have gone on to only reinforce this ambivalent attitude towards materiality are also charted. These include the perception of religion as characterized by qualities such as interiority, belief, experience and the division of the social world into the sacred and the profane.

To complement the first section this chapter then provides an introduction to some of the main practical problems that archaeology has in recovering religion from the material record. This serves to equip the reader with an understanding of some of the general and recurrent issues, or hindrances, relating to religion and materiality that commonly arise in archaeological theory and practice. Perhaps, the most striking and influential of these general hindrances is the profound lack of discussions about religiosity to be found in archaeological writings, or published attempts to reconstruct religion from the material record. This is a situation that is a direct complement to studies in religion's distinct lack of discussions on materiality. Practical problems with uncovering disembodied and abstracted 'religion' from within the material record are also explored, specifically the tendency for generic material categories, such as funerary monuments or graves, to be associated automatically with religion, to the exclusion of most other forms of material culture. The resulting bias in which the archaeological record is divided into 'normal' functional artefacts and 'abnormal' non-functional religious artefacts and objects is also discussed. These practical issues with identifying religion in the material record are then coupled with accompanying theoretical hindrances, especially the condition of modernity under which archaeologists work and the subtle but profound prejudices of secularism. It is argued, however, that if archaeologists do not attempt to examine religion in the past then others who are often less qualified, more self-interested and practising forms of religiously engaged pseudoarchaeology will do so instead.

The main aim of this chapter then is to show that there is a problematic conceptual mode relating to the categories of 'religion' and 'materiality' common to both the multidisciplinary field of studies in religion and the discipline of archaeology. Yet, it is argued that this problem is not sufficient cause to leave religion out of archaeological interpretations of the past, or material culture out of studies in religion. Having presented this problem from the perspectives of both academic fields, and explored some of its intellectual origins and characteristics, this chapter opens the way for a detailed examination of various archaeological schools of interpretation and their posited relationships between religion and material culture presented in the Chapter 3.

The problematic nature of material culture in studies in religion

There is a marked aversion to examining material culture in the academic study of religion. Commonly the spiritual and the material have been treated as being the antithesis of one another and this has been to the detriment the examinations of human religiosity presented and published within the field. Overwhelmingly, the studies in religion community, and historians of religion especially, have placed material objects and things outside of their usual field of inquiry, or at least shifted them to one side of it. This has resulted in a situation where material objects are perceived (if they are perceived at all) as almost irrelevant, or at best a distraction, from the other more important elements of religion under consideration (Kieschnick, 2003, pp. 19–21; Coleman and Collins, 2006, p. 32).

Non-material elements of religiosity such as religious experiences, beliefs, philosophies, psychologies, doctrines, textual history, literature, ethics, mythology, folklore, and so on, are common areas of specialization. The specifically material aspects of religion, however, are either examined under the rubric of religious art or architecture (or perhaps 'iconography' or 'symbolism'), or are engaged peripherally as mostly unacknowledged elements of larger studies in sociology or anthropology, or under considerations of ritual within the social sciences. When materiality is noted specifically, it has usually been done so in the context of discussions on Marxist cultural materialism and the long history of the resulting reductive approaches to human religiosity (Kunin, 2003, pp. 6–15). In such cases, religion is ultimately explained as one consequence of unjust inequalities in the consumption of (usually) material resources. Material objects, including the religious, may certainly be seen as cultural signifiers of social class and status (Veblen, 1925), as objects of value and prestige, but considerations of Marx style 'materiality' have generally had the effect of reducing religion to the position of a secondary phenomena in the 'real' material world, rather than opening up possible examinations of its material embodiment and interactions with material culture.

The contradictory values given to materiality (as opposed to text) by the emergent and barely distinguishable fields of anthropology and studies in religion during their origins in the mid- to late nineteenth century are outlined in a later section. It is enough here to note that nobody in the long line of well-known and popular theorists on religion, comprising Spencer, Tylor, Mueller, Frazer, Marx, Durkheim, Freud, Jung, Otto, Eliade (and onwards), have stated explicitly that 'most religion is in some sense technological' (Trompf, 2005, pp. 207–8). Nor have they examined specifically the material world as primary to, rather than secondary to, the realm of religion.

Recent major synthetic writers on human religiosity have faired little better. Ninian Smart focused on the religious experience in his classic *The Religious Experience of Mankind* (1969), and did not include material elements in his list of the dimensions of religion in human life, preferring to include instead non-material categories such as the mythological or the ethical. In fact, the closest he came to commenting on the material elements of religion was to mention the need for 'temples and churches', and these only in so far as they acted as containers for rituals and ceremonies had their effects on human interior experience (Smart, 1969, pp. 15–16). Cantwell Smith (1963) argued that the very term 'religion', and certainly the individually named world religions, were largely anachronistic modern constructions when applied to a pre-Enlightenment past in which there was little comprehension of 'religion' as a separate or self-defined sphere of life. Yet, his holistic conception of the religious past and his emphasis on a general and non-sectarian form of 'faith' as the basis of human religiosity did not include any consideration or notice of the material elements of such a religiously embedded domestic world (Asad, 2001). Later, Hudson Smith focused on the psychological, even mystical, elements of religious life. The mind must be, he argued, released from the shackle of simple reduction to the brain, and this dualism between mind and matter is reflected in an equally harsh split between the qualitative soul, even spirit, removed from the non-sanctified world of quantities, materialities and objects (Smith, 1992). This is just a small, popular, sample of attitudes to the material world that are common to the field as a whole, and too numerous and repetitive to list exhaustively in a work of this size.

This lopsided attitude has not gone unnoticed within studies in religion discourse. For instance, it has been argued that the omission of the material substratum of human life from considerations of religion has been partly an unconscious attempt by scholars to diminish their own discomfort with the 'messiness' and alien nature of visceral materiality, especially that of foreign and unfamiliar cultures and times (see Maffly-Kipp, 2005, pp. 76–8). Yet, the near ubiquitous nature of this apparent antimaterial bias, its very subtlety and ability to go unacknowledged, suggests that its causes may be more deeply ingrained in the history and culture of European scholarship.

The perceived irrelevance of material culture to studies of religion may stem partially from a perception, traceable in Christianity at least as far back as the Reformation, that religion is spiritual, carried out through the mind and the soul, experienced and expressed through interior faith and belief, and not primarily concerned with objects or externalities (Maffly-Kipp, 2005; Asad, 1993). The privileging of individual 'interior' spirituality over the bodily performance of ritual, or engagement with the material aspects of religious life can be traced back to Luther and the privileging of personal spiritual belief over empty ritualism. Protestant reformers such as Zwingli and Calvin preached and taught against 'externalism' and demanded a return to original textual sources in order to ensure true spiritual advancement, and this contrast appears to be reflected in the later Cartesian emphasis of mind over body and matter (Harvey, 2005a, p. 3).

However, the privileging of the insubstantial 'spiritual' in favour over the grossly 'material' within Christianity may also be foreshadowed much further back, to the Pauline division between spirit and matter (see Brown, 1988), the

Manichean antimaterialist flavour of Saint Augustine's theology, and even to the general, but by no means ubiquitous, anti-imagistic, even iconoclastic, character of the Judaeo-Christian–Islamic religious traditions (Besancon, 2000).

There does certainly appear to be some connection between the antimaterialism seemingly inherent in the academic study of religion, and the nature of the subject matter. For instance, this lack of engagement with material culture appears to take the form of an actual bias against material objects by those engaged in the study of religion. This is in contrast to historians who do not generally claim that material objects and artefacts are irrelevant to the study of human past, but rather that they are simply unfamiliar with the material. Certainly, very well-known historians like Fernand Braudel (1981) have compiled extensive historical examinations of a constellation of mundane material objects and discussed their influence on short-, medium- and long-term historical trajectories. Yet, the overwhelming attitude within the academic field of studies in religion has been that 'to dwell on relics, icons, and holy water is to waste one's time on peripherals, epiphenomena better left to antiquarians than the specialist in religion' (Kieschnick, 2003, p. 20). The use of the term 'epiphenomena' in this context is revealing. It is a direct reflection of the trend, common in archaeology (contemporary antiquarianism), to dismiss and discount religion as an unimportant and subsidiary 'epiphenomena' to their examinations of the material past. The term 'epiphenomena' was first used by cultural anthropologist Leslie White in *The Science of Culture* (1949), a book that went on to influence the new processual archaeology of the mid- to late twentieth century.

Certainly, the academic arenas of studies in religion and archaeology share much in common, not only in regard to their perceived split between the spheres of materiality and religion. For instance, both archaeology and studies in religion (at the time the anthropology of religion) arose together in the mid-nineteenth century in response to a series of similar impetus. Expanding geographical and temporal horizons, the rise of a scientific and materialistic worldview, the popularization of historical thinking and, crucially, Charles Darwin's principles of evolution all contributed to the emerging self-awareness of both disciplines (see Schnapp, 1996; Sharpe, 1986). Such influences were reflected in their shared emphasis on the importance of origins, on evolutionary schemes and on the assumption about the nature of progress and human cultural evolution (Trompf, 2005). Similarly, both worked in tandem to break down the received Christian worldview by pushing the temporal depth of their respective fields and awakening Christian culture to a greater knowledge of non-Christian religions, in particular their age and sophistication. For instance, the translation of the Rosetta Stone by Champollion after 1809, the discoveries of the spectacular material remains of the ancient cultures of Assyria and Babylonia by James Rich and Henry Layard from 1811 onwards, all led to a great expansion of the historical consciousness of European Christians. However, these material discoveries did not 'by the nature of things' (Trompf, 2005, p. 20) lead to scholars drawing general conclusions or speculations about the nature of ancient religions, or their comparative study, from the accumulating material evidence. Although the triumphs of each field did further the work of the other, archaeologists did not make major attempts to explore ancient religion, nor did the early anthropologists of religion attempt totalizing examinations of ancient religious materiality. Instead, it is their strikingly similar views on the opposing relationship between material culture and religious 'spirit', for want of a better word, and to their prioritizing of texts over matter, that we must now turn in order to understand the present dichotomy between the material and the religious that remains in both fields of academic enquiry.

The origins of the distinctive scholarly interest in the study of religion, comparing of religions, and history of religion as a general principle were firmly grounded in the linguistic and philological breakthroughs of the early nineteenth century, especially the Indo-European focused studies of the comparative similarities between Sanskrit, Persian, Greek and Latin (Sharpe, 1986, pp. 21–3). As exemplified in the works of the highly influential Max Mueller, the creation of a 'science' of comparative religions was predicated on a link between language and culture (Trompf, 1978). So, in its origins, the field of comparative religions was dominated by a philological approach to religion, where textual material was seen as of primary importance. Text and language was the clue that allowed not only ancient religions to speak once more, but for their age, mutual interconnections and perhaps origins to be eventually divined by the patient scholar. Other data, such as elements of material culture, when considered at all, was supposed to reflect lower forms of savage religiosity, a fallen materialistic degeneration from the sophisticated textual traditions of antiquity (Sharpe, 1986, p. 47). As we will see, after some time the material elements of religion came to be thought of as 'totems', 'fetishes' or the crude objects of 'animist' worship and were simultaneously used to both classify entire cultures, and also to diagnose their level of religious development and progress towards an enlightened text-based goal. Material culture was central to the emergent anthropology of religion, as it allowed religions to be catalogued, compared and ranked according to level of civilizational development, but at the same time it was simultaneously derided as of secondary consideration to text and as a sign of savage backwardness.

This early and primary focus on text over matter, however, went a long way to hinder the succeeding study of the materiality of religion by academics both in the West and abroad. For example, in her examinations of predominantly Protestant views of Chinese religious practices in the late nineteenth-century America, Laurie Maffly-Kipp has revealed the wider practice of European scholarship creating a disembodied and dematerialized form of the religions that it studies (Maffly-Kipp, 2005, pp. 72–97). Through contrasting early scholarly translations of Confucian classical texts produced for the educated public, with journalistic and tabloid reports on Chinese religious practices, she has showed how two very different representations of Chinese religiosity were created. One a scholarly, rarefied version of a textual religion produced and consumed by elite philosophers made comprehensible and familiar for Christian readers. The other an alien realm of largely incomprehensible religious rituals embedded in a tactile, corporeal and apparently disordered collection of rites and material paraphernalia. She goes so far as to suggest that the sensationalized and often racist newspaper descriptions of Chinese religions, which dwelt upon the strange and the exotic – rituals in dimly lit rooms crowded with incomprehensible objects, suffused with incense, strange smells and sounds, and all the 'exoticised materiality' of the orient – in many ways provided the reader with a truer view of Chinese religion than that produced by textual-focused scholars (Maffly-Kipp, 2005, p. 80). It was a world drawn as materially engaged, this worldly, strange and immediate, rather than philosophically rarefied, elite, distant and abstracted towards interiority.

This de-emphasizing of the engaged and material aspects of Asian religions in favour of an intellectualized and predominantly textual essence, stems, according to Maffly-Kipp, from Protestant missionary activity. Missionaries, attempting to convert a foreign religious culture, repeatedly rendered that religion into a form similar to textual Christianity. This was in order to present to their brethren, and one would assume also to themselves, a vision of exotic and mysterious Asian cultures that was not only relatively easily comprehensible, but also sympathetic and potentially redeemable (Maffly-Kipp, 2005, p. 75). Such a focus on the 'high' intellectual and textual traditions of Asian religions is notable in much of the work from Max Mueller to Mircea Eliade. In their attempt to compare religions 'they looked within Asian cultures for something recognizable to them as a religious tradition' (Maffly-Kipp, 2005, pp. 77–8). This often resulted in the traditions under interpretation ultimately sharing a series of characteristics (for instance, a charismatic authority, central textual cannon, ethical prescriptions, answers to metaphysical questions about the origins and ends of the cosmos), which resembled the Protestant Christianity these scholars were most familiar with. Certainly, eighteenth-century Europe tended to view Chinese culture in terms of Enlightenment rationalism, as a quintessentially philosophic, humanistic and rational civilization. While, in the early nineteenth century, the religions of India were understood by a Europe influenced by Romanticism as existential traditions, focused on inward, personal spirituality and heightened emotional experience and even gnosis (Clarke, 1997). This commonly held view of Asian religious traditions as being based primarily on interior experience, perhaps termed 'spirituality', and disembodied from the material world have yet to be completely arrested.

Archaeology has also, from its earliest inception, commonly dealt with texts as an important, and surprisingly often the primary, form of evidence. The archaeology of Old World civilizational centres such as Egypt, Mesopotamia, and the Classical and biblical worlds did much to reveal the past pre-Christian religious systems of the Mediterranean and Near East to a awestruck nineteenth-century Europe. The recovery of these, sometimes prebiblical, religious cosmologies began primarily as a historical pursuit concerned with the recovery and translation of new texts, to which the proto-archaeological explorations of Egypt, Mesopotamia and the Mediterranean world soon added considerable data, as well as objects of art–historical interest (Demarest, 1987, p. 372).

Then, as now, much archaeology was conceived as a support for historical knowledge, a way of testing the truth or falsity of historical accounts. Such 'textbook archaeology' was used mainly as an adjunct to history. Usually, it was historians who formulated the original questions to be asked about the past, while it was the archaeologist's role to corroborate historical scholarship in terms of material culture (Ray and Sinopoli, 2004, pp. 2–21). This direct-historical approach to material culture relied on matching the evidence from the past to similarities with later ethnographic and historical records, to let the material past speak for itself in the most straightforward manner.

A similar form of historical–textual archaeology, using material evidence to re-evaluate historical sources, has until recently been the most important form of archaeology used to explore the early stages of the Classical and documented Old World religious traditions, and is still highly influential in the archaeology of Asian religions, especially in South Asia. The archaeology of Buddhism is a good example, where material remains of religious architecture, sculpture or ritual practice have mainly been interpreted via textual or doctrinal means and that there has been little independent archaeological study (Coningham, 2001; Chakrabarti, 1995; for the opposing view, Schopen, 1997). This is still, especially, the case in the archaeology of Indian religions in general, especially Hinduism, where there have been numerous, sometimes notorious, attempts to prove the historicity of religious myths, such as the Mahabharata and the Ramayana, through archaeological fieldwork (see esp. Lal, 2002b; Ray, 2004).

Yet, although both archaeology and studies in religion, in their formative periods, prioritized text over matter, material culture was nevertheless of central, if sometimes unacknowledged, importance, since it served as a tangible connection between the researchers and the topics of their research. For archaeologists, material things, such as preserved texts and inscriptions, art objects, lost sites from the history books, were always the primary lure for investigation. While for those engaged in the anthropological study of religion, especially those based in European institutions, the various objects and material things collected from abroad were often their most direct connection with the people they were attempting to study.

In many ways, the contemporary academic arenas of both studies in religion and anthropology emerged as attempts to classify growing collections of material objects, in particular the vast assemblages of material objects collected in the nineteenth-century museums (Larson, 2007). Material culture 'provided a direct, indisputable link between subject and scholar; made and used by the people who were being studied, objects travelled, seemingly without distortion, into the hands of the anthropological "weaver" at home' (Larson, 2007, p. 94). In such surroundings, curators such as Henry Balfour of the Pitt-Rivers Museum at Oxford engaged in the almost heroic categorization of material culture in the manner of natural scientists. Such examinations were analytic, classificatory, typological and evolutionary, fixated on the search for origins and overall, were exceedingly similar to early attempts at classifying and interpreting the archaeological artefacts recovered through excavation. Although this early fixation with material culture began to dissipate in the twentieth century, when anthropologists became more direct in collecting material through actual immersion of the lives of inhabitants, the evolutionary and classificatory methods used to order and rank material things remained influential in the resulting typologies used to sort and talk about different peoples, cultures and religions under observation.

For instance, late nineteenth-century anthropology was heavily influenced by the 'three-age' system developed within the emerging field of prehistoric archaeology. This classificatory scheme, devised in 1836 by the Danish proto-archaeologists Thomsen and Worsaae (and first made available to an English speaking audience in 1848), allowed one to rank chronologically material items according to their technological form and substance; namely whether they were of Stone Age, Bronze Age and Iron Age. Although, in its origin this classificatory scheme was based not on the actual material substances used in the artefacts, but rather in the depth of the layers of silt in which they were uncovered in bottom of a Danish lake (Daniel and Renfrew, 1988), the method of judging the type, and hence the age, of a culture based upon the types and materials used became widespread outside of archaeological circles. Not only could museum collections be divided into Stone, Bronze or Iron Age depending on the material objects present, but whole living cultures and societies could be so as well. A cultural categorization was based almost entirely upon the types of artefacts that they manufactured, and the materials that they used.

This material-based classification scheme was closely related to the then-current anthropological theory of survivals, in which the 'primitive' came to be equated with the 'prehistoric' (Trompf, 2005). Extant cultures in remote parts of the world that still used relatively simple technologies manufactured out of materials such as stone or bone, people like the Andaman Islanders or Tasmanian Aborigines, were perfunctorily considered to be living remnants of ancient cultures, living snapshots of human evolutionary history. This misguided and overly simplistic equation of material object with cultural sophistication with cultural age, led to a number of early anthropologists of religion such as Tylor and Frazer positing that, in studying the beliefs and practices of 'savage' and 'primitive' peoples, they were in fact in direct contact with the religion of 'Stone Age Man' (Sharpe, 1986). In short, a direct analogy had been created between the development and nature of material culture and the development and nature of social culture, including religion. Such an approach was most prominently adopted in the work of Edward Tylor (1871), where he posited that 'primitive', low-technological cultures were a direct reflection of 'savage' religion and vice versa. For Tylor, 'levels of material culture must correspond exactly to levels of intellectual, moral and religious culture, and . . . survivals in one of these areas must inevitably correspond to survivals in another' (Sharpe, 1986, p. 58).

The influence of Charles Darwin's proposed principles of evolution (1859) was central to this thinking about material things and human religions, based upon ideas of progress and typology. Examinations of stages of cultural development and the classification of all sorts of typologies became the norm through much of the emerging human sciences. In archaeology, evolutionary thought encouraged Pitt-River's organizational schemes for the evolution of artefacts, which gave rise to the whole method of chronologically arranging artefacts according to developmental sequences, or typology (Bowden, 1991). While for the study of religion, the construction of progressive and evolutionary schemes of religious development became the base of most examinations of comparative religion well into the twentieth century. Material culture, however, faired badly in these schemes vis-à-vis the disembodied concept 'religion'. For instance, in most of the subsequent proposed typologies of religious progression, although material culture was used to chart the religious evolution of a culture, it was only through the gradual dissociation of the religious life from the material world of things and objects that a culture's progression from savage to civilized, from merely superstitious to approvingly enlightened, was charted. Material culture, although central to the diagnosis of relative religious sophistication, was characteristic of a lack of religious development, of backwardness, and of somehow being frozen in the past.

This was true even before the influence of Darwinian evolutionary thought. As early as 1760 the term fetishism, coined by Charles de Brosses in his *Du Culte des Dieux Fetiches*, was used to replace the old Christian idea of 'paganism' as a description of all the many and varied religious beliefs and practices of the world's preliterate peoples. It was based on the idea of fetishes, or material objects, either manufactured or found, that were supposedly worshipped by 'savage' people. Preliterate people's fetishism was characterized as infantile ignorance and contrasted with the enlightened and rational scientific knowledge and mastery over the material world that was increasingly characterizing European thought (Sharpe, 1986, pp. 18–19). For Max Mueller, in the early decades of the nineteenth century, it was the apprehension of natural phenomena that was the origin of the human appreciation of the divine. This was proved by the new linguistic discovery that the names of the Vedic gods were originally the names of great natural forces such as the wind and storm (Indra), fire (Agni), wind (Vayu) and sun (Surya). As the names of the natural materialized forces became more abstracted from immediate reality, and the gods became abstract forces rather than personifications of concrete events, the religion became progressively more sophisticated and enlightened.

John Lubbock's *Pre-Historic Times* (1865) first introduced typological and cultural–historical ideas fashionable within the emerging scholarly field of prehistoric archaeology to a wider English speaking public (see also Daniel and Renfrew, 1988). In it he ingeniously used a Darwinian scheme of progressive history to posit the linear evolution of religion in the past as a direct correlation with a culture's technological development. His six-rung typology of religious development was one of gradual dissociation of religion from the materiality of the world. Cultures began with simple object worship, or fetishism, then progressed to a wider appreciation of nature worship (totemism), then to human mediation with the natural and spirit worlds (shamanism), onwards to the veneration of specially created anthropomorphic models (idolatry), and finally to text-based ethical monotheism. The 'material' and the 'spiritual' were increasingly seen as two ends of a spectrum of religious development and evolution, where if a culture moved into a closer relationship with one end it naturally distanced itself from the other.

Following Lubbock, Edward Tylor (1871) adopted evolutionary thought in his own religious typology, which also posited a progressive disengagement from the materiality of the world. Tylor used the term *animus* to refer to the vitalizing element that was thought to inhabit physical bodies by those who practised the most 'primitive' forms of religion, whom he termed animists. The attribution of life and understanding to inanimate things, plants or animals was for Tylor and many of the Victorian anthropologists who followed the defining attribute of a primitive culture. Animistic people made the category error of thinking that non-organic material things were animated by life and had souls or spirits. Like children playing with toys, they could not distinguish between animate and inanimate objects (Tylor, 1871, pp. 470–80). In this way 'animism' came to replace the earlier 'fetishism' to denote the materialistic and ignorant religions of preliterate and primitive peoples. Basically, it was their veneration of material things that made them primitive. Tylor posited a progression from animism, or the worship of souls or spirits that reveal themselves in nature or things of crude manufacture, to polytheism where similar forces are writ large and further personified, to transcendent monotheism. For Tylor, material things, which he referred to as *realien* or 'hard' forms of evidence (Larson, 2007), were most important for interpreting accurately the religious development of differing cultures. He equated animism, the most materially embedded of his typology, with 'Stone Age religion' (Harvey, 2005a, pp. 5–9) and used megaliths in India and the forms of 'simple and primitive' indigenous religion practised by their makers to indicate the primitive religion practised by the megalith builders of Stone Age Europe (Tylor, 1871, p. 61). Other anthropologists of religion such as James Frazer adopted similar grand narratives of social and religious advancement and progress, but without the use of archaeological evidence or the association of religious evolution with decreasing levels of material embodiment.

The limited number of practicing archaeologists who speculated on the origins and character of early religion during this period largely followed this cultural–historical mode. Religion was assumed to have evolved progressively according to the theories of the early anthropologists of religion, and to have followed a typology, similar to that used by archaeologists on their artefacts. Notable and influential early examples included Tiele's work on ancient Zoroastrianism, Egypt and Mesopotamia, especially his *Outlines of the History of Religion* (1877) and Reinach's *Orpheus: A History of Religions* (1909).

For some archaeologists however, such as Pitt-Rivers, there was a direct correlation between evolving human religiosity and material technology (Pitt-Rivers, 1906). As will be seen in Chapter 3, this assumption that religious development necessitated a progressive distancing from the material aspects of life, led directly to the functionalist archaeology that was in ascendant during the mid-twentieth century and assumptions about the irreconcilability between religion and material culture. These ideas also formed the base of influential schemes for the archaeological interpretation of religion vis-à-vis other cultural traits, in particular Hawkes' Ladder of Inference (Hawkes, 1954, pp. 161–2). But it must be noted that these specific typologies of religious evolution were only adopted by a limited number of archaeologists, drawn from those few who chose to write on religion at all. However, archaeology as a discipline, did embrace the concept of social evolution that they were based upon, for instance, the social evolution from band-tribe-chieftain-state (Service, 1972). In addition, it could very well be argued that the tendency for archaeologists dealing with the Palaeolithic (Old Stone Age) to refer to 'shamanism' in their discussions of society (Mithen, 1996; Van Huyssteen, 2010, p. 111; see Sidky, 2010, for a good critique of this perspective), those dealing with the Neolithic (New Stone Age) to more commonly focus on 'ancestor veneration' (Tilley, 1994), those who deal with Bronze Age societies to traditionally include some form of 'priest-king' in their discussions of state formation (see Wittfogel, 1957), and for the Iron Age to be the locus for the emergence of monotheism and the contemporary world religions, is a contemporary, if unacknowledged, example of an evolutionary approach to religious history reminiscent of that of Lubbock, Pitt-Rivers or Tylor.

Overall, this early anthropological phase of the study of religion, up until say the 1920s, was dominated by an evolutionary model of progressive religious development from 'crude' materialistic worship through to 'sophisticated' transcendent monotheism. Religious history was seen as a general progression from a 'primitive' appreciation of some form of power inherent in the material world through to the less crude and more refined reification of this supernatural power into anthropomorphic spirits, deities and eventually an ethical theistic god.

Yet, as the twentieth century unfolded, this impersonal, historic and evolutionary understanding of religious culture shifted to a focus on religion as being more satisfactorily understood as an individualistic, interior and personal pursuit. In these schemes, however, materiality remained distanced from 'true' religiosity. Early psychologists who considered the problem of the seemingly cross-cultural appearance of religious perception within the human mind, such as James (1902) and Starbuck (1899), emphasized not just the individual over the social group, but the individual experience of religion and its interior, even mystical, elements. This was paralleled during the early twentieth century by a renewed interest in the personal, the Romantic, the transformative and the spiritual elements of religious experience, as well as a reawakening of interest in religious practice and mysticism (for early examples see Underhill, 1911; Woodroffe, 1919). This move is perhaps best characterized in the works of Christian and mystically inclined scholars such as Rudolf Otto and Mircea Eliade (both examined in more detail in Chapter 4).

In fact, Rudolf Otto (1924) was influenced by the work of Robert Marett, who in his *The Threshold of Religion* (1902) looked for the emotive and uncanny presence that lay behind the experience of Tylor's animism. Marett named this fearful appreciation of the awe-inspiring aspects of the natural world after the Melanesian term *mana*. This referred to the impersonal power that could be apprehended through material objects, but was, like Eliade's and Otto's sacred, not *of* the material world. Materiality was obviously connected in some intimate way with religious experience and understanding of members of the non-Western cultures drawn upon to inform the early anthropological attempts to create totalizing theories of religion, but as in the case of mana, and later Otto's holy, the material context for the arising of the experience was increasingly downplayed. Overall, the move towards psychology-based paradigms in the study of religion further marginalized the material aspects of religious life in favour of the interior, the experiential, the existential, the spiritual, the insubstantial and the transcendent.

Closely connected to the increasing understanding of religion as interiority, was the overwhelming tendency to privilege individual belief and thought in the explanation of religion, over other aspects such as embodied action or praxis (for this argument in regard to Hinduism see Michaels, 1998, chapter 1). As early as the 1870s, Tylor's definition of animism (and hence of all religion) as a *belief* in spirits or non-empirical beings privileged the interior mental aspects of religion over other more external and physical forms (Tylor, 1871, p. 425). Others, such as Spencer and Frazer, also saw religion primarily as a belief system, even as a prescientific way of thinking about causality in the world that attempted to make sense of and control material nature. This emphasis on misguided belief (and rationality) in 'explaining' religion is highlighted in predictions that religious 'belief' would naturally disappear as the benefits of modern secular and scientific understandings of the natural world and human social life spread across the globe from a Europe increasingly disenchanted with religious belief and revealed doctrine.

As already noted, the contrast between the material and the spiritual was foreshadowed in the traditional division long held within Christianity between embodied 'ritual' and disembodied spiritual 'belief'. This modern intellectualist view of religion as a belief system served to reinforce this pre-existing dichotomy between religion, as interior belief, and the material world that it attempted to explain and control in the manner of a primitive natural science.

It can be seen that this dichotomy between ritual and belief has affected both religious practice in Europe as well as the academic understanding of religion in general. The very concept of 'belief', long privileged within Christian tradition, is problematic and does not necessarily translate across cultures. Lopez (1998, p. 33) has made this point well, stating that 'the category of belief is not so easily transferred from one society to another. . . . Belief appears as a universal category because of the universalist claims of the tradition in which it has become most central, Christianity.' As early as 1897, Friedrich Max Muller made the still valid observation that 'the idea of believing, as different from seeing, knowing, denying, or doubting was not so easily elaborated, is best shown by the fact that we look for it in vain in the dictionaries of many uncivilized races' (1897, p. 228).

This dichotomy between privileged religious belief and relatively overlooked alternative ways of expressing and experiencing the religious has had negative consequences for the academic appreciation of the material elements of religious life. A way of thinking has dominated in which 'materiality must be separated from true religion', and the veneration of the material aspects of religion such as 'masks and statues', relegated to the perceived inferior and crude level of idolatry or fetishism (Harvey, 2005b, p. 3). In fact:

> The very idea that 'belief' is an inner affirmation or affiliation that should take precedence over all outward behaviour is itself among the most invidious and pernicious of the doctrines of a particular culture that

pretends to universality. . . . The problem is that the supposedly diffident project of academia has often accepted this understanding of ritual and belief uncritically. It has acquiesced to the implication that religion (a matter of private and personal beliefs sometimes contaminated by ritualisation) is separate from politics, economics and a variety of other allegedly autonomous spheres. (Harvey, 2005b, pp. 14–15)

This list of spheres of life thought to be separate from religion could just as easily be extended to include objects, artefacts and the whole material world. At the same time, archaeology could be added to those forms of academia that have perpetuated such a blinkered attitude towards religion.

It should also be noted that this subtle but pervasive equation of religion with 'belief', to the exclusion of action, practice or embodiment, has also been detrimental to the attempts by archaeologists to successfully identify religion from within the material record. Archaeologists have traditionally equated religion with intangible belief, while the material record is equated with the residues of tangible action. Physical actions such as ritual are thought to leave empirical traces that can be materially identified, while intangible religious belief is very difficult for archaeologists to identify materially; it 'occupies an invisible realm beyond the bounds of reasonable inference' (Garwood et al., 1991a, pp. v–x). As will be further explored in a later section, this ontological subtraction of religion from the engaged world of material things, and subsequent confinement of it to the rarefied and intangible realm of thought or belief, has created a significant conceptual barrier preventing many archaeologists from attempting to examine religion and material culture together.

Exceptions do exist however, often originating from archaeological examinations of non-Judaeo-Christian–Islamic contexts. For example, Bacus and Lahiri have suggested that Hinduism may be a religion particularly amenable to archaeological examination, as it has been more concerned with what people do, rather than what they think. This emphasis on practice and action in Hindu religious life ensures that a study of its texts will emphasize only certain aspects of that religion's character. Hence, because of this materialized, rather than internalized, character they ascribe to Hinduism they postulate that archaeology may be a particularly fruitful exercise in the Hindu context (Bacus and Lahiri, 2004).

Yet, before completing this overview of the history and nature of the polarity between materiality and religion, brief mention must be made of the sociology of religion, especially the early influence of Emile Durkheim (1926). This is important for at least two reasons. First, following Durkheim, the sociology of religion has predominantly focused on religion as embodied practice rather than belief and, in a similar way to archaeologists (who have oft times modelled themselves on the social sciences), those in the social sciences have generally directed their attention to ritual rather than religion per se. Second, certain characteristics of the work of Durkheim, such as the polarity between the realms of the sacred and the profane, have widely influenced later work in the study of religion, as well as the discipline of archaeology.

Robertson Smith in his *The Religion of the Semites* (1887) described ritual and practice as the sum total of ancient religions, and suggested that religion was a body of traditional shared social practices rather than an abstract system of beliefs. His emphasis on practice rather than belief greatly influenced Durkheim and, through him, the sociology of religion (see Sharpe, 1986, pp. 80–1). However, this emphasis on practice did not automatically result in an interest in the material aspects of religious ritual as primary expressions of religiosity. Instead, religion, ritual, and via ritual the material elements of religious praxis, all became illustrative of a greater reality – that of an abstracted 'society'.

For Durkheim, and the many that he influenced, religion, ritual and material things were all secondary and reflective in nature, utilized as mediums for expressing greater social truths. Material things especially could be receptacles for human categories, but they were ultimately passive and reflective in nature (Latour, 1993, p. 52). A ritual object used by Australian Aborigines could represent and objectify a greater reified social concept, such as customary authority and tribal law, for example, but this ritual object would not, according to Durkheim, 'act back' on that society with any autonomous agency. Material objects could be important participants and props in the social expression of religion, but they did so through mediating human concepts, never by acting in and of themselves. This methodological disregard for the possible primary importance of the material elements of society is reflected in subsequent research. 'Social' sciences have focused their attention on the immaterial world of disembodied culture while treating the material world as the concern of the 'physical' sciences (Dant, 2005). At best, material things are examined as being reflective or symbolic of particular forms of social communication, while the actual embodied relationships between subjects and the material world is ignored, and any notion that material things may play primary and active roles in social life have, until recently, been omitted. This is not to say that aspects of the material world have not long been studied and written on by sociologists, most notably the human body, consumption (see Chapter 3), pilgrimage (see Chapter 4), but rather that this realm of materiality has traditionally been seen as having been reflective of abstracted social relationships, rather than as being primary and active in their creation. This perception of ritual and religion, and their material correlates, as reflections of human society, and utilized as expressions of ideology, is explored in detail in the following chapter and it is enough here to point to its existence.

Similarly, Durkheim's conceptualization of human social life into a strict duality between the realms of the 'sacred' and the 'profane', and its extensive influence on postprocessual archaeologies of landscape, is the subject of Chapter 4. It is sufficient here to note that this dichotomy between two radically separate realms of social experience was, for Durkheim, absolute; 'All known religious beliefs, whether simple or complex . . . presuppose a classification of all things, real or ideal, into the classes or opposed groups . . . profane and sacred' (1926, p. 37). There was a 'logical chasm between the two' (p. 40). Revealingly, this strict polarity appears to have been informed by Durkheim's own perception of a strict duality and hierarchy between the material body and the insubstantial soul or spirit. In his *Elementary Forms of Religious Life* (2001 [1926], p. 194), Durkheim states that:

> [W]e are thus really made of two beings . . . one of which dominates the other. Such is the underlying meaning of the antithesis that all people have more or less clearly conceived between body and soul, between the sensate being and the spiritual being that coexists within us.

This primacy of the soul over the body is reflected in, and even equated with, the macrocosm of society at large, for:

> [T]here really is a part of ourselves that is not immediately subordinate to the organic factor: namely everything inside us that represents society. The

general ideas that religion or science imprint in our minds . . . do not follow in the wake of the body. . . . This is because . . . the world of representations in which social life unfolds is overlaid on its material substrate and does not originate there. (2001 [1926], p. 201)

This is an example of Durkheim's wider interest in the quintessentially immaterial aspects of society, such as a disembodied religion, or social solidarity, which is examined through intermediary structures or institutions such as kin networks or the legal system. In such a fashion he treats the material elements of society as either unimportant or already understood.

As already noted, this dichotomy between the sacred and the profane in archaeological interpretations of material culture is the subject of a future chapter. We can, however, complete this introductory overview of the disjunction between the material and the spiritual in the academic study of religion, with a brief examination of the work of perhaps the most important later commentator on religion who was influenced by Durkheim; the Romanian writer Mircea Eliade. Eliade's focus as a historian and perhaps phenomenologist of religion (Rennie, 1996), rather than a social scientist, brought him into constant engagement with the material world. In fact, Eliade's phenomenology of religious experience relied utterly on the division of space, and hence materiality, into hierarchical levels of the sacred and the profane (1957), as it did time (1954). His division of space into centripetal schemes where central sacred 'hierophanies' were marked off and bounded by peripheral zones of the profane, was influenced by South Asian Hindu/Buddhist schemes of sacred geometry and methods of architecturally embodying the experience of the sacred in concrete material form through architecture, temple building and other material delineations of space (Eliade, 1969, pp. 112–13 and 118–19 esp.). Hence, for Eliade (1957, p. 116), material culture or 'nature', is the primary locale for an experience of the sacred:

For religious man, nature is never only 'natural'; it is always fraught with a religious value. This is easy to understand, for the cosmos is a divine creation; coming from the hands of the gods, the word is impregnated with sacredness. . . . The gods . . . manifested the different modalities of the sacred in the very structure of the world and of cosmic phenomena.

Yet, for Eliade, this sacredness is of another order, removed from the realm of profane materiality. The sacred only appears in the material world as a special hierophany, as an act of manifestation:

> For religious man the supernatural is indissolubly connected with the natural, that nature always expresses something that transcends it. . . . [A] sacred stone is venerated because it is sacred, not because it is a stone; it is the sacrality manifested through the mode of being of the stone that revels its true essence. This is why we cannot speak of naturism or of natural religion in the sense that the nineteenth century gave to those terms. (Eliade, 1957, p. 118)

The sacred, although appearing in the material world, is of a radically different order and does not belong to the normal profane world. This is the very reason why it is considered sacred. For the realm of the material to hold interest for the academic researcher it must either be organized according to some plan that maps out otherworldly sacred incursions, or it must be perceived by an individual under the effect of an overwhelming experience of the numinous:

> A sacred stone remains a stone; apparently . . . nothing distinguishes it from all other stones. But for those to whom a stone reveals itself as sacred, its immediate reality is transmuted into a supernatural reality. In other words, for those who have a religious experience all nature is capable of revealing itself as cosmic sacrality. The cosmos in its entirety can become a hierophany. (Eliade, 1957, p. 12)

So, although for Eliade's phenomenology of religion, and those it has influenced (see Chapter 4), the sacred is connected to the material world, his emphasis on a strict duality between the realms of sacred and profane ensures that the sacred can never be *of* the material world. By extension, the familiar duality between materiality and religiosity is perpetuated. In Chapter 4, it will be shown how this polarity between the sacred and the profane, itself traceable to the Catholic tension between spiritually effective 'sacraments' and rituals and regular profane action (Harvey, 2005b, p. 4), has caused archaeologists to assume that the material record must be divided between ritual practices, associated with some insubstantial religion, and normal or mundane practices, associated with functionality and utility. It will be shown just how detrimental Eliade's concept of the spatially mediated sacred and profane dichotomy has been to archaeological attempts to recover religion from within the material record.

It can be seen that material culture has been marginalized in the academic study of religion. From their inception, both archaeology and studies in religion have implicitly treated material culture as secondary to textual sources. Its function, if considered at all, was to reflect and perhaps corroborate textual truths. However, in both disciplines material culture was also central in diagnosing peoples and cultures, often as part of a progression along a cultural–evolutionary series. This influence of the idea of progressive evolution ensured that material culture could act as a diagnostic of cultural and religious sophistication. But also, because of biases that privileged religious belief and interiority over action and external materiality, schemes of cultural evolution simultaneously depicted any religious 'progression' as a gradual but distinct dissociation from the material world.

This rarefied vision of religion as dissociated from the material world has contributed to a state of affairs in which materiality and religion are perceived, often almost unconsciously, as being quite naturally at odds. This perceived polarity between the two is repeated from the opposite perspective, in the work of archaeologists, who have not only failed to interpret religion from within the material record, but who have also often failed to even consider looking for it. It is to this other side of the problem of the relationship between religion and materiality that we shall now turn.

The problematic nature of religion in archaeological studies of materiality

This section explores the common and mysterious absence of religion from the great majority of archaeological interpretations of the past. It serves as a general introduction to the problem of the troubled relationship between archaeology and religion, a way of beginning to think about the issues involved. It is argued that this state of affairs, while having substantial causes, is nevertheless unnecessary and perhaps even irresponsible.

First, it is important to boldly and clearly state the problem. Overwhelmingly, archaeology as a discipline has failed to engage sufficiently with that category of human experience termed collectively 'the religious', and which forms the focus of the interdisciplinary academic programme of studies in religion. The reasons for this lacuna have been many and varied, some justified and some less so, but inevitably it has resulted in a blinkered attitude to the past, one in which religion has been devalued or ignored. This applies equally to notions of religion as a personal as well as a social phenomenon; as a mode of personal, private experience for the individual actors in the past, or as a public element of past social life. In addition, on the occasions when religion has been seriously considered by archaeologists there have been a number of problems with the way that it has been presented and dealt with.

For instance, during the early and premethodological period of archaeological theorizing, before the emergence of the 'new' archaeology in the mid-twentieth century, religion was frequently thought of as a relatively simple area of investigation. Some early archaeological approaches to religion were often remarkably naïve, either adopting an evolutionary model (as explained above), or presenting themselves as straightforward archaeological adjuncts to normative text-based historical scholarship. The best example of this naïve approach is the work by Finegan, *The Archaeology of World Religion* (1952), in which he expresses the archaeology of Buddhist and early Hindu India as an attempt to find material correlates to places mentioned in well-known religious texts in English translation. Examples include the elaboration of the archaeology of places central to the life of the Buddha, such as Bodhgaya and Sarnath, or the identification of the sites visited by Rama and Krishna, in what amounts at times to almost an archaeological tourist guide to exotic historical religions (see, for example, Finegan, 1952). Religion has faired little better in the more recent and methodologically stringent times that have followed the mid-century attempts to bring archaeological theory and practice closer to that of the social sciences. As will become clear, in this context religion has for the most part remained misunderstood, largely untheorized, ignored and omitted from archaeological literature. When the term, or one of its virtual synonyms used in the social sciences such as 'ritual', has been noticed it has, more often than not, become shorthand for that which is non-functional, irrational, or simply insufficiently understood.

Archaeologists have often been accused of borrowing from other disciplines in order to synthesize their interpretative methods (Insoll, 2004a, pp. 33–4), yet, in the case of religion there has been a distinct lack of attempts to borrow from the academic study of religion. In one of the few articles touching explicitly on the relationship between the disciplines of archaeology and studies in religion, Demarest claimed that the two disciplines have maintained 'a close but unsteady relationship' over the past century, but that this relationship has 'matured into a mutually supportive one' (1987, p. 372). However the evidence suggests, instead, a history of mostly ignorance or outright rejection. Archaeologists attempting to engage with religion have either ignored the academic study of religion outright, or have rejected certain subdisciplines of the field, such as the sociology of religion, psychology of religion or history of religion, as either irrelevant or hopelessly idealistic.

For instance, in his article on the possibilities of a cognitive archaeology of religion Colin Renfrew acknowledged that a broader perspective was needed in order to inform what exactly the phenomenon of religion was, but he looked to nineteenth-century cultural anthropology for an answer and did not mention religious studies (1994a, p. 47; Parker-Pearson, 2001, pp. 206–7). Another archaeologist interested in religion, Timothy Insoll, initially considered the various subdisciplines of studies in religion, under the supraheading *Religionswissenschaft* and concluded that the history of religions under this umbrella encompasses a 'wealth' of relevant ideas and methodologies that might benefit archaeology. He even went so far as to initially suggest that the overarching framework of history of religions offered a multidisciplinary superstructure under any archaeology of religion could function. Three years later, however, Insoll's initial overemphasizing of the methodological unity of history of religions, and his overly optimistic evaluation of its progressive and teleological narrative to human religiosity, caused him to rethink his initial attraction to the field. Now, because (according to Insoll) the history of religions looks for a normative essence of religion, exemplified by the work of Eliade, any archaeology of religion should not be subsumed within such 'an idealistic supra-discipline'. Unfortunately, this approach shows a misunderstanding of the nature of studies in religion, and overreliance on one single subdiscipline to the exclusion of many others (Insoll, 2001; 2004a, pp. 38–41).

One result of this methodological lapse has been that the archaeological engagement with religion has lagged behind most other areas of specialization (for instance, subsistence, technology, economics, politics, diet, gender, art) within the overarching discipline of archaeology. One reason for the lack of substantial and serious attempts at any 'archaeology of religion' has been the insufficient theorization of religion by archaeologists. One notable recent exception to this theoretical lacuna has been the work of Timothy Insoll, most notably his *Archaeology, Ritual, Religion* (2004a). Insoll's work on the archaeological identification and understanding of religion, and his holistic view of the embedded nature of religion in human social and material life, will be examined in some detail in Chapter 4. At this point, it is necessary only to note that his work is one of the few explicit attempts to begin to rectify this previous neglect and to serve 'as an introductory statement/ opening dialogue on the theory and methodology of the archaeology of religion' (Insoll, 2004a, p. 4).

This difficult interface between archaeology and religion has been described as characterized by 'immature methodologies' (Demarest, 1987, p. 372), with theoretical perspectives on the place held by religion in the archaeological record being 'few and far between' (Insoll, 2001, p. 4). This has applied to both the role of religion in individual and social life in the past, as well as the relationship between religious action and the material residues that make up the archaeological record, the primary evidence for archaeological interpretation. Also, the possible relationships between religion and other spheres of social life in processual debates about the nature and reasons for cultural change have been almost entirely ignored (Renfrew, 1994a, p. 51).

Yet, it has not only been the lack of theorization of religion that has prevented the creation of viable archaeological approaches to the religious. A series of inadequate, incomplete or partially unconscious assumptions about the place of religion in the past and the relationship between religion and materiality have contributed as well. Broadly speaking, early writings by archaeologists on the topic of religion were often superficial, general and reflective of the premethodological role played by archaeology as an adjunct to history. They were often concerned solely with one particular religion or religious tradition, and usually adopted a concept of religion that relied on a historical and textually based understanding (for Christianity, see Frend, 1996; for Buddhism, see Coningham, 2001; for Hinduism, see Chakrabarti, 2001; for Islam, see Insoll, 1999). Later explorations of the religious elements of past life have often fallen back on narrow definitions such as equating religion with a particular form of belief (Renfrew, 1994a, p. 49; Parker-Pearson, 2001, pp. 203–19), or have been published as conference proceedings covering a wide array of themes or perspectives. The earliest of these, the conference on archaeology, ritual and religion held at Oxford in 1989 (Garwood et al., 1991b; for a second major conference see Insoll, 2004b), was convened in recognition of this theoretical lacuna. In its published proceedings, the failing of archaeologists to adequately recognize and theorize the social significance of the 'religious', here mainly termed 'ritual', and its possible material identification, was a central concern (Garwood et al., 1991a, p. v).

However, in this particular case, although the absence of appropriate theory was noted, it was so in regard to the narrower term 'ritual' rather than 'religion'. By doing so, the bigger picture of religion as a broad category of individual and social life, one that encompassed non-ritual domains, and as an interesting area to theorize and study on its own terms, remained elusive. This reduction of the concept religion down to a subsidiary term has been, and remains, problematic, albeit exceedingly common in archaeological writing.

In general, archaeologists use the term 'religion' very rarely. Instead, religion has been commonly quietly subsumed beneath one of its partial synonyms such as 'rites', 'symbolism', 'ideology', 'ideational', 'psychology', 'phenomenology' and, most commonly, 'ritual'. This preference for narrower, more functionally explicit, terms, in place of the more inclusive but less specific, and possibly less definable, term religion, reflects the social scientific tendency for the social functions of religious behaviour to be of most interest to archaeologists, rather than the wider nature of religion as a significant domain of human life, and even less commonly the specifics of past religious beliefs or worldviews. This has been certainly true of many Marxist influenced archaeologists, more concerned with the mechanisms of past power, social control and negotiation than religion per se, and who have hence used the terms 'ideology' or 'symbolism' to describe the cognitive or non-utilitarian aspects of past social life (see esp. Tilley, 1991; Shanks and Tilley, 1992).

It must be reiterated that there are understandable reasons for archaeologist's traditional reticence to engage with the religious. One reason for the wariness towards applying the term religion to the interpretation of archaeological data has been a reluctance by archaeologists to set up a category of meaning in the past which is not only difficult to materially identify and examine empirically, but which may distort the very past archaeologists attempt to reconstruct. One of the most fascinating and challenging aspects of archaeology is the absolute need for prior categories of meaning to be applied to the mute past. The reconstructions that archaeologists painstakingly create are heavily dependent on their decisions to use particular terms and look for specific types of social activity. The often untheorized categories that they use at the outset like 'economic', 'political authority', or 'religion' will become the foundations for whole cultures and the basis for ideas about the basic function and nature of society.

For instance, the 'new' or scientific archaeology of the 1950s, as well as the processual archaeology that followed, in attempting to generate objective methodologies for interpreting the past, assumed a view of past cultures that was reliant on generalized universal cultural 'laws' across space and time (see Chapter 3). In such a climate, using the indefinable and vaguely amorphous term 'religion' in the interpretations of the data could result only in the creation of a static, essentialist, and ahistorical account of human psychology and culture in the past. Certainly, such an interpretation held little or no explanatory power or attraction for the scientifically, even positivistic, minded. Yet, later, with the gradual adoption of more relativist and contextualized methodologies by postprocessual archaeologists, and the rejection of such universalizing and essentialist interpretative schemes, religion appears to have become problematic for exactly the opposite reason. If differing peoples and cultures have all acted and thought differently and contingently, then imposing the term 'religion' on the archaeological data may assume contemporary categories of thought in the past where they are not applicable.

In fact, the term 'religion' is conspicuous in its absence from the works of many post-1950s archaeologists, regardless of their interpretative persuasion. Where it is used, it is usually as a catchall phrase to denote either the unexplainable or non-functional. This point is further elaborated and expanded upon in the historical overview of archaeological attitudes to religion in the material record provided in Chapter 3. This is true certainly of the work of most contemporary postprocessualist archaeologists, even in the cases where they claim to be attempting to transcend modernist assumptions about the past and to open their interpretations of the archaeological record to alternative non-modern lifeways. Two notable examples, each dealing with the 'landscape archaeology' of prehistoric Britain, and that both read as being centrally concerned with the reconstruction of religious lifeways but without ever considering the term are Bradley's *An Archaeology of Natural Places* (2000) and Edmonds' *Ancestral Geographies of the Neolithic* (1999). Ian Hodder and Scott Hutson's hugely influential distillation of postprocessual archaeological epistemology and method, *Reading the Past* (2003), neither considers religion in the past, nor has an entry for religion in its index. While, the classic anthology of key postprocessual texts, *Interpretive Archaeology: A Reader* (Thomas, 2000), includes index entries on feminism, ideology and functionalism, but nothing on religion. One of the foremost theoreticians of postprocessual or interpretative archaeology, Julian Thomas, in his *Archaeology and Modernity* (2004), has directly and at length convincingly argued the need for contemporary archaeologists to escape contingent modernist and secular paradigms of thought in order to recapture the authenticity of the past, but without once ever using the word 'religion' in this context.

However, if the term 'religion' has not been utilized or considered to any great extent by archaeologists, there have been many other terms that have been applied to the material data in a seeming attempt to archaeologically engage with an analogous area of human life. By far the most common synonym used in religion's stead has been 'ritual'. 'Ritual' has been useful to archaeologists in a way that 'religion' perhaps never could, predominantly because ritual can be described as an embodied practice that may leave distinct and durable material traces. It is an area of social life that may be largely grounded in the material world of things, bodies and objects, while the broader and less concrete term 'religion' has often had connotations of interiority, thought and insubstantial belief. In this way, rituals may be thought to leave material clues for the archaeologist to uncover, and hence they may be recognizable and observable in the material record, while religion may not. In practice, however, the adoption of the term ritual over the larger and more inclusive category of religion has sometimes led the two concepts to be conflated in the archaeological literature, with the whole sphere of human religiosity being steadily and imperceptibly reduced to the single act of ritual (see esp. Garwood et al., 1991a). In this case, there has been a tendency to mistake the part for the whole, to define implicitly the larger category of religion by only one of its elements. The concept of ritual, when used in religion's stead, or without any reference to the wider religious context within which ritual occurs, often leaves the archaeological literature populated with a dehumanized series of ritual actions, performed by mindless human actors existing in a seemingly secularized and functionalist world devoid of any levels of religious meaning, value or experience (see esp. Tilley, 1996a).

Hence from the outset, it can be seen that there are real, substantial and numerous theoretical and practical difficulties in attempting to reconstruct traces of religion from within the archaeological record, to 'make speechless bones and ochre say something about religious belief' (Trompf, 2005, p. 240). These difficulties centre on the problem of the material identification of religion, and its derivatives such as ritual. Most importantly, this attempt to extract the larger (religion) from the smaller (its material correlates), has led at times to a conflation of the two in archaeological thinking and writing. At worst this has resulted in the concept of religion as a dynamic and immediate system of beliefs and practices, as a lived phenomenon, and the problem of its identification through material residue becoming fused as one. At times, the result of this conflation of categories has been the creation of a methodological confusion as to what religion is.

For instance, particular material categories such as graves, ritual objects and monuments have been linked commonly with the disembodied terms 'religion' or 'ritual'. This 'terminological shorthand' (Garwood et al., 1991a, p. vii) has created a confused baseline of empirical correlates that says much about archaeologist's presuppositions and assumptions about religion, but has done little to offer a way of theorizing the natures and roles of religious life in the archaeological past or its identification in the material record. Referring to ritual, Garwood and colleagues (1991a, p. vii) make the point that the unthinking correlation of material categories with abstract concepts of ritual allows little scope for a useful definition of ritual or theorizing about the role ritual played in past social life:

> [T]he material identification of ritual, for archaeological purposes, is really a methodological problem predicated upon the particular conceptions of ritual and the particular theoretical understanding of material culture that are adopted. Though material matters must dominate archaeological thinking, the starting point for such thinking clearly lies beyond the immediate material domain.

Religion must be theorized as a realm of human life and social behaviour that exists in and off itself, and to do this archaeologists must look beyond easy assumptions about its material identification.

As noted, this conflation of religion as a living system that encompasses many aspects of human individual and social existence, and its material correlates has led to a linking of particular aspects of the archaeological past with the religious. Such aspects have classically included graves and burials (including grave goods), monuments, and art, which have then been considered as generally 'non-functional' according to modern economic and utilitarian benchmarks. This particularistic approach to the material identification of religion has resulted in other spheres of human life such as economics, diet, subsistence, domestication, urbanism and trade as being most commonly thought of as having little, if anything, to do with religious life. Rather, they are interpreted according to 'functional' rationales.

Ian Hodder's work at Catalhoyuk (2006; 2010a; 2010b; Hodder and Meskell, 2010) presents one notable and recent move away from this overly narrow approach to religion in the archaeological record. Drawing on an interdisciplinary team of archaeologists, natural scientists, anthropologists and theologians, Hodder remarks that many of the spheres where religious activity was eventually tentatively identified were not at all obviously associated with religion in the minds of the archaeologists at the outset (2010a, p. 26). Hodder's painstakingly detailed and meticulous excavation of the domestic homes at Catalhoyuk has revealed a series of mostly self-contained and largely self-sufficient houses that each appear to memorialize elements of the wider cosmos through ritualized activities that were part of everyday life. Evidence for these rituals includes the periodic application of plaster and wall art, the inclusion of parts of hunted, dangerous animals such as bull's horns within the walls and internal features, the deposition of valuable objects such as obsidian flakes in 'hidden' hoards, and the burial and sometimes reburial of corpses under homes, including the plastering of human skulls. Religious activity appears to be so prevalent throughout the archaeology that 'the houses at Catalhoyuk and all the activities that took place in them were seamlessly religious, social and practical' (Hodder, 2010b, p. 17; 2006, pp. 135–40). This implies that information about religious activity and life may be recoverable from a much wider spectrum of the material past than many archaeologists might at first suppose; the crucial step is to make the decision to look for it.

However inspiring Hodder's research program at Catalhoyuk may be, in the vast majority of cases where only certain types of archaeological material data have been examined as pertaining possibly to the religious, this has resulted in a partial and particularized view of the past, a view that has been detrimental to the potential for the interpretation of larger religious worlds.

It should be noted, however, that easy assumptions as to which particular categories of archaeological and material data may pertain to the religious have by no means been unique to the discipline of archaeology. As we have seen above, those who study religion have also, at times, been blinded by prejudices relating to religion vis-à-vis materiality. In his consideration of the origins of religion Trompf (2005, p. 189) notes the dangers of an approach that looks for some single material signs of religion in prehistory, and which then delimits religion to a few technologically primitive signs indicating its origins and early existence. These attempts to define religion too narrowly can be seen as a reflection of the systemizing endeavours of the nineteenth-century anthropological theorists of religion such as Tylor, Spencer and Frazer which may 'come flooding back in cramped situations like this' (Trompf, 2005, p. 189). In fact, in looking at the prehistoric forms and origins of religion, Trompf considers much wider categories of evidence than many in either the disciplines of study in religion or archaeology are accustomed. For instance, tool manufacturing, signs of ritualized conflict, payback, the socio-ethical dimensions of early food sharing, trade, and the cooperative basis needed for the remarkable human migrations from Asia to far South America and crossing by sea to Australia are all considered prior to turning attention to more particularistic and commonplace aspects such as rock art, cult, burial and monuments (Trompf, 2005, pp. 205–24). His notion that the earliest religion may have 'crystallized' to some degree around the necessity of violence, group solidarity, hunting and the warrior ethos is interesting as a balance to the overly narrow and particular approaches to finding religion in the material record, utilized commonly by archaeologists.

One classic example of a sphere of the material past that has been commonly identified as pertaining self-evidently to religion, to the exclusion of most other spheres, is the archaeology of death, in particular of burial. Archaeologists have at times treated death as the sum of all religious life and religious belief in the past (see Insoll, 2004a, p. 66) and this has resulted in a diminishing of the visibility and importance of religion in the great majority of archaeological record. Not only has religion effectively been marginalized from other non-death contexts, but the very concept of the importance and position of religion in the past has subtly been shaped by archaeologist's views on the social role and meaning of death (an emotional experience that in the West is usually apprehended with fear), with funerary rituals (public performances of wealth and status) and funerary monuments (public performances of wealth and status ossified, made permanent and given materiality). A brief examination of the changing attitudes of archaeologists towards the social function and role of death and burial will serve to illustrate this point.

The relationships between processual archaeological theories of social life and religion will be explored in detail in the next chapter, but we can note here that both classic processual and most postprocessual considerations of the role of death in the archaeological record emphasized the nature of funerary rites and funerary monuments as being symbolic of social status, or embodied and material means of social negotiation, rather than as indicative of elements of religious life. For instance, the influential work of Ucko in the 1960s interpreted burial and funerary rites as a set of primarily symbolic social acts that enhanced the status and prestige of the person or people who were doing the burial, rather than the wider religious life of the society or deceased (Ucko, 1969). In a number of studies, Ucko used ethnographic material collected from Australian Aboriginal cultures from the Western Desert to interpret a wide collection of funerary remains from mid-second millennium BCE north Wales. The impression from his and later accounts is that the paraphernalia surrounding death and burial in the past (the rites, the rituals, feasts, displays of consumption) were performed primarily in order for those left behind to secure their rights to the property or social capital of the deceased/ancestor. This sociological interpretation of the 'function' of the material remains of death in the archaeological record was taken up by influential proponents of processual archaeology such as Lewis Binford (see Binford, 1971; 1972a), and remained a central interpretative paradigm through the succeeding decades.

According to such functionalist interpretations, death and burials, although being acknowledged as spheres of life somehow connected with the religious, were interpreted as symbolic of the dynamics of power within social life. In the manner reminiscent of Durkheim's sociology of religion, ritual and religion served to mask and further other, more essential, social functions, rather than being a valid category of cultural life sui generis. Hence, one of the most exciting methodological developments in archaeology in the 1970s was the idea that the materiality of death and burial could be used to elucidate social structure. As will be explained in the following chapter, one related circumstance was that the place held by religion, under the rubric 'ritual', in archaeological reconstructions did come to be theorized explicitly by processual archaeologists. Yet, this theorization was based upon a reductive scheme where ritual, and by implication religion, came to be considered as primarily a form of social communication that functioned to ensure social equilibrium.

From the 1980s there was a move in archaeological theory towards looking at how the rituals and monuments of death and burial actually mediated the ongoing creation of social life, rather than simply reflecting a reified harmonious society. For some Marxist inspired archaeologists, funerary rites and the materiality of burial were seen as systems of social non-verbal communication that could be interpreted not only as fossilized testaments to past social structure, but as active players in the ongoing creation and perpetration of that social structure in the past (for the classic text, see Shanks and Tilley, 1982). These methodological approaches to the archaeology of death were influenced by Marxist theory that saw the ritual elements of ancient death and burial as manifestations of ideology and social control. Classic examples of this approach were Parker-Pearson's examinations of changing Victorian burial practices in England, and the changing material nature of burial in Jutland between 500 BCE and 500 CE (1982, pp. 99–113; 1984). Both of these case studies saw changing types of burial being related to changing ways of legitimizing and perpetuating the shifting socio-economic order. So, in such cases the archaeology of death became an examination of how the material culture of death and burial became an ideological 'resource' or 'weapon' used by the elite in the constant creation and perpetuation of unequal modes of social life.

Importantly, Parker-Pearson did acknowledge the primary need for an archaeologist to know something of a culture's beliefs and attitudes towards death and burial, their religious views, before they could hypothesize the roles of burial rituals and monuments in wider social life. He termed this knowledge of how a society structured and thought about its world 'c-transforms', and noted its importance in looking at the burial practices of Cambridge, a highly differentiated society that nevertheless buried its dead in an egalitarian, unostentatious manner (Parker-Pearson, 1982; for a discussion see Hodder and Hutson, 2003, pp. 2–5). Basically, to understand the role of the materiality of death and burial in cultural change one must have some prior understanding of some of that culture's attitudes to life, death and the relationship between the two. Such knowledge clearly implied an understanding of a culture's views on the nature of the human being and their relationship with the wider cosmos both before and after death, basically their *religious* worldview. Parker-Pearson has subsequently applied, with great success, a similar perspective to the megalithic ritualized landscape surrounding Stonehenge, Woodhenge and Durrington Walls in southern England. However, the term 'religion' itself was still not used, and once again, religion, by implication, was reduced to one secondary subsystem in a larger process of social communication and negotiation.

This particularistic approach, which has reduced past religion to the domain of death and burial, can be seen as having been taken to its logical and extreme conclusion with Parker-Pearson's suggestion that it was the fearful appreciation of death itself that provided the very origins of religious belief in the past. This mono-historical vision of the archaeology of religion, and even the origins of religion, rested upon the hypothesis that it was the human emotional apprehension of death that became the very existential impetus for the origin of religious belief in general and the various world religions in particular (Parker-Pearson, 2001, pp. 203–19). Through examining a cross-section of the archaeological material culture surrounding death, such as graves, grave goods and monuments, Parker-Pearson suggested that the emotive experience of death, fear especially, was not only the original cause of religious belief, but determined later religious change as well. In support, he traced an evolution of the material culture of death from the Neolithic through to the end of the Bronze Age. In doing so he suggested that there was a progression from ancestor figurines and a 'cult of skulls' in Neolithic Jericho which gave way to the worship of deistic figures in early state and urban Mesopotamia and Egypt, through the medium of heroic human ancestor gods. He also noted that the creation of the cosmic cities and monumental edifices of religious power of Bronze Age Mesopotamia and Egypt, where a celestial cosmic sphere was reflected materially on earth, might have originated in the building of graves and monuments to the dead. Parker-Pearson's implied suggestion that it is the changes in the actual materiality of death (graves, figures of deities, monuments) that drive new modes of religious consciousness is novel in granting an element of creative agency to the material culture of death and burial. However, more apparent is the conviction that religion is characterized by interiority and belief. Also apparent is the extremely particular approach of this extreme example, where literally the whole spectrum of human religious life, both individual and social, is reduced to its most easily identifiable material correlates (the archaeology of death and burial) and grounded in a particularly modern interior and emotive appreciation of death characterized by fear.

It can be seen that religion has mostly been left inadequately theorized by archaeologists, and that it has been subsumed by derivative terms such as 'ideology' and 'ritual' and that its identification in the past has been reduced to commonplace assumptions about the material record. Still, the least useful but possibly the most familiar, situation in which 'religion' has been inadvertently abused by archaeologists is when it has been used indiscriminately to describe that which is not understood. In such cases, religion and its supposed synonyms, such as 'symbolic' and especially 'ritual', have been employed to describe and categorize material artefacts and relationships in the archaeological record that either defy rational functionalist interpretation, or are just plain baffling. In such situations, the religious has become a descriptive category for that which is difficult, and religion is useful only as an 'all-purpose explanation used where nothing else comes to mind' (Bruck, 1999, p. 313).

This use of religion as a last resort for the perplexed archaeologist is so notorious as to have become a cliché, cited most memorably in Paul Bhan's humorous, but at the same time perfectly serious, observation that a confounded archaeologist can always use the terms 'religious' or 'ritual' to explain away the objects which they cannot otherwise explain (1989). As Renfrew has noted, if an artefact or feature cannot be explained in rational functionalist terms then it may well be given a ritual function, with 'ritual' then becoming a residual category defined by the absence of 'a good alternative explanation' (1994a, p. 52). In such cases, religion is correlated covertly with everything that is non-functional, irrational, strange, inexplicable or simply odd, and can quickly become the 'dustbin' for any inexplicable data (Hultkrantz, 1978, p. 27, quoted in Insoll, 2004a, p. 12).

Although flippant, such remarks underlie a very real and specific way that many archaeologists have perceived artefacts and sites that may have potential religious frames of meaning attached to them. Recovered material objects and things that are not understood, that have no apparent use or function, are categorized as being useless or functionless (Hodder, 1982a, p. 64). In such cases, terms such as 'religious' are used as a form of negative empiricism, to define as non-functional all that is not understood and, by extension, to describe as 'non-religious' all that is utilitarian and explicable. In such cases an equation between the polarities functional and non-functional, domestic and ritual, secular and religious or even profane and sacred is established and maintained effortlessly. Such attitudes have led commonly to a situation in which the religious, and hence non-functional and even irrational, realm is passed over by empiricist archaeologists as 'speculative and non-scientific' (Hodder and Hutson, 2003, p. 26). Speculative it certainly is, as is all archaeological interpretation, but why it should also be seen as being somehow non-scientific is problematic.

Overall, then, it can be seen that religion has lagged far behind other areas in archaeological theorizing. Certainly, the great majority of post-1950s social scientific and methodologically self-conscious archaeologists have tended to ignore the possibilities for an archaeology of the religious. The term 'religion' has been dropped quietly from much archaeological literature, if it happened to be included in the first place, and the religious spheres of human life have been reduced down to a number of smaller and more specific terms such as 'ideology' or 'ritual'. When religion and its correlates have been considered, there have been difficult and serious problems with their archaeological identification from within the material record.

Particularly problematic has been the adoption by archaeologists of overly narrow definitions, or implicit assumptions, as to the nature of religion, for instance, the equation of religion solely with death and burial. These can be seen as mono-explanatory understandings of religion that confine the religious life to a limited sphere of human activity such as death, burial and the afterlife. In such cases, certain rarefied, usually somehow extraordinary or abnormal, elements of the archaeological data are recognized as being in some way concerned with religion. This comfortably leaves the great remainder of human life in the past to be interpreted according to functionalist logic, usually in accordance with a reductive theory that considers religious life as a secondary derivative of somehow more real and underlying economic and technological processes. Hence, at its most serious this absence and misuse of the term religion has led to both implicit and explicit reductive and functionalist perceptual schemes (Lane, 1986, pp. 181–92) that have coloured and severely disfigure the types of pasts archaeologists reconstruct and write about. This can be seen in situations where terms such as 'ritual' or 'religious' have been abused in much of the archaeological literature by serving as catchall terms used to classify unclassifiable material without any apparent function. In such cases, religion, if any elaboration is made at all, is reduced to specific and limited spheres of life in the past characterized by their abnormality or discordance with the larger sum of archaeological evidence and narrative.

Yet, practical issues are not the sole reasons for the unwillingness of archaeologists to look for religion in the archaeological record. A priori conceptual assumptions about the nature of religion appear to play as much a role in removing religion from the archaeological past as do the physical and theoretical problems with its material identification. In fact, as suggested above, practical problems with the identification of religion in the archaeological record often rest upon assumed methodological theories, or implicit and even unconscious biases, about the nature of religion and material culture.

The failure of archaeologists to uncover religion in the material record is not simply the result of the manifold difficulties in identifying religious behaviour from within the archaeological data, although, as noted above, such practical problems are real and have played an important role. The philosophical context within which archaeology arose and has continued to be practised has also hindered archaeologists in addressing the existence and role of religion. An a priori concern with a particular form of objectivity, one that excludes the religious elements of human life as subjective, irrational and somehow irreconcilable with science, has been particularly detrimental to attempts at creating archaeologies of religion. In effect, and perhaps with justification, archaeological attempts to envision an objective past have, until recently, privileged a secular worldview, one in which religion is absent or, at most, devalued greatly. Yet, this neglect of religion in archaeological interpretations has presented the present with a critically inadequate and thus distorted impression of the past, a past that has sometimes been created in seeming mirror image of the idealized secular and modernist 'now'.

Although archaeology as a discipline has made great advances in its methodologies and practical skills, archaeologists may often lack a self-awareness of the intellectual and cultural contexts in which they practise their discipline in the present: what Gadamer (1975) has called the tyranny of hidden prejudices. It can certainly be argued that the absence of religion in archaeological reconstructions of the past is as much a reflection of the practitioners themselves as it is of any limitation in the evidence they discuss. This is to say that modern academics might not deem religion important or useful in understanding humans, in understanding the *real* processes and drives that propel individuals and societies through time, and hence it has been omitted from archaeological vocabulary.

Certainly, the data that archaeologists examine is constrained not only by the real, objective world independent of its observation, but this data is also dependant on an archaeologist's own theories and assumptions about this world, how they wish to observe it and how they wish to categorize it (see Hodder and Hutson, 2003, p. 18). In brief, the theories that archaeologists espouse about the past are constrained and dependant on their own cultural contexts, their social and cultural worldviews. So, in attempting to understand just why religion has been so inadequately represented in archaeological literature, the condition of modernity, under which the majority of archaeologists function, must at least begin to be taken into consideration. The modern paradigm most archaeologists work under is one that usually excludes various forms of meaning from the material that they study (J. Thomas, 2004), religious meaning being one of these.

One of the fundamental filters that condition how moderns view their world is the Cartesian dichotomy between the subject and the object, under which it is assumed that the object, the external world, is neutral and value free up until the point when a rational subject, our internal consciousness, imposes its own meaning upon it (Crosby, 1997). The method of giving meaning to the world is characterized as the dispassionate, rational and analytical examination of neutral and value-free material phenomena. The world is a 'blank sheet' to be rationally and dispassionately examined, and any other relationships that human minds may have with things, symbolic, ethical, sentimental or religious, are built 'on top' of this primary rational and dispassionate examination of a neutral backdrop. Religious, ethical, symbolic and emotional modes of experience are secondary and derivative: they occur after the fact. These modes of experience are seen rarely as being primary, immediate or coactive with the very act of perception itself, as suggested in post-Heidegger phenomenology (Heidegger, 1962, p. 101). Julian Thomas has argued that the aim of archaeology, a discipline connected intimately to modern experience and indeed a 'distillation' of a modern sensibility, is to first strip away these religious, aesthetic, sentimental relationships with the world prior to any objective and scientific account being made (2004, p. 59).

If this is the case, then the archaeological method, in being scientific, dispassionate and based upon Cartesian rationality, will struggle to be able to provide interpretation of meaning or value in the past, least of all religious meaning. Instead, archaeological attempts to give objective, rational, dispassionate order to things produce a system of knowledge that is profoundly modern and, as such, secular and non-religious. Such methods provide much valuable and crucial data on rational abstractions about the past, such as chronology, manufacture, underlying social 'functions' (concepts of which the inhabitants of the past themselves would most likely have had little notion), but it cannot give us information about other frames of meaning such as the religious.

Again, Julian Thomas (2004, p. 65) argues:

Ethics, law or aesthetics are difficult to reduce to pure rationality, and this means that in order to comply with the demands of the Enlightenment they must be emptied of their content or be declared to be non-scientific. What this means is that human knowledge must take a form that can be addressed using an abstract and formal epistemology, or it must be relegated to a lesser category of thinking, alongside rhetoric, superstition or fantasy.

One could quite justifiably add religion to this list.

The sheer extent to which modernist presuppositions have managed to erase all considerations of religion from the work of most archaeologists can be illustrated by the very work of Thomas himself, who explores this problem and minutely details its origins and conditions, but still ignores religion in his examination of archaeology and modernity. Thomas acknowledges that the philosophical outlook of modernity is concerned with the decline of religious conviction, at least in the Western world. He argues explicitly the ways in which philosophy, science and the kind of secularized rationality (even archaeology itself) have come to replace religious meaning and tradition as the predominant and commonsense way of thinking about and giving meaning to the world, and he acknowledges how modern assumptions have hobbled archaeological attempts to recreate radically different pasts (J. Thomas, 2004, p. 40). Yet, he completely ignores religion as a possible field of expanded archaeological enquiry and, in a fashion typical of the discipline, the term 'religion' is barely mentioned in his writing.

The intellectual procedures of modernity, when used outside of a modern context, may be inappropriate for reconstructing past worlds in a faithful manner. Archaeology uses its methods and philosophical assumptions to seek to establish an order among the data it uncovers. However, there is a strong possibility that this may be an order, an imposition of meaning, which the people who inhabited the past would have found strange and meaningless. It is certainly useful for archaeologists to acknowledge the past as having possibly been other and different from the secular present. In order to begin to approach religion in the archaeological record it is perhaps necessary to be mindful of the differences between the contemporary world of secular modernity and that of traditional societies where many aspects of life may relate to explicitly religious cosmologies and themes. Certainly, it would seem prudent to do so when framing specific imaginative and speculative hypotheses about the roles and natures of the material evidences they uncover from the past. For:

> [T]he past is dead and we cannot reconstruct it 'as it was'. There is always a gap. It was the recognition of that gap and its intellectual consequences that led David Clark to suggest nearly thirty years ago that archaeology had lost its innocence. Since then, we also seem to have lost out nerve. We have lost sight of the fact that, for all of our technique and our rhetoric to the contrary, the study of the past is an act of the imagination, bound by conventions and by evidence, but creative nonetheless. (Edmonds, 1999, p. x)

However, this is not to argue that archaeologists should attempt to practise 'non-modern' archaeology, or attempt to engage with the past through non-empirical means, such as naïve empathic phenomenological intuitions or schemes of revealed knowledge derived from a supposed transcendent source, in order to access past religious systems. It is not the place of archaeologists to experience the past religiously, although it could be argued that this is to some degree inevitable. However, what is worrying is that this 'blinkering' effect of modernity does determine *the types* of knowledge that archaeologists will most readily and commonly search for in the past. The danger is that religion has been seen as a lesser category of thinking, experiencing, practising and doing, one that is inferior and less important than rational, objective or scientific understandings of the past.

Indeed, in not acknowledging the possibilities for interpreting essentially religious frames of meaning in their data, archaeologists may actually contribute to the continuation and proliferation of hidden assumptions. No matter how objective, scientific and rational archaeologists may attempt to be in their reconstructions, they always at some point have to *interpret* the data. Yet, if the types of meaning that they impose on the past through their interpretation are founded by their own assumptions about the world (capitalistic, rational, secular, for example), archaeologists may not be sufficiently self-critical to realize that this is colouring their view of the cultures they are recovering and reconstructing through their careful scientific method.

The shifts in the reading of prehistoric landscapes and monuments in northwest Europe is a case in point. The development of postprocessual landscape archaeology is examined in some detail in Chapter 4, but it is instructive to note here the shift that has taken place in intellectual understandings of the function of megalithic monuments from the Neolithic and pre-Celtic periods. Early and middle twentieth-century authors, such as Childe (1925) and Renfrew (1973), working under utilitarian models that privileged explanatory factors such as the projection of political power and coercive control, regularly interpreted the function of prominent megaliths in the landscape as territorial markers, embodied semiotic reference points that controlled and marked ownership over surrounding resources. More recent interpretations have stressed instead the use of monuments as not solely markers of controlled territory, but also of memory, kinship and myth (see esp. Edmonds, 1999). This change in interpretative style is explored further in Chapter 4, it is enough here to note the central importance of archaeologist's worldview flavouring the supposedly objective interpretation of data.

Frameworks of meaning are imposed upon the 'neutral' data in even the seemingly simplest and most self-evident forms of archaeological interpretation, all of which involve the application of imaginative speculation and hermeneutics (Hodder and Hutson, 2003, pp. 26–8). Taking a clay vessel as an example, the function of such an object, even its seemingly simplest utilitarian function, cannot be determined without some idea of the ends involved in its use, and these ends will be ranked according what the interpreter considers to be more or less important. Is the function of a vessel to store food stuffs for later human consumption, or as an offering to an ancestor or deity, or both? A self-evident frame of meaning may suppose that the vessels function as a receptacle for this-worldly sustenance is more important than that of a receptacle for storing otherworldly sustenance, but this is a position based upon contingent values and assumptions. In addition, before function is addressed, categories of objects must be ascertained, and such categories are already laden with meanings. For instance, pots for holding food for human consumption are categorized as 'storage vessels', rather than 'vessels of communication' between human and non-human realms, 'votive offerings', 'sacrifices', or 'cosmological symbols' (see Astor-Aguilera, 2010, for the alternative interpretation). Similarly, even the hypotheses as to these categories and function of an object will imply some assumed suspicion of its meaning. Hence, no matter how practical and utilitarian the attitude is adopted by the archaeologist, it involves an unavoidable act of hermeneutics, of interpretative guessing about the nature of the inhabitants of the past, of accessing vicariously their minds. In such cases, it is doubtful whether speculation on religion can ever truly be avoided.

For instance, Claude Levi-Strauss when visiting the archaeological sites of the Indus Valley at Mohenjo-Daro and Harappa noticed the planned, regular streets, the neat drains, identical dwellings, and, to his eye, utilitarian and flimsy art and general lack of decoration and embellishment in the material culture. He saw it as an 'art devoid of mystery and uninspired by any deep faith' (1973, p. 163). His somewhat intuitive interpretation of what he saw as utilitarian material culture was certainly a product of his own modernist position. Yet, all these 'non-religious' characteristics of Indus Valley material culture can, and have, been interpreted as evidence for an early proto-Hindu/Buddhist religious system, one that valued ritual purity through ablutions, order, mathematical planning, the depreciation of the human form, and the recapitulation of the divinely ordered macrocosmos to the human microcosmic world through the creation of ordered urban planning (for a critical discussion, see Kenoyer, 1998).

So, it appears that archaeologists, like all academics, will never be able to be completely value free and 'modern' in their approach to interpretation. The very approach of modernism will inject implicit biases into their methods and conclusions. If archaeologists have ignored religion because of their modern and secular prejudices, then their interpretations given may at times say more about modern archaeologists and the present than they do about past worlds. This is certainly true if one examines the development of archaeological theories and methods over the past century, and charts the long line of modern interpretative frames (functionalist, Marxist, economic reductionist, cognitive psychological, socio-biological to name a few) that have been used to 'explain away' past religious belief and practice (see Chapter 3).

The other side of this question needs to be considered as well. It could well be argued that the very attempt to archaeologically identify past religion is itself but one more interpretative filter, this time derived from the world of late modernity where religion appears to be reasserting itself. Religion is again becoming more visible and perhaps important on the world stage, and there is a resurgence of interest in issues relating to religion, if not religious belief itself (Dillon, 2003; Lincoln, 2003). Examples include the increased interaction between religion and national politics (see Berger, 1999; J. Thomas, 2004), religious fundamentalism (Santosh, 2004), the influence of postmodern and subjective epistemologies, new religious movements and the 'new age' (Possami, 2005). It must be noted that in all of these spheres archaeology itself plays an important role. Hence, it is likely that in time archaeology will increasingly mirror these larger cultural currents. A brief consideration of the phenomenon of 'pseudoarchaeology' will serve to illustrate both the resurgence of a species of 'religiously engaged' archaeology in response to contemporary issues, as well as the problems of an attempted archaeology *of* religion becoming, instead, archaeology *as* religion.

From the 1960s onwards there has been a global increase in pseudoarchaeological interpretations of the past, especially in North America, Europe and South Asia (Lefkowitz, 2006). Difficult to define, pseudoarchaeologies include wide variety of various 'new age', utopian, fundamentalist, politically motivated or nationalist interpretations of the often religious past made through a limited and non-contextualized 'picking and choosing' of often misinterpreted, archaeological data. Unlike the majority of published work produced by academic-based archaeologists, pseudoarchaeology may self-consciously appeal to the imagination of the reader and its claims often attempt to provide some existential meaning for the individual, to have 'some meaningful connection with . . . religion' (Lefkowitz, 2006, p. 197; Rountree, 2001).

In addition, pseudoarchaeological work often defines itself in antagonistic opposition to orthodox scientific and rationalist archaeology, and its interpretation of the past often presents the viewer with an exciting and esoteric vista 'replete with arcane knowledge and significance' (Jordan, 2006, p. 109). Pseudoarchaeological interpretations appear to appeal to both the general human attraction to the fantastic and exotic, as well as to actually provide quasi-religious, even spiritual, narratives about the relationship between the contemporary modern world and its religio-historic origins. Pseudoarchaeology often produces a cosmological religious narrative in modernist for, including fantastic origin stories, mythic fables about the rise and fall of Golden Age civilizations, divine retribution, mysterious wonders and the ability to use the hidden wisdom gleaned from the archaeological past to 'redeem' the present. Examples of quasi-religious cosmological narratives in pseudoarchaeological works are numerous and varied, ranging from serious retellings of Plato's political metaphor of Atlantis, to examples of exceedingly creative contemporary mythmaking. The best-known example is, of course, Erik von Daniken's *Chariots of the Gods?* (1969), in which aliens, rather than angles, appear to hold the secrets of human origins and ends, which they have secreted throughout the world's archaeological record.

This is not to claim that all religiously motivated or 'spiritualistic' interpretations of archaeological data should necessarily be labelled as pseudoarchaeological. Different readings of the material past, say between neo-Pagans, secular archaeologists and committed Christians, can often be interpreted as examples of contested narratives cohering around a particular, usually high profile, site, such as Stonehenge or Catalhoyuk (for a case study that focuses on the contested site of Stonehenge, see Blain and Wallis, 2007). In such cases it is not necessarily always correct to state that a religiously motivated reading of a particular site is incorrect. For example, contemporary goddess followers may agree with the rather fantastic interpretations of the Neolithic Anatolian 'town' Catalhoyuk proposed by the archaeologist Mellaart, rather than that proposed by a far more rigorous and multidisciplinary researcher like Hodder (Rountree, 2007), although most archaeologists would probably claim that the evidence suggests otherwise. The contestation of sites of contemporary spiritual appeal should not necessarily be seen as a negative phenomenon in which the objectivity of archaeology is threatened by subjective religiosities. Instead, it may sometimes be a symptom of the enduring mythological and spiritual appeal that many archaeological sites continue to have in the present day. This can be reinforced by the absence of notable public attempts by archaeologist to breath religious life into their reconstructions of the past, to reaccess the religiously significant elements of the modern experience of such locales (for discussion, see Carmichael et al., 1994, pp. 3–21), a reality that many archaeologists are increasingly aware of and proactive about addressing (see Hodder, 2006, chapter 1).

However, the dangers of the pseudoarchaeological overemphasizing of the religious characteristics of the past must be noted. These include the commonplace tendency for well-known ancient cultures to become the religious 'other' for modern commentators, repositories for comforting religious fantasies and cultural myths. An example of this is the ancient Maya. Since its discovery, the archaeology of the Maya has been a prime 'emotional Shangrila' for those looking for a place where they can pin their own religious hopes and fantasies (Webster, 2006). It was only with the decipherment of Mayan language and script, actually a move away from pure archaeology, that comforting assumptions, almost cultural myths, about the Maya (priest-kings, a symbolic and mystical script, a peaceful and unwarlike culture, pyramid urban centres as hierophanies) began to be dispelled (Webster, 2006, pp. 143–53). A similar process could be outlined in the history of the archaeology of many cultures. Ancient Egypt has had its archaeological remains interpreted as the repositories of religious, mystical and esoteric knowledge (gnosis), for far longer than the discipline of archaeology itself has existed (see Jordan, 2006). The pre- or proto-historic remains of the Indus Valley culture in Pakistan and India are good examples of this process of religious projection today (Larson, 1995).

This connection between archaeology, religion and contemporary identity raises the issue of explicitly 'religious' or 'confessional' types of archaeology. An example is committed religious insiders doing archaeology (or more commonly interpreting archaeological data) with the express purpose of either validating the truth claims of certain religions, or even of unearthing religious insight (see Insoll, 1999, p. 8). Practitioners of religious archaeology come from many differing perspectives, from biblical scholars (for a recent history, see Davis, 2004) to neo-Pagan archaeologists (Wallis, 2002; 2003), and it is difficult to do justice to this complex topic in so limited a space (see Wallis, 2003). It must be stated though, that in such cases archaeology can become subordinate to a religious worldview and find itself being used as a tool of a specific religious tradition rather than a way of understanding a range of past realities, including human religiosity.

On occasion this has led to archaeological research being used as a weapon or tool in religious controversy and violence, often closely tied to contemporary nationalism. A case in point is the corruption of the archaeology of South Asia by politically motivated religious groups. Hindu revisionist historians in India have used archaeological reports of continuities of material culture from the Neolithic, through the Indus Valley culture and up unto modern times to imply a level of cultural continuity, nationalistic unity and eternal Hindu hegemony over the landscape of India, as embodied in the stories of deities such as Rama or the Pandava brothers (Witzel, 2006). Through imposing a modern and anachronistic form of Hinduism on to the archaeological past, revisionist historians have identified particular ethnic and cultural groups and religious traditions with the very land of India, and thus reaffirm those people's and culture's superiority in the modern political arena. In such cases, archaeological data has been used to supplement historical texts that condone or promote the exclusion and even victimization of non-Hindu religious groups (Cunningham and Lewer, 2000). B. B. Lal (2002a; 2002b), the former Director General of the Archaeological Survey of India, has used the term *blut und boden*, a patriotic connection between one's blood and the soil of one's homeland, in connection with supposed religious continuity in the archaeological record of the subcontinent.

It can be seen that without a committed attempt by archaeologists to engage with religion in the past, and especially with religious plurality and change, the material can be misinterpreted to serve nationalistic, and even quasi-fascist, ends (for the Nazi use of archaeology for similar ends Arnold, 2006). In light of such cynical and extreme misuses, the neglect of religion in the discipline of archaeology is unhelpful in that it prevents both the understanding of past human religious life in the archaeological record and leaves this field of enquiry entirely wide open to the speculations of others. Practitioners of pseudoarchaeology have exploited these gaps, a few of whom have malevolent motivations. Although such pseudoarchaeological attempts to breathe religious colour into the archaeological past may consist of fantastic and imagined fictions, or consist of creative forms of contemporary myth-building and appropriations of the past by new religious movements, they may also be motivated by opportunistic nationalistic, exclusivist or chauvinist politics. Parker-Pearson put this problem well when he stated: 'If archaeologists abandon their efforts to reconstruct the big picture through their own master narratives they will be trampled underfoot by the many others who are far less concerned with honest evaluation of the actual evidence and more determined to impose their politically and motivationally suspect visions of the past and thence the future' (2001, p. 217). Archaeologists cannot really afford to leave consideration of religion outside of their examinations of material culture. Religion and materiality are not mutually exclusive. In fact, materiality and religion have never been separate, and to acknowledge this is to widen the horizons of archaeological research.

* * *

In this chapter, we have explored the received polarity between material culture and religion from the perspectives of both disciplines. It has been shown how a disjunction between religiosity and material culture has been common to the intellectual climate within which the academic fields of archaeology and studies in religion both emerged. The ambivalent nature of material culture, where it was used as a diagnostic tool in ascertaining the cultural and religious progression of differing cultures while at the same time being a sign of their spiritual backwardness, was noted. It was also shown how privileged visions of religion as interiority, belief and sacred experience, played a role in furthering this polarity, where true religion was seen as being a state of mind emancipated from the material world of action and embodiment.

For archaeologists, during the early premethodological days of the discipline religious cultures were either viewed within the prism of normative cultural–historical scholarship, or prehistoric cultures were ranked according to a cultural–evolutionary progression according to the nature of their material culture. Attempts at any archaeology of religion were scarce, however, even during this early period. Subsequently, the term religion was for the most part dropped from the great majority of archaeological writings and interpretations. Since this time, there have been a number of major epistemological barriers for any archaeological attempt at addressing religion within the material record. For instance, overly narrow visions of religion as pertaining to only one sphere of life have limited the nature of the evidence archaeologists have examined when considering religion, and the pervasive association of religion with belief has made it difficult to theorize how it may relate to the material world.

Practical problems certainly do abound for the successful archaeological uncovering of religion. It has been noted that the absence of theoretical hypotheses as to the relationship between religion and material culture has led to a situation in which a material category such as death has been assumed to relate to religious life according to the unacknowledged, intuitive assumptions held by the archaeologists themselves. This example can be extended to other forms of particularization surrounding material categories such as art, monuments and votive objects. Furthermore, such conflations of specific material categories with 'ritual', and hence with 'religion', have created a situation in which the certain elements of the material past have been assumed to pertain to religion, while the remainder does not. This tendency to divide the material record into 'functional' and 'religious' spheres has also allowed archaeologists to commonly label as religious any data which they are otherwise unable to categorize, that is, give a good utilitarian explanation for.

Furthering this problem, a priori assumptions about the nature of the past and the need to impose 'commonsense' rational and secular interpretative frameworks to its interpretation have revealed the deep and pervasive role that the biases of modernity have played in erasing considerations of religion from the material record. However, in the context of the world of late modernity, 'the religious' may itself be becoming a timely interpretative paradigm that filters the nature of archaeological interpretations. In this context, archaeologists do have a responsibility to the present to provide a balanced and disinterested image of the religious past. This is important, if merely, for the fact that it may help prevent others with less scrupulous agendas, such as those who utilize the archaeological record for profiteering or nefarious political and nationalistic ends, from doing so instead.

There has been a long-standing perception of contradiction between religion and the material, and this polarity is a problematic conceptual mode common to both studies in religion and archaeology. Yet, this historical and conceptual baggage is not sufficient cause to leave religion out of archaeological interpretations of the past. Having presented this problem and explored some of its intellectual origins, we have opened the way for a detailed examination of various archaeological schools of interpretation and their relationship to religion and material culture explored in Chapter 3.

3

Archaeologies of Religion

In order to understand the troubled relationship between archaeology and religion it is useful to look in at the history of archaeological attitudes and assumptions regarding the materiality of religion over the course of the twentieth century. Various schools of archaeological interpretation, such as the cultural–historical, anthropological, processual, environmental, cognitive and early postprocessual, are presented in this chapter and examined sequentially. The relationships between archaeology, religion, ritual and material culture are examined together, with the place held by religion in social life, and its interaction with materiality, considered especially. The overall failure to address religion in the archaeological record is attributed to theoretical assumptions drawn from Durkheimian functionalism and Marxist ideology that have coloured how both religion and material culture have been thought to act in society. Through the following pages these theoretical hindrances are examined in the context of the successive understanding of material culture that they have facilitated. In such a way, the problematic concepts of 'material culture' and 'religion', identified in the last chapter are looked at further and in more detail.

Throughout the twentieth century and beyond an emphasis on 'functionalism' in regard to religion, where religion is seen as a symptom of a larger social reality, and 'Marxism', where religion is conceived as an intrinsically false manifestation of other social processes, most usually ideology (see Lohse, 2007, p. 3), have both effectively prevented archaeologists from examining religion in its own terms. Unfortunately, this has meant that material culture has been theorized as either reflecting ossified belief-systems, or used as a medium of relatively inert ideological communication and contestation. These sometimes hidden theoretical assumptions have prevented the archaeological record from being examined as a locale of other forms of autonomous religious action and experience. They have also reduced the role of material culture in human social life to communication, to the transfer of discursive information. The emotional elements of human engagement with objects have been ignored, and instead material culture has been interpreted as being simply a signifier or solely symbolic. Other possible modes of perception that material things can evoke such as the immediately emotional, the somatic and even the numinous have been ignored.

It will be shown here how even newer cognitive and postprocessual archaeologies of religion have not escaped a functionalist or a Marxist position when addressing religion in the past either, and that to find a genuinely useful attempt at archaeologically engaging with the materiality of religion, one has to examine the phenomenology of landscape, which is the subject of Chapter 4.

The Marxist and functionalist context

Marxist and functionalist assumptions were the major influences determining how archaeologists treated religion during the first half of the twentieth century, as the discipline emerged out from the cultural–historical context of the late nineteenth century. Broadly, it can be generalized that a reliance on Marxist economic and ecological theory dominated archaeology in the half-century from 1900 to 1950, while a Durkheimian focus on culture as primarily a functionalist and adaptive mechanism dominated the 'new' and processual archaeological theories from 1950 to the 1980s.

From this period onward, interpretative and postprocessual archaeologists reworked these Marxist and functionalist themes in order to focus more specifically on issues of power, agency and contestation in the material record. For instance, the relationships between ideology, material culture and social reproduction were increasingly thought to be important and open to archaeological investigation through the 1980s and into the new millennium.

During the period up until the mid-1980s, however, these Marxist and functionalist biases effectively reduced archaeological considerations of religion, and largely erased them from a major portion of the archaeological record. An emphasis on functionalism in regard to religion, where religion was seen as symptom of larger social processes that acted to provide a 'hidden' social function, and Marxism, where religion was seen as an intrinsically false manifestation of social consciousness, a mostly unimportant by-product of larger social truths, both served effectively to prevent archaeologists from examining, or even considering, religion in its own terms. The persistent polarization between religion and functionality discussed in the previous chapter, which resulted in the flippant assumption that if the use of an artefact could not be determined then it must be somehow 'religious', was bolstered by the general functionalist assumptions of the early Marxist archaeologists. This served to confine supposed religious artefacts to the category of non-functional aberrations. Concurrently, Marxist inspired suspicions equating religion and ritual with hidden ideological communication and repressive social control have echoed down through all the major schools of twentieth-century archaeological theory through to today. In general, the result has been that religion has been ignored as either being irrelevant or unrecoverable.

But it is important to be aware that neither functionalist nor Marxist assumptions were theorized explicitly as formal archaeological methods until after the mid-century transformations in which archaeology attempted to recreate itself as a methodologically coherent discipline in the character of the social sciences (Watson et al., 1984). Functionalist assumptions formed the basis of processual systems theory, which reduced religion and ritual to a homeostatic regulating device (see Clarke, 1968). A Marxist bias towards materiality, and a consideration of religion as an unfortunate but useful by-product of inequality, was formalized by postprocessual archaeologists into distinct theoretical understandings of ritual as a repressive ideological tool utilized in the subjugation of populations by Machiavellian elites (Shanks and Tilley, 1982). So, for the bulk of the twentieth century, until at least the very late 1960s, both 'functionalism' and 'Marxism' must be understood, in the main, as generalized theoretical assumptions, or conceptual 'baggage', rather than as explicit methodological stances taken by researchers.

Such generalized Marxist attitudes can be traced to Marx's own views on the significance of religion in human life. Marx focused on religion as a secondary social institution rather than an autonomous sphere of human life of interest in itself: 'Man makes religion, religion does not make man' (Marx, 1844). In addition, Marx assumed that religion was an inward, belief-centred, emotively expressed phenomenon that appeared in response to inequalities in the material relations of production and consumption between people:

> But man is no abstract being squatting outside the world. Man is in the world of man, state, society. This state and this society produce religion, which is an inverted consciousness of the world, because they are an inverted world. (1844)

This religious, ideological, superstructure was secondary to and derivative of the material economic infrastructure. A cognate view can be seen expressed in the classic early twentieth-century works of Australian archaeologist Gordon Childe. His books *Man Makes Himself* (1937) and *What Happened in History* (1942) are some of the earliest attempts in archaeology of presenting a dynamic explanation of the underlying processes that shape culture. This active and empowered ethic ('Man makes himself') echoes clearly Marx's own efficacious perspective. Childe, however, did acknowledge human spiritual experiences, but was not optimistic about the ability of archaeologists to identify them in the past (1945), and his references to religion do not go beyond 'commonsense' material embodiments such as graves, temples and monuments. In fact, Childe's attitude to religion was very similar to Marx's own who, unlike many have supposed, was not unsympathetic to expressions of religion in themselves, and did not morally dismiss them as drug-induced illusions. For Marx (1844):

> Religious suffering is at one and the same time the expression of real suffering and a protest against real suffering. Religion is the sigh of the oppressed creature, the heart of a heartless world and the soul of soulless conditions. It is the opium of the people.

Opiates were, it should be remembered, used as a medicinal cure-all well into the twentieth century, and their use is still common today. Religion was all very well and good, it just wasn't as interesting or important as the underlying economic and material conditions that precipitated it.

Religion may be visible in human history, but for Marx this very visibility was a manifestation of false consciousness, and so religion was neither as influential, primary nor causative as the real materialist history that it masked. Yet, for Childe, the exact opposite was true. An archaeologist's spade had the ability to access directly the true 'material' stuff of history, the real bones of the past social leviathan, and so who, in this context, really needed to consider aspects of false consciousness such as religion (Childe, 1942)? If religion masked real materialist history, then archaeologists had the advantage of being able to dispense with the mask in their interpretations of the primary material evidence. Considerations of past religiosity would only obscure the truth, in the characteristic way that religion had done during all those long millennia until Marx had come to redeem the world.

Such a position certainly reflected a modernist presupposition that religion was somehow a false or derivative force in social life that holds no inherent explanatory power, or interest, in its own right. It was implied that thoughts, ideas, belief-systems, religious experiences and meanings, rituals, practices and expressions, all the 'superstructure' of a culture, were determined wholly by the productive and economic base, or the environmental and technological 'infrastructure', of a society. However, there was as yet no suggestion that religious behaviour was 'ideology', or a covert form of social communication through which differing levels of society, or classes, attempted to assert their will over one another, as was later proposed by Althusser (1971). Nor is the related concept, first suggested by Veblen (1925) and adopted widely in the disciplines of anthropology and archaeology, that material objects can act as cultural signifiers, suggestive of social status and able to be utilized as weapons of ideological competition, apparent either. In fact, the early Marxist influence on religion in archaeology was limited to a simple privileging of the material elements of history above the 'ideal', and an implication that these material elements were somehow equal to the material culture archaeologists uncovered. The further equation that religious life was necessarily removed from such material contexts was derived instead from the general functionalist assumptions current at the time, and which were themselves also influenced by Marxist suppositions.

From the beginning, archaeological examination of the material past has been primarily concerned with the identification of particular material artefacts and objects with their past use, or function. The dichotomy in archaeological interpretation, whereby identifiable utilitarian function was opposed to unidentifiable religious non-function, was introduced in the previous chapter. Hawkes furthered this dichotomy with its transformation into a specific theory of archaeological epistemology. His 'Ladder of Inference' attempted to create an explicit theoretical interpretative formula for archaeologists to apply to the material, and in doing so it both summarized the pre-existing archaeological bias against religion and also connected it with a hierarchical vision of functionality and epistemology. In Hawkes' (1954, pp. 161–62) opinion:

> To infer from the archaeological phenomena to the *techniques* producing them I take to be relatively easy. . . . To infer to the *subsistence/economics* of the human groups concerned is fairly easy. Operationally, of course, it is laborious. . . . But its logic is simple and needs never be anything but straightforward. . . . To infer to the *social/political* institutions of the groups, however, is considerably harder. . . . To infer to the *religious institutions and spiritual life* may seem superficially perhaps, to be easier . . . [but] in general, I believe, unaided inference from material remains to spiritual life is the hardest inference of all.

This division between separate spheres of human activity assumes that they are inherently different, and can be organized hierarchically in relation to one another 'leading up from the generically animal in man to the more specifically human' (Hawkes, 1954, p. 162). Not only does this reflect the earlier cultural historicism of Pitt-Rivers or Lubbock, where the overtly religious occupies the bottom rung of the ladder, but it explicitly plots this progression against both the potential for such traits to be archaeologically identified in the material record, as well as their relative function and utility to society (Bradley, 1984, pp. 1–4). Hawkes' interpretative scheme is based upon a negative empiricism, and this stress on an absence of evidence leading to an evidence of absence, has resulted in the creation of a covert epistemology in archaeological attitudes to the religious. So the Ladder of Inference can work as a 'ladder of understanding', a mode of interpretation in itself, in which technology and subsistence are easier to identify materially and, therefore, they are also considered to have been the prime movers in social life.

This covert epistemology hidden in Hawkes' generalizing 'law' also reveals an implied functionalism where all possible functionalist explanations, framed in terms of the technological and/or economic, must be exhausted before more generally social, political, aesthetic or religious explanations are considered. For Renfrew:

> If a given practice, which might otherwise be taken to have a religious function, can be explained in other, 'functional' terms, such an explanation is the preferable one. I am not confident of the logical strength of that assertion but it certainly reflects the prevailing process of archaeological inference. (1994a, p. 52; see also Renfrew, 1985)

In addition, this polarization of the material record into that which is functional and obvious and that which is non-functional and 'hidden' has allowed later archaeologists to assume that ritual and religious artefacts are solely ideological in nature (see Shanks and Tilley, 1982; 1987). For instance, the meaning of some types of activity, such as the economically functional, is thought to be more archaeologically self-evident than others, such as the 'religious and spiritual life'. However, as Lane has observed (1986, pp. 182–3), because the religious is characterized as obscure it is capable of having obscure and 'hidden' meanings, it can therefore be termed 'symbolic'. Yet, through being defined in contradistinction to the less obscure and more archaeologically visible realms of the technical and economic, a polarity is created whereby that which is visible and self-evident has practical and functional meanings while that which is hidden and obscure has more esoteric or symbolic meanings. Early postprocessualist archaeologists adopted this position and went on to link it with Marxist concerns about ideology and social control (see below). Religion is understood to mask unspeakable social truths; it is false consciousness.

Furthermore, post-Hawkes, all symbolic and religious meaning can be stripped from that which is functional, while 'normal' practical and pragmatic meaning is not naturally given to the obscure or religious realms. In such a case, the polarity between the functional and utilitarian domestic contexts of 'normal' archaeological excavations and the symbolic and non-functional 'ritual' contexts is deepened. In this case, the use of the terms 'ritual' and 'domestic', or 'religious' and 'functional', may 'introduce a set of largely ethnocentric, and frequently andocentric, assumptions which serve to reinforce and reproduce an appearance of mutual exclusiveness and opposition between these two aspects of human action' (Lane, 1986, p. 181). This subject is explored further in relation to the use of the sacred and profane polarity in Chapter 4.

Overall, it can be seen that during the early part of the twentieth century the possibilities for religion to be uncovered in the material record receded due to a number of influences. First, Marxist materialist thought privileged the material, economic and technical over the false and secondary phenomenon of religion. This general and pre-existent equation of religion with non-materiality was furthered by an explicit theorization of the material record in which religion was seen as being both the antithesis of function and at the same time non-recoverable from a material context. Utilitarian processes such as economic, technical, even political spheres of life were characterized as being materially visible as well as important, while religion and the 'spiritual life' was thought to be invisible and largely unimportant.

Archaeology as a social science

Beginning in the late 1940s a new mood regarding the limits and possibilities for the archaeological interpretation of the past began to emerge in Britain and North America. The first stirrings of what would become a mid-century transformation in archaeological theory, method and practice were concerned mainly with attempts to formulate self-conscious methods for interpreting the material past that were more objective, scientific and certain than the impressionistic cultural–historical mode that had gone before (Lyman et al., 1997). New scientific and overtly methodological forms of archaeology began to appear following the First and Second World Wars. They were influenced by the same epistemological disenchantment and felt need to find a new rational foundation for knowledge that spurred on wider philosophical attempts to reground knowledge at this time, such as logical positivism (J. Thomas, 2004, p. 68). Initially, this new mood in archaeology had similar reductive implications for how the materiality of religion was to be addressed.

Archaeologists such as Taylor and Steward attempted to escape the direct-historical approach to the past by forging a close connection between anthropology and archaeology. In their methods they defined themselves in opposition to the proceeding cultural–historical school of archaeological theory and practice. Generally, cultural–historical archaeology had produced narratives within which cultures acted as individual 'characters' who progressed through time and space, and in doing so influenced each other through the mutual diffusion of cultural characteristics and technological innovations (see Forde, 1930; for a later account Piggott, 1968). Steward was especially critical of the earlier cultural–historical archaeology and its undisciplined and impressionistic interpretations of cultures that were often based upon normative text-based assumptions (Steward, 1955). In the new climate the occasional premethodological willingness to speculate on the possible religious roles of their data was considered undisciplined and naively speculative. For Steward, showing a functionalism reminiscent of Hawkes', religion was an essential aspect of human behaviour and social life, but its appearance in the archaeological record was assumed generally to be too overly complex and obscure to be recovered through a study of material traces (Steward, 1955).

Taylor, especially, advocated the use of ethnographic analogy and anthropological comparison in attempts to interpret the material past (Taylor, 1948), a direction later furthered by Lewis Binford and the 'new' processual archaeologists of the 1960s. The work of the cultural–evolutionary anthropologists was particularly influential on Taylor, especially Leslie White, who, in his *The Science of Culture* (1949), dismissed religion as cultural epiphenomenon. White's chapter on Akhenaton argued that the history, events and general 'cultural evolution' of later Egyptian society would have been no different if the heretic Pharaoh Akhenaton, who during his reign briefly deposed the priestly establishment, had 'been but a sack of sawdust' (1949, p. 279). The contradiction here is that one can take this reductive and absolutist argument as either an indication that religious fervour in the past was either too weak to affect the overall cultural history of a society, or that the organized religion of the Egyptian priests was too strong. But for the emerging archaeological sciences the influence of positivistic forms of anthropology served only to further distance archaeologists from unnecessary speculation on difficult peripherals such as religion.

With the mid-century revolutions in archaeology, specifically its attempts to become a science and develop a body of independent theory and methodology, religion was increasingly ignored, or relegated to being materially unidentifiable, as well as largely undesirable. In part, this reaction against theorizing on religion in the past, and turn instead towards the objectivity of the hard sciences was a result of the undisciplined speculation on religion carried out on the fringes of the discipline in the early days of archaeology. Certainly, in Britain there was an element of residual unease about the 'treasure hunting' and 'druid finding' of the early antiquarians, and this may have helped turn a new generation of archaeologists more firmly away from questions of religious life in the past (Piggott, 1986). Instead, they moved closer to the physical sciences in their understanding of the material record.

The dissatisfaction with cultural–historical views of archaeological cultures as being monolithic entities, reified to resemble human individuals with personal traits and defined characters, was continued into the 1960s with the beginnings of the 'new' archaeology. Rather than looking at cultural typologies, temporal phases or issues of cultural diffusion, societies were instead conceived as organic functioning systems of interacting variables that were constantly in a state of change and adaptation. Cultural change was not an abnormality, or single event, but rather an ongoing process, one that constantly adapted a culture to its role as a mechanism of ensuring social equilibrium, organization and control (Meltzer, 1979). Archaeologists increasingly saw their role as identifying these underlying social processes, hence the label 'processual' to the emerging new science of archaeology.

This 'new' or processual archaeology of the 1960s was an attempt by archaeologists to catch up with the social theory of the early twentieth century, and in many ways processualism was an explicit endeavour to make archaeology into a social science, rather than a colourful, romantic and inexact adjunct to history (for an early explanation, see Binford, 1964). For cultural–historical archaeology, epistemology could be quite simple; an adequate description of the past was, by and large, an adequate explanation. Instead, processual archaeology attempted to remove subjectivity from the process of evaluating archaeological claims and adopt a problem-based and problem-orientated approach to knowledge creation (Binford, 1964). For instance, the use of a hypodeductive approach to the evidence was widely advocated (Metzer, 1979, pp. 646–9), and there was also an attempt to utilize new forms of emerging technology, especially statistics and computers (for the classic example, see Renfrew, 1973; more recently Fagan, 1988).

This period of methodological self-introspective did serve to allow some of the various 'new' archaeologists to begin to theorize for the first time on the possibilities of recovering information on religion in archaeological interpretations of material things. This was especially true of the prehistoric.

Hawkings (1970) originated the subdiscipline of astroarchaeology by looking at the astrological alignments of British monuments and megaliths and musing on their original cosmological significance. In a similarly imaginative manner, Marshack (1971) explored the patterning and placement of simple European Palaeolithic art and interpreted it as recording, in notational style, significant astrological lunar rhythms, which he saw as also having mythological and ritual bearing. At the same time, by bringing archaeology closer to the social sciences and also drawing theoretical paradigms from the broader humanities, the work of those such as Weber, Levi-Strauss and Eliade began to infiltrate some of the earliest archaeological thinking about the wider dimensions of material culture and its relation to the non-functional aspects of society. For instance, archaeologists such as Paul Wheatley drew on the work of Mircea Eliade and Louis Mumford to chart schemes of bounded sacred space, possibly indicating preurban ceremonial centres in archaeological settlement patterns across Eurasia. His work was based upon the concept of the hierophany, an incursion of the experience of the sacred into the material world of mundane space. This irreducible experience of the sacred centre was then expressed through the built environment through the erecting of large non-functional city walls, buttresses and embankments. Wheatley, while drawing on Eliade for his theoretical basis, gathered historic evidence for similar schemes of bounded urban planning drawn from historic India and China, and then attempted to impose this framework on the archaeology of early Mesopotamia and Mesoamerica. His thesis was that religious sensibilities were as important as economic factors in the origins of much early urbanization, and that many early cities, such as Ur and Uruk in Sumer, were extensions of Neolithic sacred centres (Wheatley, 1971). While Leroi-Gourhan (1968) used structuralist principles, developed from the work of Levi-Strauss, to order Upper Palaeolithic art into binary oppositions representing cosmological dualities.

These developments notwithstanding, the major early influence on processual archaeology, however, was cultural–evolutionary anthropology. This was especially the case in the adoption of anthropological classificatory systems whereby societies could be ranked on a scale from simple to complex according to an evolutionary understanding of cultural change. As such, cultures were generalized and ranked in different hierarchical levels depending on their social complexity, from egalitarian bands, to tribes with hereditary leadership, to chiefdoms and finally states (White, 1949). During this period archaeologists did not adopt, or readopt, a similar cultural–evolutionary view of religious progression and development, in the vein of the nineteenth-century anthropologists of religion discussed in Chapter 2 (Parker-Pearson, 2001). This most probably reflected the general lack of consideration of religion rather than any unwillingness to use progressive and evolutionary teleologies. The only sign of the existence of such a scheme in the 'new' archaeology was the previously mentioned generalized division of Palaeolithic, Neolithic, Bronze Age peoples into shamans, monument building ancestor venerators, and the exploited subjects of despotic priest-kings. However, such evolutionary religious typologies were to return in the work of the later cognitive processual archaeologies that speculated on questions of mental evolution and the origins of religion.

Although there were moves in the 'new' archaeology to examine the archaeology of religion, in general religion had little place in processual examinations of social change largely because the cultural–evolutionary anthropology of the time did not consider it to be a crucial phenomenon in social life. For those who followed anthropologists such as White, culture was primarily a mechanism for facilitating group adaptation to the physical environment. Lewis Binford, perhaps the main innovator behind the new archaeology of the 1960s and many of its subsequent developments, defined culture as the 'extra-somatic means of adaptation of the human organism' (1972a; 1972b). In light of this environmental reductivism, methods of subsistence, economics and trade took on the central role of important variables in cultural change. As early as 1967, Binford argued that the capabilities of archaeologists could be broadened through the use of anthropological and ethnographic comparison and statistical methods using computers. Archaeologists could draw on ethnographic analogies with contemporary 'hunter-gatherer' peoples such as the Saami in order to create hypotheses that could then be tested through statistical means against the archaeological data. Although denying that religion held any explanatory value, archaeologists, and ethnoarchaeologists in particular, at this time perpetrated other illusionary narratives. For instance, they portrayed contemporary Saami people as equivalent with premodern tribal people who still followed an exclusively hunter-gatherer economy. Yet, functional and utilitarian rationales prevailed as to determining which cultural traits were important in effecting change. So, although this use of ethnographic analogy and prolonged exposure to non-secular traditional peoples did at times facilitate a greater interest in the religious aspects of human culture, Binford was committed to a functionalist understanding of social science and was personally unsure how to go about recovering these religious dimensions of past society (Robin Torrance, personal communication).

Binford's attempts at dividing a culture up into a set of archaeologically identifiable subsystems, and then examining the interaction between these subsystems and the resulting influence on cultural change, was one of the earliest attempts by an archaeologist to apply systems thinking to the material record (see Taylor, 1948, for an earlier attempt). In doing so, Binford became one of the first archaeologists to theorize explicitly on religion in the material record by including religion as a subcategory in his systems approach. As noted, Binford (1972b) defined culture as the 'extra-somatic means of adaptation of the human organism'. In this same paper, he listed some of these particular cultural systems that functioned as adaptive devices. One of these was the 'ideological sub-systems' made up, in part, of 'ideotechnic artefacts', which included 'figurines of deities, clan symbols, symbols of natural agencies etc' (1972b, pp. 218–20). Binford makes it clear that these ideotechnic artefacts played a 'primarily functional context in the ideological component of the social system' (1972b, p. 220), but exactly how ideology related to environmental adaptation, was not at this point made clear. So, in the main, Binford's vision of culture as an adaptive mechanism to a hostile environment served only to promote a reductive view of human culture that was dependent completely on ecological determinism. It also perpetuated, and enshrined in theory, the pre-existing functionalist bias inherent in any reconstruction of material culture that prioritized technological innovation as primary.

Binford furthered this reduction of human culture down to the level of a mechanism for environmental adaptation in his later work, forging it into the subdiscipline of environmental archaeology. Under this rubric, archaeology became an almost entirely positivistic attempt to make large-scale systems-wide generalizations about human populations (for an early example, see Binford, 1965). There was an explicit attempt to remove considerations of human subjectivity from archaeology, and instead focus on the macroscale interactions of demographics, environment, resources and climate. Attempts were made to synthesize universal cultural covering laws, under which the individual and their psychology, their religion thoughts and actions, had little relevance to the workings of the human population en masse (see Binford, 1981).

However, it was the focus on cultures as combinations of discrete characteristics organized into systems that was to become the dominant theoretical model adopted by processual archaeologists. Most completely developed by Clarke, this systems view was modelled on the general systems theory (GST) originally proposed by the biologist Ludwig von Bertalanffy (1968), in which numerous complex entities such as organisms, ecosystems, societies or computer programs could be abstracted as wholes made up of a number of discrete interacting parts. According to the systems approach adopted by Clarke (1968), society was made up of a number of discrete, but interacting, subsystems such as the social, psychological, economic, material and religious. The economic, subsistence, political, environmental and technological systems all interacted in a web of relationships that together formed a cultural whole at any one point in time. However, in accordance with the epistemological bias perpetuated by Hawkes, Clarke's systems theory equated the most important social systems with those that were most easily identifiable to an archaeologist (such as economic subsistence and technology). For Clarke, religion was one element within the larger socio-cultural subsystem, itself subordinate to a nexus of more important functional systems. In this way, religion was again marginalized not only in terms of material identification, but also in terms of its very importance in human social life.

Clarke defined religion as 'the structure of mutually adjusted beliefs relating to the supernatural, as expressed in a body of doctrine and a sequence of rituals which together interpret the environment to a society in terms of its own percepta' (1968, p. 110). Hence religion was one element in a culture's extraphysical means of adaptation to the external environment. Although Clarke did not elaborate significantly on how exactly religion helped relate a people to their environment, he appears to have assumed that ritual acted in some way as a homeostatic device effecting group cohesion, predictability and social equilibrium. Later, the anthropologist Rappaport suggested that religious concepts were reinforced concretely and backed up periodically through private and communal rituals, and in this way rituals acted as a communication system ensuring the social integration and cohesion of a society. However,

Clarke's and the early processualists' positions on the specifics of this matter is unclear.

But what is clearly apparent is that this highly reductive and functionalist concept of religion was reinforced and amplified in Clarke's musings on the origins and value of religious rituals and structures of belief in archaeological cultures. For Clarke, religious rituals and propositions were the ossified remnants and survivals of the past choices a cultural group had made in its adaptation to the pressures of the hostile world. As part of the socio-cultural system of a culture, religious motifs could be seen as shadowy memorials to the systemic trajectories made by a culture in the past. 'Long after the situations that prompted specific adaptations have passed, they may survive in such [socio-cultural] systems – especially embalmed with the conservative memory of the religious subsystem' (Clarke, 1968, p. 112). For instance, the apparent 'fixation' with bulls and horns in late Minoan religion is proposed to have been the preserved memory of an important adaptive period in early Minoan culture, a time when giant wild cattle were common on Crete and a 'living part of an economic and religious equilibrium' (Clarke, 1968, p. 113). Although, just what the nature of this 'equilibrium' was, and how exactly any specific religious beliefs or rituals originally assisted in the supposedly primary act of managing the important economic resource of these prehistoric cattle is neither suggested or explained. Surely, it must have been more sophisticated than the enshrining of cattle in religious rituals, art and iconography simply in order to remind people to keep eating them.

There are a number of criticisms that can be made of this systems approach to culture and religion. First, as we have seen, the way that a society was broken down into subsystems was not empirical, but in fact reflected biases general to processualism's reductive and functionalist approach to cultural anthropology. Material subsystems (in a Marxist sense of the term) were privileged as primary. Also, it is difficult to impose such systems back in time to non-modern contexts. Where would something as ubiquitous as a group of village women bathing and collecting water for a household fit in a systems approach: economic (the collection and transportation of resources), subsistence (providing sustenance), social (gossip), political (gossip), religious (ideas of purity and bathing), ideotechnic (are their pots decorated), and so on? Furthermore, according to such a method, all culture, including religion, was determined by the productive economic base of society. Cultural meaning was produced through the relationship between people and their environment. Any examination of religion or ritual in the past would always involve a reference to another activity or subsystem outside of itself. Religion was never self-generating or irreducible (Hodder and Hutson, 2003, p. 42), and in fact it would always be, in the final analysis, economics. This systems assumption that religion was primarily reflective of something greater neatly combined Marxist and Durkheimian thought together, to the detriment of any potential archaeology of religion.

As the materialist philosophy of Marx was in some respects a reaction against the abstract idealism of Hegel, so too was Durkheim's conviction that religion could only ever be understood in terms of its social function a reaction against the 'psychologically orientated individualism' (Sharpe, 1986, p. 83) current in late nineteenth-century anthropology. As we have seen, the view that religion was an inward existential reaction to an unknown cosmos, an emotive individual perception, was characteristic of the work of Tylor and the nineteenth-century anthropologists. And in a similar way to Marx, Durkheim's more sophisticated position, that religion was a group reflection and actualization of social life, in effect reduced religion down to merely the surface appearance in a society, a mask to the real forces that are the better focus of academic and scientific study. By theorizing that religions are group performances played out by a community in order to externalize a sense of group affiliation and solidarity, he effectively coupled both functionalism and Marxist ideology together. Durkheim's work gave religion a function, in that it could now be seen as a method for social group creation, and it also saw religion in a Marxist guise, in that its role was essentially that of a communicative device, diffusing useful ideology in order to perpetuate group cohesion. According to such a 'symbolist' view (Giddens, 1984), religious beliefs and actions are not taken seriously or literally as expressions of religious meaning and value, but rather a reductionism is applied to religious belief and ritual, in which they are understood as primarily fulfilling a greater social function.

In the same way that religion and culture were perceived as being symbolic or reflective of other processes, processual archaeology in general treated material culture as reflective and secondary in social life also. Systems theory did acknowledge that, in principle, changes in material culture were linked to changes in social organization, economy and ideology. Material remains were seen as a reflection of the functioning of a society, and so material culture was useful for more than simple classification of typological change. It could act as a reflection of societal change and a diagnostic of cultural process. For instance, the adoption of cultural–evolutionary anthropological schemes, and the law-like generalizations systems theory made about a culture to explain empirical observations of the material record, introduced a series of assumed objective and cross-cultural laws or generalizations (Binford, 1983). These covering laws, also termed 'middle-range' theories (for a good example, see Rathje, 1992), were used to provide formulaic links between the observations of recovered material data and the living culture that produced it originally. Basically, for processualists the patterning of material culture could be correlated with the patterning of human society. However, the assumption was that human behaviour effected material culture according to law-like systems, leaving an ossified record of this behaviour in the archaeological record. The direction of influence between society and materiality was solely one way. Material culture was reflective of human action and played a passive role in social life.

It will be seen below that this lack of agency given by processualist archaeologists, both to individual human subjects within their overarching systemic cultures, and also to the very materiality of the past that they were examining, were two of the greatest concerns that led eventually to the postprocessual reactions against early processual theory. Cognitive processual archaeology, on the other hand, was an attempt to reinsert the human, the subjective, and even the religious, back into the past, to abandon the macroscale cultural–evolutionary approach of positivistic anthropology, and it is to this development that we shall first turn.

Cognitive, or cognitive processual, archaeology is a stream of archaeological method that developed out of the context of processualism. It was an attempt to redress some of the perceived excesses of early processualism, especially its sharp environmental reductivism and relegation of the mind and subjectivity to the sphere of epiphenomena, and the perception that the individual was powerless and insignificant in the face of an all-encompassing monolithic 'culture' (Renfrew and Zubrow, 1994). Instead, cognitive archaeology attempted to put the individual and their thoughts back into interpretations of the material record, and to do this usually through the application of cognitive psychology, the science of mental processes and perception. Cognitive psychology views the human being as an intelligent decision-making creature who achieves goals through 'complex hierarchical systems of information processing' (Segal, 1994, p. 23). Accordingly, the mind is understood through primarily an evolutionary framework, which 'explains' it as having developed in response to adaptive and selective pressures (a view similar in some ways to the classic processual understanding of culture). Because all humans share the same evolutionary heritage, the cognitive psychological approach has, at times, claimed to be capable of generalizing universal, and not culturally specific, insights into ancient subjectivities (Peatfield, 1993).

Perhaps, uniquely in processualist systems, religion does have a definite, even central, place in some cognitive archaeology (Renfrew, 1985; 1994a). As we will see there has been a focus on Palaeolithic art and iconography, on shamanism, and questions of the origins of religion in the human mind, and its evolutionary function. There has also been an evolutionary and socio-biological emphasis on culture as an information processing system that carries adaptive advantages further than the biological realm. In a similar vein to Clarke or Binford, culture is understood as a way of processing information about existence in the world in ways that maximize the potential for survival. As such, cognitive archaeology adheres to functionalist biases in regard to religion, which it understands primarily in terms of its adaptive value (or not) for an individual or culture.

This neo-evolutionary approach, whereby cultural innovation is interpreted as a function of biological selection and adaptive processes, was most exemplified in Mithen's *The Prehistory of the Mind* (1996). As noted, cognitive archaeologists interpret the human mind as being the result of innumerable adaptations to selective pressures from the external environment. This is similar to the classic processual understanding of culture as a collection of adaptive strategies serving to ensure homeostasis. This similarity is furthered in Mithen's description of the mind, ancient and modern, as an evolved system composed of a number of distinct subsystems, which are referred to by cognitive psychologists as 'modules'. For Mithen, these modules developed through natural selection as responses to the functional needs of hunter-gatherer humans during the Pleistocene, when much of the evolution of the mind took place. Each module was connected with a particular domain of practical activity, and together they interacted to a limited degree and grouped 'around' an early hominid general intelligence. However, originally these modules were all mostly separate and self-enclosed and operated in isolation from one another. But, eventually the barriers between the several specialized intelligences broke down, creating a new mental fluidity as knowledge began to flow between cognitive domains (Mithen, 1996, p. 69). At this point, the four domains of practical/technical knowledge, environmental intelligence, social intelligence and linguistic intelligence, somehow came together to form cognitive 'fluidity'. And it was this new fluidity between formally discrete systems that allowed humans to begin to do lateral things with their minds, to create metaphor, art, symbolic thought and, hence, religion.

For Mithen, this was the source of the Upper Palaeolithic 'revolution' in artistic and cultural life, and was also the original fount of human religiosity. It is suggested that it took place in two stages, with vague totemic and anthropomorphic thought developing about 100,000 years ago as a result of the integration of the social and natural history intelligences (the material world was mistaken for the social world). Then, about 60,000–30,000 years ago, the addition of technical knowledge to this cognitive mix gave rise to animism, leading overall to Mithen's confident assertion that 'religious ideologies as complex as those of modern hunter-gatherers came into existence at the time of the Middle/Upper Palaeolithic transition and have remained with us ever since' (1996, p. 202). The hunter-gatherer worldview, originating in the Upper Palaeolithic was one in which the social world (thought), the natural world (matter) and technical knowledge (the application of one to the other) were connected together by links of analogy and metaphor. For, do not Palaeolithic cave paintings, such as the 'birdman' of Lascaux or the 'shaman/sorcerer' of Les Trois Freres, depict people and animals mixed together to form conglomerated supernatural beings (see Sidky, 2008, for a critical perspective on these romantic assumptions)?

Not only does such a scheme repeat the cultural–evolutionary religious typologies of, say, Lubbock almost word for word, it also attempts to explain the very origins of religion as the mistaken mixing of the material and social realms. For Tylor and Lubbock, the earliest and most primitive religions were those that were most manifested in the material world. For Mithen this was because religion basically began as a short-circuiting of the brain, whereby things (objects) were mistaken for people (subjects). Religion is a confusion resulting from the mingling of the material and mental realms. Although Mithen does not state it directly, in a manner altogether reminiscent of Tylor he certainly implies that contemporary 'survivals', that is, hunter-gatherers, animists, people of a religious persuasion in general, are under the sway of an original cognitive category error. Religion is an accident, a happy by-product of more important processes that occurred at a relatively recent period of human cognitive evolution. For Mithen (2001), 'religious ideas have no natural home in the mind. There is no evidence that they came into existence until very late in human evolution.'

It can be seen that Mithen has made a sincere and ingenious attempt to acknowledge and explain the existence of religion, as a complex and dynamic sphere of human life (thought), in the material record. However, by attempting to define it as a discrete cognitive phenomenon he has unfortunately repeated the totalizing errors of nineteenth-century anthropology by narrowly defining it as an aberration to more usual functional and sensible modes of being. Also, in attempting a definition of religion that rests upon biology, he has necessarily assumed that, not withstanding a deplorable childlike mistake in mixing the material and social worlds, people in the past thought like, interacted with their world, and perceived in much the same way as people do today. His theory of religion is characteristic of cognitive archaeology in general, in that it attempts to access an essentialist, universalist and static concept of the human mind in the past. By definition, Mithen's conception of religion is primarily a cognitive experience, meaning that religion is always, and can only ever be, a form of interiority, and this prolongs the easy and limited equation of religion and interiority in the Western academic tradition.

A similar approach can be illustrated in the work of Renfrew, especially his attempts to suggest an archaeology of religion and cult. Because he was interested in an archaeology of the mind and of cognition, Renfrew dispensed with the usual processual emphasis on religion as a social practice, as ritual, and instead focused on questions of religious belief and experience. By focusing on individual belief and experience Renfrew has been one of the very few archaeologists who have actually consistently used the word 'religion' rather than one of its synonyms (1994a, p. 48). Renfrew acknowledges that different cultures interpret their world differently according to their own structures of thinking (1994b), and he attempts to avoid imposing culturally constituted notions about past religions as 'coherently codified . . . authoritative systems of belief' onto the archaeological evidence (1994a, p. 47), even warning about the utility of the very term 'religion', as a separate social domain. He also highlights the dangers of using intuitive jumps in ascertaining the meaning of particular iconographic symbols and objects in the past. However, as a 'cognitive' archaeologist, he also claims that his own experiences are not radically dissimilar to that of all other human beings (Renfrew, 1994b), and his interpretations are necessarily grounded in a reiteration of assumed dichotomies such as the functionalist/symbolic, domestic/ritual and profane/ sacred, which are projected onto the material record.

In fact, Renfrew grounds the religious experience on Rudolf Otto's concept of the numinous 'Holy' experience, that all modern *Homo sapiens* have access to the irreducible, universal and emotive interior experience of a mysterious non-human numinous power seeming to originate outside of themselves (Renfew, 1994a, p. 49; Otto, 1924). Religion is experienced and performed according to the template of the sacred and profane dichotomy, and can be identified archaeologically if material culture adheres to forms common from the history of religions. Renfrew lists obvious material objects that may indicate that a site or collection of artefacts had a religious significance in the past, including spaces with natural associations such as springs, caves, hollows and special buildings such as raised platforms and temples, cult images, abstract representations of deities, and animal symbolism (1994a, pp. 51–2). So although Renfrew's attempts to access religion in the archaeological record, and to put religiosity back into the past, are laudable and striking in their virtual isolation, it can be seen that his attempts do not go far beyond the 'commonsense' interpretations that led to the dichotomy between the functional versus the non-functional. In this way, Renfrew's interpretations of material culture are similar to Mithen's, in that it can be given a religious identification only if it is symbolic or evocative of a religious experience familiar to the contemporary archaeologist.

In the next chapter, we will explore some of the concerns inherent in adopting any form of universal 'middle-range theory' of material culture that is based upon uniformitarian and ahistoric assumptions such as the dichotomy between the sacred and the profane. Here it is enough to state that, by adopting essentialist and universal criteria for the 'religious' as opposed to the 'functional', cognitive archaeologists can only discover in the material record that which they already expect to find, while simultaneously perpetuating functionalist and reductive assumptions about the bulk of the material past. For instance, although Mithen and Renfrew both base their theories of mind on cognitive psychology, alternative approaches to a cognitive archaeology have used other criteria, with similarly predictable results. Nash, for example, has used a concept of mind based upon Jungian archetype theory, in his examination of prehistoric landscapes. Although his attempts to access the 'surreal or fantastic quality' of the material record, and explore a 'wealth of transcendental knowledge' (Nash, 1997, p. 57) are an exciting and refreshing change to much archaeological literature, his view of past religious experience is static and universal, rigid and inflexible.

Also, and more seriously, for cognitive archaeologists religion is seen as 'palaeopsychology' (Fritz, 1978; for the argument against, see Binford, 1965). It is a system of beliefs, thoughts and experiences that are located predominantly in the interior of the mind. Mithen (2001) described the mental realms of religious belief as a cognitive adaptation to complex human interaction with the environmental and social world through symbolically structuring experience. But by privileging 'belief', 'mind' and 'experience' over 'action', 'body' and 'practice', cognitive archaeologists also favour a vision of religion that relates it most strongly to the transcendent, non-empirical or supernatural rather than the worldly, normal and relational. For Renfrew, religion is defined not simply as belief, but as a certain special type of belief that must not be about the world or the way that it works but about supernatural forces that go beyond the world and transcend it (1994a, p. 48).

It can be seen that for cognitive archaeologists material culture may reflect religious belief, as with Renfrew's list of material patterns that correlate with religion or Mithen's Palaeolithic paintings of half social, half natural objects. Certainly, the problems of identifying the mind's 'ideals when all that survive are material things', are acutely recognized (Parker-Pearson, 2001, p. 203). For Mithen, Renfrew and other archaeologists influenced by the cognitive perspective, such as Parker-Pearson, it is only when the mind has directly shaped the material world in a symbolic fashion that its contents can then be 'read', that palaeopsychology can be attempted. For, 'beliefs and faiths that have moved spiritual mountains have also constructed edifices of enduring permanence, size and complexity' (Parker-Pearson, 2001, p. 203). However, these attempts to recover cognitive information from material patterns rest upon a universal measurement of mind, upon assumptions about the nature of the religious experience. They also rest upon an assumption that this 'spiritual' dimension is distinct from, and separate to, any considerations of the material world, which can only ever be a symbolic reflection of insubstantial belief and palaeopsychology.

To sum up, cognitive archaeology has made unique and important attempts to consider an archaeology of religion. For cognitive archaeologists, religion may be a natural and crucial (if accidental) element of the human condition, and an important aspect of any archaeological reconstruction of the past. Rather than seeing ritual and religion as purely communicative devices and mechanisms for the social exchange of information, as processual and postprocessual archaeologists commonly do, some cognitive archaeology acknowledges the transformative, immediate and effective nature of the religious experience on individuals (Peatfield, 1993). But as an archaeology of the mind, cognitive archaeology attempts to create universal and ahistoric rules about culture and religion. Also, it sees religion as primarily a mental construct, a belief-based and mind-orientated phenomenon, and this distances it further from the realm of material culture. Religion is looked for, and found, in the usual places, in accordance with the particularism outlined above. The realms of art, death, burial are seen as being the only 'natural' places that materially can symbolically reflect religious life because they are seen as being the closest material reflection of mind available for archaeologists to access. The polarity between the bulk of the archaeological record revealing functional use, and a minority reflecting hidden symbolic religious behaviour remains and is entrenched.

Interpretative archaeology

Undoubtedly the largest reformulation of archaeological method in the second half of the twentieth century began in the mid-1980s with the rise of interpretative or 'post' processual archaeology from within the context of processualism. Postprocessualism defined itself in opposition to processualism in the same way that 'new' archaeology defined itself against the perceived faults of the earlier cultural–historical archaeology. Sometimes termed 'interpretative' (Thomas, 2000) or 'contextual' (Hodder and Hutson, 2003) archaeology, postprocessualism emerged as a series of disparate attempts to widen the sorts of information archaeologists could gather from the past.

Never a unified field or discipline, it was, and is, rather a general rejection of the perceived scientism, false objectivity, universalism and lack of agency characteristic of processual archaeological interpretations of material culture. This has allowed postprocessualists to place themselves in the convenient position of being able to label any and all new, innovative and interesting approaches in archaeology as 'post' processual (Thomas, 2000). Matters of individual thought, action and belief in the past, as well as the importance of symbolism, art, ritual, metaphor and power have all been significant aspects of postprocessual theory that have separated it from earlier forms of archaeology. Although this has in part served to free potential archaeologies of the religious from the conceptual straightjacket of processualism, overall the majority of postprocessualist considerations of ritual have failed to escape functionalist and Marxist assumptions regarding religion. In fact, in many ways, early postprocessualist concerns with religious ritual as an ideological support to competing social groups have been a direct continuation of earlier processual assumptions that religion was one subsystem acting in unison with others to ensure a society's ongoing function and adaptation to external and internal pressures.

Although postprocessualism is largely indefinable, except for its conception of itself as apart from processualism, certain common ways of approaching the material record may be singled out in a tentative fashion. For instance, postprocessualist archaeologists often advocate a plurality and multiplicity of views on interpretation, and a diversity of approaches to the past. Such approaches can be grounded in the use of complex ethnographic analogy that goes beyond the simple law-like scientism of processualism (Hodder and Hutson, 2003, chapter 8). Ethnographic analogy can be used to inform contemporary archaeologists of potential past realities that do not conform to modern perspectives, to suggest contrary, alternative and non-modern ways of looking at the archaeological record. Also, a focus on individual agency, rather than abstracted and overarching social institutions, or cultures allows for the reintroduction of individuals and their agency into the past (for the earliest discussion of individual agency and social reproduction, see Barrett, 1994).

Most importantly, considerations of material culture as playing an active role in social life, rather than just being a passive reflection of past social actions, have allowed some postprocessualists to move beyond a symbolist and reflective approach to materiality. Material things may be interpreted as having biographies, and adopting roles in society beyond that of simple commodities (Kopytoff, 1986). Things, objects, sites and landscapes may be active participants in the production and constant reproduction of social structures, as well as their subversion, and therefore cannot be interpreted as direct reflections of past monolithic societies in a processual mould. The ability of symbolic and ritual objects to play roles in the negotiation of social life is explored below, while the material structuration of social life, and its consequences for possible archaeologies of religion, is explored in Chapter 4.

Many of the common characteristics of the postprocessualist approach to archaeological interpretation do appear to open up the archaeological record to considerations of the materiality of religion. In a similar way to processualism, however, the term 'religion' is very rarely used by postprocessualist archaeologists 'even if [they are] guilty of stressing the symbolic aspects of human action at the expense of the practical' (Insoll, 2004a, p. 77). This has been partially because of an interest in the ideological and symbolic elements of social life, to the exclusion of alternative and wider social landscapes such as the religious. In addition, despite a perceived concern with fluid, multiple, and subjective interpretations of the past, an understandable wariness of attracting the label 'fringe' or 'pseudoarchaeological' prevents overly ambitious interpretations of the religious past. Partly, this may be because of perceived connotations between unwarranted interpretations of the material record and alternative archaeologies such as neo-Pagan beliefs surrounding megalith sites, pyramids, goddess worship, and so on.

Instead, the term 'ritual' is most often used in postprocessual archaeology, and its symbolic and material nature examined, rather than the more vague and less theorized term 'religion' (for an early example, see Hodder, 1982a). This is despite it being often unclear and rather vague as to what is meant by 'ritual' in much of this literature. As noted previously, ritual may be concerned with human action in embodied relation to material culture, while religion is a more complex phenomenon that also incorporates connotations with subjective belief, thought, emotion, myth, story and much more. Certainly, it is the social aspects of past religion that are easier to identify archaeologically and of the most interest to postprocessual archaeologists, rather than the specifics of past religious beliefs or worldviews. In the majority of postprocessualist archaeology, the ritual and symbolic dimensions of material culture are examined within the framework of the roles that they may have played in social reproduction.

An ideological and symbolist approach to ritual, where it is examined primarily as a communicative and symbolic system in social negotiation was common in much of the earlier postprocessual archaeology, especially of the British Neolithic. Through the medium of authors such as Veblen, Althusser and Rappaport, a form of neo-Marxism became very influential in early postprocessual theorizing on the role of ritual. As such, when the majority of postprocessual archaeologists have touched on religion it has been commonly understood as merely an expression of ideological communication, usually manipulated by elites so that they can uphold their control over a society. So, religion is once again understood primarily as a form of ideology, as referring to a series of ideas put into political action by individual agents (Friedrich, 1989, p. 301). Lohse has defined the use of the term ideology within archaeological interpretations as pertaining to a series of 'communication based strategies for maintaining the various social positions that archaeological subjects clearly held . . . for the purpose of shaping social relations' (2007, pp. 6–7). Yet, it can be seen that the term 'ideology', when implicitly used as a concept through which to understand the nature and function of religion, simply reinforces some unwarranted assumptions, such as religion referring primarily to interior belief and being primarily a form of communication.

Shanks and Tilley (1982) examined a series of Neolithic burials and tombs from Britain, and argued that evidence for ritual activity in reality illustrated the cynical use of ideology by elites in the past to hold onto power. For example, the practice of collectively burying the disarticulated skeletons of many people together as one mass in tombs may in reality have been an ideological statement on egalitarianism that cleverly masked the reality of a non-egalitarian society. Hence, material culture such as tombs, burials and the human body itself was used by those with power to hide this reality from the wider society and project, instead, an ideology that supported comforting notions of social equality. Ritual was ideology, and ideology communicated a false consciousness to the masses.

Well expressed here is the postprocessual critique that societies are not wholes that function as rational superorganisms, in the mould of processual systems thinking, but rather are collections of multiple social groups, often with competing interests. Drawing on Foucault (1977), Shanks and Tilley made a strong structuralist critique advocating a theory of dialectical power between individuals, social groups and material structures to effect multilinear social change (1987; see especially their manifesto on power in the appendix). However, Shanks' and Tilley's assumption that only a Marxist reading of material culture can give archaeologists access to the permutations of this social world is simplistic. In their interpretation, Shanks and Tilley imply a cosmological scheme and the social values that it is thought to embody and promote.

The assumption is that ritual, and the symbols used in ritual, reflected an ideal image of the world and, in turn, this gives the archaeologist a view of the idealized social structure. This reconstruction of a whole society, based upon funerary data, is ambitious. The very concept of 'ritual', based as it is upon Durkheim's overly stark and ambitiously cross-cultural sacred and the profane dichotomy, is problematic. More so is the assumption that ritual will necessarily reflect shared 'beliefs' that are universally understood by the performers and audiences of the past. Discursive understandings of ritual may be multiple and contested, if they even exist at all. Catherine Bell (1992, p. 183) made this point well:

> [A] community's ritual life, can be very unclear to participants or interpreted by them in very dissimilar ways . . . this suggests that some level or degree of social consensus does not depend upon shared information or beliefs, and ritual need not be seen as a simple medium of communicating such information or beliefs . . . they focus on common symbols, not on statement of belief . . . ritualized practices afford a great diversity of interpretation in exchange for little more than consent to the form of the activities . . . ritual does not necessarily cultivate or inculcate shared beliefs.

Shanks and Tilley's method of interpretation is even more questionable when a central assumption is that truth can only be gleaned if the canny archaeologist turns any immediate or intuitive message of that data on its head and reads it instead as an ideological example of masking unequal power relations. Shanks and Tilley do not consider that if the funerary data is symbolic then its referents may be more ambiguous than a simple one-to-one inverse relationship to the social order (for criticisms, see Garwood, 1991; Lewis, 1980). In different contexts, the human corpse may have had multiple symbolic meanings or associations, been purposefully misleading or not, had various meanings to different people, sexes, ages or totems. The very concept of symbolism, as opposed to signalling, suggests multiple broadening levels of association, rather than strict univocal meaning.

This supposed connection between ritual and symbolism, ideology and social reproduction must be examined in detail in order to understand the early postprocessual approaches to religion. By focusing on the function of religion as a support for ritual, which itself is a support for the ideology used to maintain social relationships, postprocessualist archaeologists have merely continued the functionalist assumptions of processualist archaeologists in regard to religion. In both systems ritual, and by extension religion, is conceived as serving purely to further a larger social function. For processual archaeologists religion, in the final analysis, mediated economic relations between a culture and its environment, whereas, for postprocessual archaeologists it masks power relations and politics between the individuals within a culture. Furthermore, the materiality of religion is conceived as a purely reflective device, one that serves only as a non-verbal form of communication: a form of communication that travels in only one direction from the elites to the masses.

As explained, systems theory was used in processual archaeology to attempt to make sense of the differing aspects of a society, and how they interacted with one another in order to ensure social stability and prosperity in the face of constant change and variability. For Binford and Clarke, religion was subsumed within a subsystem that served in some not-quite-specified way to regulate the relationships between a society and its external environment. At roughly the same time as Binford and Clarke were producing their major works in systems analysis the anthropologist Roy Rappaport, coming from a cultural ecology stance, was theorizing how exactly religion could act as a symbolic communication system concerned with the regulation of the social and ecological variables of a hunter-gatherer culture. For Rappaport, both ritual and religion communicated information about food resources and their availability to a social group. The social conventions current in a hunter-gatherer society regulated how its members, as a whole, negotiated the economic, ecological and social variables they faced in their day-to-day life. Conventions, such as those concerned with harvesting certain types of resources, intermarriage between families or relations between the sexes, had to be accepted and adopted by all the members in a society and, for Rappaport, religion/ideology was one of the mechanisms that ensured that this occurred (1968; 1971; 1979).

Rappaport's work was highly influential on the archaeologist Robert Drennan, whose ideas on the relationships between religion, ritual and society have influenced much subsequent archaeological literature (see esp. Renfew, 1985; Renfew and Bhan, 2000, p. 406). Drennan (1976) drew on a flowchart of Rappaport's that explained the social function of religion by dividing it into three mutually supporting categories; 'Ultimate Sacred Propositions', 'Rituals' and 'Religious Experience and Feeling'. In it, ultimate sacred propositions served to direct the faithful to perform rituals, which then induced a perception of religious experience and feeling, which in turn supported the ultimate sacred propositions ad infinitum. So, for Drennan, ritual induced a set of religious experiences that supported social conventions and thus ensured social harmony. In formulating this scheme he also drew upon Durkheim's idea that while common sets of religious beliefs integrate people into a social whole, ritual was the performative means of creating and ensuring such social solidarity. These 'rituals of sanctification' imprinted in a physical and experiential way the authoritative nature of religious dogma on to aspects of social life, and this made peoples' actions and expectations predictable and ordered, which in turn contributed to the smooth running of society.

For instance, Drennan suggested that as societies become increasingly large and complex, such as the transition from a hunter-gatherer economy to a sedentary-agriculturalist system, new social regulations were needed to mediate between individuals, the group and the environment. As society increases in size and complexity, literally more religion and ritual were needed to keep it together. Material culture was at least reflective of this transition. Drennan found an increase in cult figurines (possibly indicating an increased amount of ritual activity) and the beginnings of permanent ceremonial architecture at about 1500 BCE in Mesoamerica, at just the time when this process was occurring. However, Drennan (1976) did not suggest that it was the actual materiality of religion that was playing new and crucial roles in the creation of social complexity, but rather, that it was the group ritual performance that was the effective agent, and the materiality of religion simply reflected this.

Early postprocessualist Marxist archaeologists adopted Drennan's idea that the 'sanctification' of ritual legitimized the contemporary status quo and led to the economic and social stability necessary for a society's ordered functioning (see Shanks and Tilley, 1982; Barrett, 1989; 1991). This facilitated an increase in interest in possible ways that archaeologists could study ritual and, implicitly, religion.

So, for processualist archaeologists religion, most often hidden within the term ritual, was a subsystem of social life that acted as a homeostatic device ensuring social stability and equilibrium. While for early postprocessualist archaeologists, ritual and ideological practice were also seen as important in that they created and maintained social hierarchy. The functionalist interpretations of the place held by religion in past social life adopted by both processual and postprocessual archaeologies, resulted in similar accounts of religion in the past. It was a functional mechanism that ensured social reproduction, despite size, spatial–temporal context, particular character, and so on. For postprocessualist archaeologists, religion was usually termed 'ritual', to distinguish its material and action-centred characteristics. Although it was given importance in the interpretation of past cultures, its role was one of being a mechanism of ideological control. Ritual and religion were first and foremost a type of symbolism and important mainly as forms of symbolic communication between peoples or groups. This represented a direct continuation of reductive and functionalist Marxist thought, from systems thinking through to postprocessualism, where ideology functions as masking the conflicts and contradictions that arise due to competitive means of production. Ideology disguises the arbitrariness of social relations by making them appear natural, eternal and inevitable. In part, material culture and ritual – the materiality of religion – were seen as valuable resources for effecting ideological control because of their conservative, durable and seemingly permanent, otherworldly and eternal nature (see Chapter 4).

However, early postprocessual critiques of the role or ritual in the past progressed only a little further than their processual forebears. Rather than seeing material evidence for ritual and religion as a fossilized reflection of past social life, they focus on the roles of ideology and belief-systems in serving the interests of the elites, perpetuating social order, equilibrium and hierarchy, and preventing social disruption and harmonizing society. But the basic approach to religion and ritual is the same: it is reductive and functionalist.

Yet, this is not the only way in which ritual was understood by early postprocessualists to have functioned in the archaeological record. Before closing this chapter, brief consideration must be made of the early work of John Barrett, especially his attempt to 'read' ritual as a text. Barrett's consideration of the nature of the material record as a 'text', capable of being 'read', influenced ideas about materiality and religion, especially the active and primary nature of material culture as an agent in religious life. They also opened the way for the specifically phenomenological modes of approaching materiality and religion, as fields of interpretation, which are critiqued in Chapter 4.

In 1985, Linda Patrick argued that there were two ways of looking at the archaeological record. First, as a fossilized collection of objects which could be catalogued, compared and sorted into types in order to identify similarities of type and changes over time. This was the descriptive method common to the much early twentieth-century archaeology. Second, archaeological data could be a 'textual' record inscribed with the meanings of past human actors that is thus pregnant with signification, and capable of being read symbolically by later researchers. An example being the attempts, critiqued above, by early postprocessualist to 'read' ideology into the material symbols of the past.

John Barrett (1991), however, directly challenged such early postprocessual attempts at interpreting ritual, claiming that Shanks and Tilley's interpretations of ideology in Neolithic mortuary practices, as a cross-cultural sociological law, could never tell the researcher anything about the past that they did not know at the outset. For Barrett, rituals did not simply symbolize the ideal world of the dominant social group and serve to impose this ideological fiction on to the unwitting masses. Rather, they provided a negotiable field of discourse, where people could control the multiple layers of symbolism of the political system by reinterpreting and re-reading the symbolic meaning of ritual performance. Just as a text is written on a durable substance, and then acts as a 'field of negotiation' open to many readers, rituals act as a partially durable set of actions on human bodies and the material world and, as such, they survive outside their original context of creation, or authorship. 'The code of ritual appears inscribed upon the physical medium through which it is expressed,

including the bodies, gestures, movements and voices of the participants'
(Barrett, 1991, p. 4).

So, for Barrett and those whom he influenced (see esp. Tilley, 1991), the
interpretation of the material culture of ritual became a form of Literary
Reception Theory, where the meaning of a text is determined equally by the
reader's context as well as the author's original intent. This was influential on
the later phenomenologists of landscape, as it opened the material record to a
plurality of meanings that depend partially on the social and cultural context
of the reader. Rather than a single ideological statement, the materiality of
ritual could have a plurality of changing meanings in differing periods and
contexts, and according to different people in the past (Holtorf, 1995; Bender,
1993).

At its extreme, this position threatens to fall into a total relativism where
archaeologists are just one more voice in a morass of equally valid narratives.
However, in its original form, Barrett drew on the hermeneutics of Ricoeur,
and especially his concept of discourse. The meaning of any speech or
text must be interpreted by the listener, and is therefore informed by their
cultural and contextual pre-expectations (Barrett, 1991, p. 4). For Barrett,
in traditional societies the meanings given to a ritual are not disembodied
and free-floating and capable of endless reinterpretation, but are instead
understood to originate from transcendent religious contexts (their 'authors'
are gods, spirits, ancestors, etc.). With enough contextual information about a
culture, an archaeologist may begin to be able to 'read' their material remains
in a similar way to the original members of the society, although it is likely
that contemporary archaeologists would also need access to indigenous
epistemologies to be able to understand what it was that they were 'reading'
(for a similar approach, see Astor-Aguilera, 2010).

Such a view introduces a dynamic view of society, similar to that proposed
by sociologist Anthony Giddens, and explained further in the next chapter.
Social life is continually brought into being and reproduced by people as they
act social roles and reinterpret their meaning. Social control comes from the
perpetual recreation of the social through performance in, and interaction and
negotiation with, the social and material world. All these can be characterized
as dialogues or discourses with the past, with memory or with concrete 'textual'
representations of established order (divine or otherwise), that are constantly
open to (re)interpretation. A single symbol or collection of symbols such as

a ritual may be interpreted from many competing angles at one time. There is no dominant power ruthlessly holding on to ideological control with an unshakable grasp. Power is instead recreated and negotiated constantly. 'A structure of social authority does not stand naked awaiting the cloak of ideological legitimacy to be thrown around it by ritual practice' (Barrett, 1991, p. 2).

Such ideas about the structuration of society are explored in the following chapter. It is enough here to round out this examination of Marxist and functionalist influences on archaeological attitudes to religion by noting that this theory allowed such presuppositions to be transcended. For the first time, Barrett's vision of ritual as a negotiable field of discourses, which is enacted within certain existential parameters but is nevertheless in a constant state of flux, allowed for archaeological understandings of materiality and religion that transcended the functionalist and Marxist presuppositions about religion as derivative of deeper social processes, and secondary to truer social rules. Neither were ritual and religion monolithic narratives imposed upon a people in the interests of social cohesion, environmental homeostasis or privileged power politics. In addition, material culture no longer had to be seen as reflective or symbolic of human action or ideology, but could be seen as a participant in social life, with materiality and society could be seen as mutually supporting.

As we have seen, for postprocessualists such as Tilley, material culture was active, but only in so far as it served an ideological function. It acted so that the system of masking inequality could function. Even whole landscapes could best be analysed as providing a set of 'symbolic resources' used by the elite in 'the creation and reproduction of structures of power' (Tilley, 1996b, p. 161). However, this approach was limited in that it reduced the role of material culture, and of ritual, in human social life to communication, to the transfer of discursive information. Other possible modes of perception such as the emotional, immediate, non-discursive experiences of ritual and materiality were overlooked. Furthermore, symbols were seen as being univocal and part of normative systems of belief. But for Barrett (1991, p. 2), material culture was:

> [T]he residue of systems of signification, a means by which people were once able to structure their actions in particular and culturally meaningful ways. [It operated] as a code through which historically specific knowledges

about the world were maintained, and which in turn guided the human subject's actions within that culturally mediated world.

Material culture, from cloths to architecture, artefacts to the entire landscape, structured this field of common experience. For Barrett, 'it frames the interlocutors' actions and guides their movements, it may be exchanged between them, it may signify cultural differences between them, and it may act as the mnemonic devices necessary to guide and structure discourse' (1991, p. 3). Material culture provides a communicative field of discourse, but as a 'signifying system' that does not simply reflect information, but that takes part in discourse. This potentially allowed for particular material things, monuments and locales to act as sites of continuing religious meaning for a society. Material things, as symbolic resources, could have their significances reworked and reinterpreted constantly, but always in the context of traditional frames of reference, for instance, through concepts such as 'ancestors', 'gods', the 'numinous' – although these problematic terms would have to be critically examined before being imposed indiscriminately onto the past. Past meanings would inform present interpretations, especially at places where a constant negotiation with the past through the act of ritual is reworked to create new symbolic codes and systems of signification (Barrett, 1991, p. 8). For Barrett, the 'meanings inscribed upon this material in one context may contribute to the meanings which are available to be recalled in another. These artefacts may be identified as "cultural objects"', a term that Barrett borrowed from Giddens (1984). Artefacts have agency and exert it as part of an ongoing dialogue with individuals, and this agency can at times be thought about as primarily a religious 'power' or 'personality', a transcendent reference point that remains somewhat stable, changing slowly as succeeding readings of the material pass through multiple horizons of interpretation. This is not a point that Barrett stressed or pursued, but is a concept closer to Ricoeur's hypothesis that some residue of the author's intention may remain fixed to the 'free-floating' text through time once it has escaped their grasp.

This universalist suggestion that material agency can be thought of as first and foremost a 'religious' power in many indigenous contexts is only true, however, if we leave behind many of the assumed corollaries and definitions of religion that depend on static concepts such as the 'sacred' or the 'supernatural', and instead define religion in the terms given in the first chapter: *a discourse whose concerns transcend the human and contingent and that claims for itself a similarly transcendent status, that includes a set of practices whose goal is to produce a proper world, and that can be engaged in by either an individual, or a community.* Material agency that is projected from a non-human source into social life, or perceived by an individual, would, by the very nature of its material and external origin, be considered to transcend the human and contingent. The examination of this idea and its consequences for any materiality of religion must be left as the subject of the next two chapters.

* * *

It can be seen that potential for any discrete archaeologies of religion has been hampered by a number of biases perpetrated in all schools of archaeological theorizing over the course of the twentieth century. Marxist and functionalist assumptions have been the major influences determining how archaeologists have treated religion during this period. An emphasis on functionalism in regard to religion, where religion was seen as a symptom of larger social processes that acted to provide a 'hidden' social function, and Marxism, where religion was seen as an intrinsically false manifestation of social consciousness, a mostly unimportant by-product of larger social truths, both effectively prevented archaeologists from examining religion in its own terms. Through the cultural–historical, evolutionary, anthropological, processual and scientific streams of archaeology, up until about the mid-1980s, these Marxist and functionalist biases effectively reduced archaeological considerations of religion, and largely erased them from the bulk of the archaeological record.

As an archaeology of the mind, cognitive archaeology attempted to create universal and monolithic rules about culture and religion. Practitioners of cognitive archaeology, such as Renfrew and Mithen, adopted an evolutionary mode for identifying religious experience and explaining religious change in the archaeological record, a mode reminiscent of the nineteenth-century anthropologists of religion such as Tylor. They perceived religion as primarily a mental construct, a belief-based and mind-orientated phenomenon, and this distanced it further from the realm of material culture. Cognitive archaeologists looked for, and found, religion in the usual places. The realms of art, death and burial were seen as being the only places that materiality could symbolically reflect religious life because they are the closest material reflections of mind available for archaeologists. Material culture was reflective, and religion simply symbolic. The polarity between the bulk of the archaeological record revealing functional use, and a minority reflecting hidden symbolic religious behaviour remained in cognitive archaeology and was entrenched. This served to deepen the polarity between the functional and the religious, allowing the religious to be seen later as solely symbolic, and a means of ulterior social communication.

For the emerging archaeological sciences of the mid-century, the influence of positivistic forms of anthropology served to further distance archaeologists from speculation on religion. Although there were moves in the 'new' archaeology to examine religion, it had little place in processual examinations of social change. This was largely because the cultural–evolutionary anthropology of the time, from which the 'new' archaeology drew much of its theory, did not consider it to be a crucial phenomenon in social life. This new emphasis on theory and method in archaeology did provide the first explicit theorizing on religion, albeit a theorization that served to virtually expel it from archaeological research altogether.

According to the functionalist bias inherent in processualism, religion had a place in human culture subordinate to more 'functional' cultural systems (such as technology and subsistence), and this subordination was reflected in the difficulties in identifying religion in the material record. Binford and Clarke's explanation of cultural as an adaptive mechanism to a hostile environment only served to promote a reductive view of human culture which was dependent completely on ecological determinism. Such functionalist assumptions formed the basis of processual systems theory, which reduced religion and ritual to a homeostatic regulating device. In short, processualism saw religion as either in opposition to that which was functional, or as a subordinate social system, the primary cultural function of which was to regulate a society and keep it in balance.

This systems assumption that religion was primarily reflective of something greater neatly combined Marxist and Durkheimian thought together, to the detriment of any potential archaeology of religion. In addition, this view that religion served a social function in regulating social life opened the way for later postprocessual and Marxist archaeologists to equate religion with ideology and modes of social control. A Marxist bias towards materiality, and a consideration of religion as an unfortunate by-product of inequality, was formalized by postprocessual archaeologists into distinct theoretical understandings of ritual as a repressive ideological tool utilized in the subjugation of populations by elites. Ritual was, like material culture, symbolic and reflective of ideological statements made by the elite. This position neither allowed for dynamic religious systems, diversity, cultural change nor positive forms of religious experience in the archaeological past. Furthermore, material culture was capable of expressing religious ideology, but it did so only as a reflection of premeditated ideology. Materiality and religion had no roles other than passive reflections of deeper social truths.

In both processual and postprocessual systems, ritual and, by extension, religion were conceived as serving purely to further a larger social function. While, for processual archaeologists, religion and material culture, in the final analysis, mediated economic relations between a culture and its environment, for postprocessual archaeologists, they masked power relations between the individuals within a culture. So, postprocessualists, by including the work of Althusser into their theory of religion and ritual, in effect reproduced a functionalist model of society, and a reductive model of religion. In fact, neither cognitive nor postprocessual archaeologies of religion managed to escape a reductive functionalist or a Marxist position when addressing the materiality of religion in the past. Instead, to find a genuinely useful attempt at engaging with religion in archaeology, one influenced by Barrett's notion that ritual and material culture could act and be read like a 'text', one has to examine the phenomenology of landscape, which is the topic of the following chapter.

4

Sacred and Profane Landscapes

Over the past three decades, archaeologists have increasingly examined ancient landscapes rather than specific sites, and this phenomenological approach to the archaeology of landscape has opened the way towards an understanding of some of the relationships between religion and material culture. This is not to say that these 'landscape archaeologists' have attempted to create a specific body of theory on the materiality of religion. The term 'religion' is used as rarely in their work as it is in that of other archaeologists. Yet, their examinations of the reflexive relationship between people and their environments and between society and landscape in the past have caused them inevitably, and somewhat vicariously, to enter into speculation on religion, and especially on the relationship between material landscapes, perception, religious action (praxis), continuity and change.

In order to appreciate how this archaeological approach has led its practitioners towards considerations of religion, it is necessary to look at how the phenomenological method has been utilized by landscape archaeologists and how this use of phenomenology to 'enter into' past worlds has led them to invariably approach past religious cosmologies, non-modern epistemologies and worldviews. It must be stated at the outset, however, that the phenomenological method is based upon the interpreting of an object or landscape through some form of mutual principle of understanding, whether this is acknowledged or not. Although archaeologists have been careful not to overtly adopt any idealistic forms of intuitive empathy with the past, they have not been able to avoid some level of preunderstanding in their phenomenologies of landscape. This has been problematic for a number of reasons.

Unfortunately, the dominant interpretative bias that has entered into the phenomenology of landscape in regard to religion has been the application of the sacred and profane dichotomy onto the material of the past. As we will see, this dichotomy forms the basis for the differentiation between the ritual and the domestic in much archaeological categorization. Implicit in the sacred and profane dichotomy is the concept of some form of essential sacred significance that is inherent in the material landscape. The use of this mode of interpreting the past must be critiqued, however, as it can only ever lead to ahistoric and essentialist understandings of both religion and material culture.

That said, there have also developed modes of landscape archaeology and ways of understanding ritual that do not rely on an application of the sacred and the profane to the prehistoric landscape. This move away from the dichotomization of the past into the 'ritual' and the 'domestic' is desirable. However, archaeological attempts to do so, and instead to see religion as a phenomenon that saturates all human action and that is embedded in all aspects of past life, have yet rarely been able to synthesize ways of identifying religion in the material past.

What these phenomenological examinations of past landscapes have been able to do, however, is to open up ways of looking at the material world as religiously active and potent, rather than as neutral or simply reflective. In particular, Giddens' theory of structuration and Bourdieu's habitus have been adopted in the context of the material landscape and this had led some archaeologists to adopt ways of looking at the material world that is amenable to it being both cosmologically infused and religiously engaged. Material things can be religious subjects as well as objects, and this is as true of the archaeological past as it is today. This consideration of the social agency that material culture can play in religious landscapes leads to the possibilities of a substantive way of approaching the materiality of religion, which is the subject of the last chapter.

Landscape, phenomenology and religion

Over the past two decades archaeologists of many persuasions, including traditional social scientific as well as self-declared postprocessualists, have become interested in examining whole regions and landscapes as cultural artefacts rather than merely specific sites or locales (for the theoretical development, see Dunnell, 1992; Ebert, 1992). The underlying rationale is that while the consideration of singular sites can reveal limited aspects of past existence, the consideration of a wider context, the geographical and cultural setting that each individual site and feature is but one small part of, can reveal many more. When the materiality of past life is extended to include a wider collection of objects beyond the usual directly manufactured artefacts clustered at specific sites, then most elements of the durable material world can come to be investigated as having an archaeological significance (Dunnell, 1992, p. 34). In this way, both natural features (such as rivers, rock outcrops, mountains) and the remains of cultural material (for instance, monuments, ruins, artefacts scatterings, inscriptions) are able to be considered simultaneously as forming the basic material constituents of any past landscape (for the archaeology of natural features see Hirsch and Hanlon, 1995; Bradley, 2000; Lekson, 1996). Where available, reports from individually excavated sites from within a bounded area may be incorporated into this 'holistic' picture of a landscape, yet frequently such archaeology requires little or no excavation but merely a thorough survey of the extant features and surface deposits of a defined region.

Often collated beneath the umbrella label 'landscape archaeology', this archaeological perspective encompasses differing views on the place held by the landscape in past cultural life and its significance to archaeological interpretation in the present. These differences are reflected in the ambiguities contained within the term 'landscape' itself.

The word 'landscape' entered the English language in the late sixteenth century as a derivative of the Dutch word *landschap*, a term which referred to a unit of human occupation, as well as a pictorial representation. Schama remarks that these origins have left 'landscape' with dual connotations of both a utilitarian area of human occupation and jurisdiction, as well as an imagined and artificial environment, mediated by human design and memory, one literally 'created' and mediated by cultural expectations, much like the Dutch countryside itself (1995, p. 10). Thomas, highlighting this blend of perception and reality, links the term 'landscape' with pictorial landscape paintings: images produced for the consumption of nostalgic, alienated urban dwellers in seventeenth-century Holland. For him, 'landscape' is connected intimately with the subject–object split characteristic of post-Cartesian philosophy, as well as the rise of elite, capitalist and gendered forms of relating to the 'objective' land (Thomas, 2001, pp. 166–9). This blend of perception and reality inherent in the term 'landscape' has, unsurprisingly, allowed it to be used in a number of differing ways by archaeologists. David and Wilson have isolated three major formulations of landscape common in the archaeological literature: a positivistic conception where landscapes are treated as objective and scientifically measurable physical entities and external environments that are independent of human subjectification or signification; an art-historical emphasis on landscapes as representations of the world, as in painted landscapes; and, finally, 'landscapes as the engagement of people in place, as experience of the world', where landscapes are 'meaningful, socially constructed places involving bodily and cognitive experience' (2002, p. 6).

It is this later concern with landscape as a conceptual category, a nexus between mind and materiality, as well as a phenomenological horizon of being and becoming, which has been at the centre of the majority of postprocessual engagements with landscape. As with much postprocessualism, this concern can be traced to a reaction against the quantitative excesses of processualism (for instance, settlement archaeology), especially the scientistic reduction of places to mere 'foci of activity' rather than 'loci of meaning' (Evens, 1985). At the same time, this shift also reflected parallel changing attitudes towards considerations of landscape in the disciplines of anthropology and geography.

For the 'new' archaeology of the 1960s, if landscape was thought about at all, it was as a neutral and 'blank' expanse of space, rather than as a collection of places. Archaeological features, sites and human patterns of distribution could be ascertained and quantified through the application of the scientific method, while subjective elements such as issues of ideology, perception or religion were irrelevant or unrecoverable. Ian Hodder was one of the first postprocessual archaeologists to critique this approach (1991), claiming that it wrongly conceived of the landscape as an abstract 'container' of human life rather than an active participant in it. Following Hodder's critique, postprocessualist approaches moved away from the science-like covering laws that attempted to chart hard material correlates between the environment and human behaviour, and instead adopted a contextual and intersubjective approach to the meaning of different landscapes (Lane, 1986). In this way, the interpretative and self-critical archaeologies of landscape drew on a parallel theoretical tradition within cultural geography (see esp. Berger, 1972).

Increasingly, the landscape was conceived to be the medium through which social actions were expressed and also, through memory and associations with the past, re-expressed to contribute towards the ongoing structuration of society. Society was conceived as a continual process, an ever-changing interaction between people and their material enculturated surroundings (Evens, 1985). At first a predominantly British affair, but increasingly influential in North America, Europe and parts of Asia (Thomas, 2001, p. 177), this creation of interpretative landscape archaeology has also been the site of what has become probably the largest and most extensive engagement with religion carried out within the discipline of archaeology.

The attitude shown towards landscape by many interpretative or postprocessual archaeologists has been broadly phenomenological in nature. It has been this attempt to effect a phenomenological reengagement with past landscapes and past worlds of meaning that has opened archaeologists to the importance and the potential for uncovering past religious perception, experience, practice and action. Hence, landscape archaeology has generally necessitated an engagement with the cultural worlds of past societies. For Knapp and Ashmore (1999), all artefacts and sites within a landscape are best seen as revealing not only the traces of past social systems such as, say, ancient economic strategies or demographic patterns but as also holding socio-symbolic, cultural and subjective dimensions that may still be accessible to the modern researcher. Thomas (2001) has taken this further, arguing that to study past landscapes is to study past mental worlds and systems of meaning, and therefore the archaeology of landscape (like all archaeology) is an exercise in phenomenology and hermeneutics. Yet, although much contemporary landscape archaeology is increasingly concerned with ancient, often prehistoric, religious perceptions, actions and cultural values, and the majority of landscape archaeologies do find themselves alluding to past religious or 'sacred' landscapes in some form, the word 'religion' still remains very rarely used in archaeological discussion of landscape.

Instead, considerations of the past cultural meaning of the landscape are often conducted under the exceedingly slippery problematic term 'phenomenology'. This term has been used in at least two distinct, yet related, ways, both of which have resulted in somewhat covert archaeologies of the religious. First, notions, drawn mostly from the work of Heidegger and Merleau-Ponty, regarding the nature of 'being' and 'dwelling' within an enculturated landscape through non-discursive and pre-intellectual bodily practice have been particularly influential. For Tilley, especially, phenomenology refers to the enculturated, meaningfully infused and prescriptive elements of residing within a landscape of continuous intelligibility. His *Phenomenology of Landscape*, consistently refers to the sacred, numinous or liminal elements of such an enculturated landscape, as well as the mundane but simultaneously 'mythic' and memory-laden elements of routine daily life (Tilley, 1994, chapters 1–2; 1996b). As a result, this form of landscape archaeology has centred on an approach based upon the determining of human routes of movement, intervisibility between monuments, sites and natural features in the landscape, and performed bodily interaction with the material world (an approach followed by Bradley, 2000; Edmonds, 1999). Also, and in characteristic fashion, Marxist archaeologists such as Tilley have examined how such material resources could have then been utilized and manipulated by elites in order to exert power on social life.

In terms of religion, these monuments, routes of movement, natural features and various other human/material relations are thought to have formalized the landscape and determined the possibilities for people to interpret their world around them, and this is described usually as having been achieved through the creation of cosmological stories, worldviews, ancestral precedents enshrined through monuments and material modifications to natural features, and so on (see esp. Edmonds, 1999; Bradley, 2005, chapters 3–4). Basically, phenomenological landscapes are assumed to have been religious, cosmic or (more usually) 'sacred' landscapes. Religion is thought to infuse and emanate from all aspects of the physical environment. For within 'a traditional society the creation of myth normally serves as the basis for the organization of society, territory, dwelling and family. The myth embodies a metaphysical doctrine and inspires every act and every artefact' (Khambatta, 1989). Or, according to Derks (1997, pp. 128–9), writing on Roman Gaul:

> The visual attention and bodily movement of the actors is presumed to be focused on a single point, whose position is bound up with certain cosmological entities (e.g. ancestors in the case of a barrow) or is found to be

linked with a particular astronomical configuration whose prime importance is in turn explained in terms of a cosmological foundation of society.

The second major way in which phenomenology has been adopted by landscape archaeologists, and still related to the first, has been to draw on the use of expanded phenomenological horizons in the interpretation of the material record. In general, archaeologists have avoided adopting the idealized 'principles of understanding' advocated by phenomenologists such as Husserl, because of a justified perception that they are overly idealistic, and dangerous to attempt to apply to the mute archaeological record (Hodder and Hutson, 2003, chapter 6; Insoll, 2004a, pp. 38–40). However, the work of Gerardus Van der Leeuw, on the relationship between power and religion, in which he attempted to enter empathetically into the phenomenon being described, rather than identifying essential characteristics of religion a priori, has been influential on many landscape archaeologists such as Thomas (Van der Leeuw, 1933; Thomas, 2001).

Considering any possible understanding of a religious expression as being grounded in the phenomenon itself, Van der Leeuw's phenomenology posited that this intrinsic 'essence' is only perceptible by the phenomenologist through first a deliberate restraint (*epoche*) and a bracketing of their subjective pre-expectations leading to the relatively open and receptive mental state characterized by *eidetic* vision. Therefore, any integration of the phenomena into an interpretative whole must, according to such a method, be arrived at *first* through the phenomenon's primary analysis and comparison. Thomas has largely adopted Van der Leeuw's phenomenology as a tool, or reminder, to encourage the archaeologist to attempt broader hermeneutical horizons, to escape from their inherent biases and perceptions, and to become more self-critical of their interpretative assumptions: to attempt, what he terms, an 'engaged' ethnography. In a sense, this is a negative utilization of phenomenology. It is not used to recreate past worlds through some preconceived formula, but rather to remind archaeologists to become increasingly aware and self-critical of their own presuppositions and to refrain from unwittingly imposing them backwards in time.

Both forms of phenomenology listed have been influential on the development of landscape archaeology, and can be labelled together as a general 'phenomenology of landscape'. Both have also been closely connected with a widespread assumption that the closer an archaeologist moves towards a valid phenomenological understanding of past landscapes as 'lived' realities for ancient human actors, the more they will begin to face the problem of needing to reaccess past religious worlds. This implicit appreciation of the phenomena of religion is based upon the likely assumption that in the absence of historical texts the specifics of ancient belief-systems can rarely be reconstructed in detail, a starting point for phenomenological interpretation is that premodern people did not perceive their worlds in the same secular manner that modern researchers traditionally attempt to (Tilley, 1994). Instead, the landscape archaeologist must at least consider an engagement with the minds of past people, minds that were most certainly foreign, strange and other – and therefore assumed to be in some way 'religious'. Whatever the validity of this assumption, archaeologists such as Thomas, Tilley, Bradley, Hodder, Richards, Edmonds and many others have made an implicit connection between ancient worldviews and religious cosmologies in their theoretical writings on the landscapes of the European Neolithic (see Thomas, 1991; Tilley, 1994; Bradley, 2000; Hodder, 1984; Richards, 1996; Edmonds, 1999). Other recent attempts to reconstruct the religious dimensions of ancient landscapes have been conducted on societies as diverse as those of pre-Columbian Central and South America, prehistoric Australian, ancient Egypt, Roman Europe and the Buddhist cultures of East Asia, among others (see Barnes, 1999; Brady and Ashmore, 1999; Richards, 1999; Tacon, 1999).

Overall, postprocessual archaeologists have examined landscapes as whole entities, and conceptualized them as enculturated material environments that provided the context for social life in the past. A people's and a society's 'horizon of intelligibility' has been generally considered to have been moulded on religious and cosmological worldviews. Through doing this, landscape archaeologists have opened the examination of materiality to a phenomenological understanding of the past, where a religious worldview is intrinsically infused in the material surroundings, and vice versa. Landscapes are conceived as being encoded with layers of meaning, memory and transhuman authority, and this allows for a view of material culture (in this case the whole material environment/landscape) as both religiously engaged and potent.

The sacred and the profane

Anthropologist Mary Douglas stated the central difficulty with any phenomenological reconstruction of landscape when she wrote that 'the organization of thought and of social relations is imprinted on the landscape. But, if only the physical aspect is susceptible of study, how to interpret this pattern would seem to be an insoluble problem' (Douglas, 1972, pp. 513–21; see also Tilley, 2006). Pure phenomenology as a method for recovering meaning from past landscapes is limited in that it rests upon the assumption that any cosmological or transcendent meanings that a religious landscape had to people in the past were predominantly subjective. They rested purely in human minds and were bound to particular historical and cultural contexts that, in the absence of textual sources or other informants, are ultimately unknowable to a modern researcher, and if speculated upon remain forever epistemologically unverifiable. To recover any past religious worlds or cosmologies, an archaeologist must make educated, but still speculative, leaps of the imagination. By far the most common speculative leap of the imagination used by landscape archaeologists has been imposing some form of sacred and profane dichotomy on to the material of the past.

Much landscape archaeology has been influenced by the supposition that there is a dichotomy between the sacred and profane in human experience, and that this dichotomy is then patterned in human behaviour and material culture. According to this assumption, 'ritual' behaviour occurs in relation to the 'sacred', while 'mundane' or 'domestic' activities are positioned within the 'profane' (for some of the influences of this categorization see Richards and Thomas, 1984). Durkheim's view of the sacred as that which is set apart in order to represent or symbolize a group's unity, and Eliade's view of the sacred as an incursion into normal reality of a wholly other order of existence have already been outlined in Chapter 2.

However, the very concept of 'ritual' as a distinct sphere of human activity, based upon Durkheim's overly stark and universalist dichotomy between the sacred and the profane has long been seriously questioned within the fields of studies in religions and anthropology. There is good evidence, for instance, that the setting aside of certain actions as sacredly significant, or ritualistic, is not common to all societies (Bell, 1992, pp. 123–4; Astor-Aguilera, 2009;

2010). Asad has suggested that ritual is best understood as merely one among many competing discourses that interact within and through the social activities of differing cultures in varying ways (Asad, 1979). That this concept of ritual is often closely associated with ideas about the sacred as a separate category of experience is well expressed by Goody (1962, pp. 36–7) who has made the point that:

> The term ritual is one that has been used in diverse ways, receiving almost as much abuse as the word myth . . . most subsequent writers, have identified ritual with the sacred, a concept that was developed by Durkheim . . . that served as his alternative to the minimum definition of religion put forward by Tylor. . . . Durkheim's dichotomy between the sacred and the profane seems to me no solution to the difficulty. One of the main grounds upon which he bases his proposal to adopt sacred as the criterion of the magico-religious is that this division is one recognized in all societies. This I believe to be no more than in the case of the natural–supernatural distinction, which he rightly notes is a categorization imposed by the European observer upon the practices and beliefs of other societies. If these ideas are not universally, or even widely, present as folk concepts, that is, concepts employed by the actors themselves, do they have any advantage . . . the world is indeed divided in two domains, as Durkheim . . . contended, but it is a division imposed by the European observer.

Certainly, this polarization of experience and activity has created a problematic dichotomy in archaeological examinations of the past, one that has continued the long established tension between the functional and the religious in archaeological interpretation. The very terms 'sacred' and 'profane' suggest some form of spatial separation and strict geographical dichotomy imposed on the world. The root *sacer* is derived from the Latin concept of setting apart and demarcating land given over to deities or the divine (see Hubert, 1994). Yi Fu Tuan (1978), however, tells us that the term 'profane' relates to earth and land set just outside of a cult temenos, perhaps a shrine or temple. Hence, the language of the sacred and the profane refers to a setting apart of one part of the world from another and the subsequent special demarcation and polarity between the two.

Similarly, for George Bataille (1989), as for Eliade, the sacred was that which was experienced as radical otherness, as a realm of antisociety where social order was upturned in a powerful holy or numinous experience similar to that of Otto. This conception of the sacred, as an incursion of 'power' in the landscape, has been widely influential in the phenomenology of archaeological landscapes. Initially, however, archaeologists adopted the notions of 'power' and 'sacred landscapes' from the fields of human or cultural geography, rather than directly from the discipline of studies in religion.

Under the influence of practice theorists such as Merleau-Ponty and phenomenologists such as Heidegger, the discipline of human geography attempted to describe and understand the importance of individuals within the landscape, including their subjective perceptions and impressions (see esp. Lowenthal, 1976; Tuan, 1974; 1977). Human geographers like Yi Fu Tuan were drawn towards questions of how religious landscapes were perceived, for instance, trying to understand the religious or spiritual connection between individuals, place and landscape, and why some places of religious significance appeared to remain unchanged in the face of significant historical change. Tuan found Rudolf Otto's (1924) mystical notion of the numinous useful for theorizing why some places appeared to have an abnormal level of power and thus attract religious activity through time. It was, he suggested, the experience of the mysterium tremendum (an uncanny and powerful sense of awe) and the numen loci (a place-bound spirit) that emanated an emotive power that created a numinous experience at certain places. These places could remain significant and 'powerful' across time, remaining potent and stable sites of popular veneration or organized religious ritual, while all other elements of the cultural and geographical landscape changed (Tuan, 1977). These popular 'phenomenological' explanation of ritual and religious landscapes, current in geographical circles, suggested that sacred places in the landscape were chosen for their inherent ability to influence experience in a dramatic or otherworldly fashion (see Otto, 1924; Tuan, 1978, Relph, 1976; Bachelard, 1964). However, it should be noted that for Otto, although the numinous manifested itself as the mysterium tremendum, an overwhelming and profound sense of otherness that projected from the material world into human perception, he did not believe that it arose *out* of the material world but only through its means. As with Eliade, there was and is a thinly guised ontological mysticism at the heart of this concept of the sacred arising 'out of' or 'through' the material landscape.

However, it was Mircea Eliade's explicitly geometric and spatial analyses of the structure of sacred space that came to influence the phenomenology of archaeological landscapes most directly. Eliade's spatially defined categorization of the sacred effectively created a strict polarity between two differing realities, the sacred and the profane. This polarity is clearly expressed in Eliade's concept of the sacred place, which was both ahistoric and cross-cultural. Eliade explained the sacred place as being a primary experiential phenomenon, which arose within the mind of *homo religiosus* (traditional, religious man) irrespective of time, space or specific religious affiliation. Manifest through a central axial hierophany (such as an *axis mundi*), and often enclosed by those who experienced it within bounded concentric rings that demarcated the sacred from the profane, it became the sacred centre of the world. This sacred place was a religious sanctuary that reconnected those who could experience it with a primordial divine timelessness and unbounded infinity (Eliade, 1957; 1986).

In his classic and influential works *Material Culture and Text* (1991) and *A Phenomenology of Landscape* (1994), Tilley used the sacred and the profane as a basis for his overly stark dichotomies between religious and non-religious space, both within prehistoric landscapes, as well as between contemporary capitalist landscapes in the present and precapitalist landscapes that were invested with meaning, myth, ritual and sacred power in the past. His categorizations of a sacred and numinous 'power' that is inherent is some locales, and his ideas on premodern man as *homo religiosus* and thus in contact with sacred experience, are all drawn explicitly from Eliade (Tilley, 1991, p. 101; 1994, p. 66). Tilley's early writings on sacred landscapes have influenced much work on the supposed 'sacred' landscapes in the Neolithic.

Colin Richards' interpretations of the prehistoric landscape of Neolithic Orkney (3300–2800 BCE) are based upon an Eliadian structure of sacred versus profane space. For Richards, such order was 'cosmologically based', and consisted of repeated concentric arrangements of space that focused in rings down on a central sacred *axis mundi* (the place of mediation between realms). These concentric circles of sacred and profane space formed a symbolic resource that structured the whole Neolithic landscape, from the arrangement and alignment of individual houses, larger ceremonial monuments and megaliths, to entire natural features such as hills and lakes. Together, this acted to create a fully 'choreographed' prehistoric landscape of the sacred and the profane (Richards, 1993; 1996). In a similar way, Paul Tacon has used Eliade's notions of the geometry of sacred space in his adoption of the *axis mundi* hierophany and its role as the connection between higher and lower worlds in his examination of the sacred landscape of prehistoric northern Australia. For Tacon (1999), such an essentialist position allows the archaeologist to organize cross-culturally material, and thus to 'see a common pattern – human-made sacred places modelled on a core set of natural places', although embellished in culturally distinct and unique ways (see also Tacon, 1990).

This focus on some kind of inherent 'power' that separates the sacred realm from the profane, and allows an archaeologist to discriminate between what is religious and what is non-religious in the phenomenological engagement with the material past has also been influential outside of purely landscape circles. As seen in Chapters 2 and 3, the polarity between 'abnormal' religious artefacts and 'normal' functional artefacts has been common to archaeological assumptions about the nature of religion in the material record. However, it is revealing to note that of the two archaeologists who have explicitly written at any length on the methodology of religion in archaeology, Colin Renfrew and Timothy Insoll, both have at times adopted a similar essentialist/archetypal notion of the sacred drawn from the theories of Eliade and Otto.

As we have seen, the centrality of personal experience in Renfrew's cognitive archaeology of religion, and the necessity for a universal and cross-cultural concept of religiosity as a common cognitive phenomenon, led Renfrew to ground his idea of the human religious experience on Rudolf Otto's idea of the numinous and the holy (Renfrew, 1994a, p. 48). For Renfrew, it was the irreducible and emotive experience of a mysterious non-human power seeming to originate outside of oneself that led to the possibility for uncovering reflections of this common apprehension in the patterning of the material past. In a similar way, Timothy Insoll has also taken note of the core, irreducible, holy or numinous experience of the sacred, and termed it the 'essence' of religion. But, for Insoll, the irreducible and indefinable nature of the numinous/sacred makes it difficult for it to be applied to archaeological contexts. He is wary of adopting it uncritically. Yet, he does state that the idea of the numinous may 'provide a starting point for a required conceptual framework' for theorizing religion in archaeology because it acknowledges the value and existence of religion in and of itself (Insoll, 2001, pp. 9–10).

Certainly, one would have to agree with Insoll's wary attitude to the use of the idea of the holy or numinous, and the sacred and profane dichotomy it presupposes, in interpretations of archaeological contexts, landscapes or otherwise. The sacred and profane dichotomy can serve as an easy theoretical underpinning of the well-used archaeological shorthand terminology that assumes oppositions between the 'ritual and domestic', 'ceremonial and mundane', 'ideological and functional', hidden and obvious', 'religious and economic' and even 'objective and subjective'. Simultaneously, the perception that the religious life of human beings is somehow connected with an irreducible quality of experience and practice is a useful counterbalance to the functionalist and reductive excesses which much of nineteenth and twentieth-century archaeology has shown in regard to religion.

Renfrew neatly referred to this contradiction when he noted that the sacred and profane dichotomy has had the effect of 'problematizing' religion in archaeology by interpreting it as a distinguishable and to some degree separate field of human activity. But he also noted that this dichotomy has at the same time facilitated archaeological interpretation of religion (Renfrew, 1994a, p. 47). As we have seen, when activities are consciously set aside for religious or 'sacred' purposes an archaeologist may be able to identify their material residue as having been either symbolic of religious action or conforming to patterns of religious experience. But if material things have other profane or secular functions and uses, then the problem of their archaeological interpretation is compounded. This may certainly be the case in material contexts such as landscapes, where religion may, like economics, be inextricably embedded within the matrix of social and material organization. Yet, although Renfrew suggests that archaeologists may, by utilizing the sacred and profane dichotomy, be making unwarranted assumptions about religion as a separate subsystem of social life in order to facilitate their reductive and functionalist interpretative categorizations, he does not wish to theorize such a problem, but rather sees it as one of the 'inescapable constraints' of a modern perspective and sums up that such 'cautionary thoughts are perhaps easier to formulate than they are to apply in practice' (1994a, p. 47).

Garwood and colleagues acknowledged this dual problem also when they used *The Sacred and the Profane* as the title for the inceptive conference on archaeology, ritual and religion, at which they attempted to recognize theoretical issues central to the interpretation and identification of ritual in the archaeological record (Garwood et al., 1991a, pp. v–vii). They showed concern that the ritual secular dichotomy pervaded most archaeological discussion on religion in the past. They saw this as problematic and their title was specifically used in order to 'bring to the centre of discussion the pivotal opposition that has structured archaeological perceptions of past social practices' and remained the implicit basis upon which most definitions of ritual and its archaeological identification had rested (Garwood et al., 1991a, pp. v–vi).

It can be seen that there are numerous problems inherent in any phenomenological approach that relies on normative formula of religious experience and practice such as the sacred and the profane. As shown above, when used as an interpretative 'principle of understanding' this formula has the effect of reinforcing a functionalist paradigm that divides the material record into a great majority that is explainable and functional and thus non-religious and a small minority that is aberrant and therefore possibly religious. Because religion is given its own underdefined sphere in human life, a mysterious, strange, unfamiliar sphere of the non-functional, set-aside and somehow supermundane, religion becomes a bewildering and unsettling thing to look for, identify or write about (Lane, 1986, pp. 182–4).

Second, this phenomenological formula imposes a necessary ahistoricity on to the material record and this can undermine the meaning of specific structures and places.

Third, there is a tendency to present the people who move in these landscapes as disembodied non-individual actors, conforming to Eliadian structures of experience, rather than as autonomous individual agents. The actions and beliefs of individual and idiosyncratic actors or agents, perhaps holding alternative experiences, upon the perception of sacred sites and landscapes are not explored or explained.

Therefore, fourth, issues of multivocality, contestation and expressions of power are incapable of being addressed. As outlined in Chapter 3, a focus on Althusserian-style ideology can lead to a reductive and overly suspicious impression of the material past, yet issues of power and contestation do have to be considered in relation to past landscapes.

Fifth, there is a general inability to determine the specifics of religious action and experience at locales in the landscape, such as the types of religious ritual or belief associated with particular places, or what kind of religious cosmology is being referenced.

Last, such formulae have little ability to address processual issues of religious change in the material record. In fact, issues of religious continuity versus change, and how this is reflected in the archaeological record, become particularly difficult once a sacred versus profane polarity is adopted.

The concept of an inherent sacred experience that is on occasion exuded by portions of the material world, is symbolized by certain predetermined forms, or experienced by people at particular places, suggests a view of material culture as being inert, passive and largely disengaged from human life. Material culture is considered functional, utilitarian and inert unless under certain special and mysterious circumstances it is able to reflect something other than itself. The idea that material things can reflect some form of agency in religious life is explored further in the next chapter, but it is important to state here that this agency cannot conform to static, essentialist or structuralist principles, but instead must be dynamic, multivocal and contextual. Questions of how material culture can take part in religious life must be taken out of an ahistoric framework for the same reasons the sacred and profane dichotomy does not assist phenomenologies of past landscapes.

The major problem is that supposedly 'sacred' landscapes appear to be monolithic, presenting a univocal religious narrative/cosmology that is fully internalized and ascribed to by everybody within a strangely one-dimensional religious society. There only seems to be one way to read a sacred landscape of this type, one dominant cosmology, and all individuals are expected to relate to their religiously infused landscape in a broadly similar manner (Asad, 1979). When applied in this unvocal fashion, the sacred and profane dichotomy appears to create essentialist and ahistoric, univocal, singular and static perception of the sacred in the past. This is especially the case when looking at particular places and locales in the landscape. Eliade's, Otto's or Tuan's theories of places of significance or structuralist spatial models reliant on universal frameworks of meaning based upon a series of analogous polarities, seriously restrict any examination of religious of cosmological landscapes as having an historical, plural, negotiated or multivocal character (Harding, 1991).

Attempts to access such universal categories of mind have often revolved around the identification of a mid-range formula, or syntax, applicable to the landscape and its built forms in order to unlock a hidden symbolic patterning. Parker-Pearson and Richards (1994) attempted to apply such a structuralist formula of spatial syntax/semantics, taken from the work of Umberto Eco (1980), to the symbolism of built structures, especially houses. But their application of a formulaic syntax were widely criticized as being universal and idealistic (Leach, 1982; Hodder, 1991, pp. 39–41; Lawrence, 1987), and resulted in an inflexible process of interpretation, similar to Eliade's repetitive interpretations of sacred space in religious history. In fact, the very structuralist syntax that they used was based upon an acknowledged relationship with the sacred and the profane dichotomy. For 'the human body's potential divisions (top/bottom, left/right, front/back, vertical/horizontal, male/female) provide a simple framework, which we impose on the world linked to concepts such as sacred/profane, future/past, and good/evil. . . . In addition the body can also represent any bounded system (like a house, a territory, a group)' (Parker-Pearson and Richards, 1994, pp. 10–11).

Indeed, the potential for there having been multiple ways of experiencing and acting within a landscape in the past must be considered. Often in phenomenologies of landscape, the importance of the individual, their context and their gender, their very identity, is viewed by the contemporary researcher as being redundant (Maclean, 2001). However, individual actions and experiences of materiality must play the central role in any examinations of landscape, for a religious landscape can only be considered so, in so far as it affected the individuals who dwelt within it. For:

> Lived landscapes are relational entities constituted by people in their engagement with the world. It follows from this that different people may experience and understand the same landscape in rather different ways. . . . [E]ach person occupies a distinctive position in relation to their landscape. . . . Landscapes might thus be said to be multiple or fragmented. It is not simply that they are perceived differently: the same location may effectively be a different place for two different people. (Bender, 1998, p. 86)

This multivocality has been difficult to reconcile with phenomenologies of the sacred and the profane which attempt to 'recover' the sacred landscape as it 'was'.

The question of multivocality within religious landscapes touches upon another important issue – that of stability, continuity and change in relation to sacred place. If a landscape contains features that are considered of sacred importance then there will be an underlying contradiction in any archaeology that looks at processual issues. This contradiction is between the idea that the sacred and its manifestations are a stable and privileged epistemological category that can be identified through phenomenology and, simultaneously, that the sacred is a facet of a living culture that is made up of a number of possibly competing narratives at any one time. If landscapes play a part in perpetuating, mediating and changing a culture through time, as postprocessualists claim they do, then they must undergo a constant process of negotiation and recreation themselves. Otherwise, both the landscape and the social system would be static and there would not be a reflexive or recursive relationship between the two. This is similar to the point made above that notions of the active presence or 'power' of materiality must extend beyond static schemes such as the sacred and profane, if material culture is to have anything other than a static and reflective influence on religious life.

Archaeologies of landscape that attempt to ascertain past religious significances must, it seems, consider an ancient landscape in much the same way as we might a contemporary one. Central to any lived landscape, past or present, will be a number of dynamic issues including ritual and religious change, negotiation, reinterpretation, different and perhaps sometimes competing practices and relationships, all being played out within the realm of material engagement. For archaeologists, of course, the unique timescale provided to them means that these issues of change and plurality may be particularly pertinent.

This raises the important issue of the reliability of archaeological evidence for apparent ritual and religious continuity in the past. In particular, whether the appearance of material continuity in the archaeological record necessarily points to continuity in religious life. If a site shows continual occupation, or if a monument is reused, reappropriated or referenced in the material culture across time, this might be taken as evidence for religious continuity. Yet, the occurrence of a marked continuity in the archaeological record, and even the wholesale appropriation of monuments and places, may in fact be evidence of attempts to create the impression of tradition and changelessness by people living through times of marked transition (Bender, 1992).

Certainly, there is much evidence for the long continuity of the use of particular natural places in European prehistory. Ritual deposits in particular seem to be present at many places from the Mesolithic all the way through until the Iron Age, and perhaps even into the Early Middle Ages (Bradley, 2000, p. 153; Allen and Gardiner, 2002). The question is whether examples of material continuity can be interpreted as also being examples of millennia-long ritual continuity and, even more difficult, the long established existence of 'sacred place'. An equally plausible interpretation would be that these apparent continuities in material culture were as much about consciously *manufacturing* and *maintaining* continuity in the face of social, economic, ritual and religious change.

Rather than seeing ritual and material continuity as a result of some imperceptible appreciation of 'the sacred', or proof of an ahistoric religious 'continuity', these sites may be taken as evidence for Giddens' (1979) concept of structuration, where the present is constantly created anew in response to the past. One religious structure may literally be built on top of another, say a mosque above a church, but this may be less about the expression of some timeless continuity of the 'sacred' and more about the use of the past by those in the present to negotiate and create ever-changing social structures. In this case, the materiality of religion (for instance, monuments, artefacts and landscape features marking place and memory) can be seen as one malleable resource constantly used by social actors to shape and negotiate the present. Religious sites may be appropriated, not because there is some phenomenology of the sacred underlying their existence, but because they are visible and significant material actors that participate in social life.

Hence, supposed sacred continuity that involves the appropriation of the past, or the invention of tradition through building on to the past landscape, may indicate religious *change* rather than religious *continuity*. Modern applications of pseudoarchaeological interpretation in order to recover the religious 'meaning' of ancient sites, the 'rediscovered' cultural significance of places such as Stonehenge for various neo-Pagan and other groups, for example, are good contemporary examples of this creative process being either consciously or unconsciously applied to the material landscape. The material past, including archaeological sites, are a primary resource in the creation of religious meaning, and it is their link with perceptions of continuity and durability that appears to give them this affordance.

As we have seen, the monolithic application of the sacred and profane dichotomy, and notions of some form of chthonic power of the *numen loci* do not allow phenomenologies of landscape to addresses issues of cultural variety, power of change. It has been suggested that a perception of an immutable sacredness may not be responsible for the existence of apparent archaeological continuity at a religious site. But such continuity does certainly exist, often over exceedingly long periods of time. Material things, including monuments, natural features and places do have the ability to attract and accrete long-lasting religious associations. As we shall see, when the sacred and the profane are taken out of a consideration of the materiality of landscapes then this continuity can be seen to be a function of material agency, rather than some other alien 'power', 'structure' or 'essence' being expressed through the material.

There are major problems with the concept of the sacred and profane being monolithically imposed upon archaeological landscapes. Not only have the sacred and the profane tended to be polarized, such schemes are ahistoric, univocal and incapable of exploring issues of religious change, or the dynamic relationship between material culture and religious life. Furthermore, this dichotomy has resulted in the polarization of the material evidence from the archaeological past into the 'ritual' and the 'domestic'. This dichotomy between the sacred–ritual and the profane–domestic is unhelpful for it fails to reflect the complex nature of relationships people have with their religious landscapes. When this dichotomy is removed, the range of possible relationships that people had with their material environment is expanded. It is now time for us to explore the potential of archaeologies of landscape without the sacred and profane/ritual and domestic dichotomies, and the repercussions for the materiality of religion.

As noted in Chapter 2, although the sacred and profane dichotomy has been commonly applied to the archaeological past, in the manner of Hawkes' Ladder of Inference, it is essentially a culturally bound and limited concept (Lane, 1986), derived in part from Otto and Eliade's Christian background, personal mysticism and covert confessional agenda (see Wasserstrom, 1999). Hawkes claimed that he found the functional easier to recover from the archaeological record than the 'spiritual', but never seems to have considered that his divisions of past life into the technological, economic and religious may have been inappropriate to the societies he was attempting to interpret. The sacred and the profane do not necessarily exist as a strict polarity, or even dichotomy, in all cultural contexts. Instead, they may be seen as complimentary, parts of a singular whole, or not existing as separate ontological or experience categories at all.

Descola and Pálsson (1996) have contrasted the contemporary West with a series of other societies where the sacred and the profane are by no means as clearly delineated. They describe such cultures as having a 'monist' worldview, as opposed to contemporary Western, or 'dualist', modes of thought. They note that in such cultures, the world may not be conceived of as a series of opposites, but rather as a unified whole, where ritual permeates many or all aspects of daily life. For instance, certain animist cultures have a conception of an interpenetrating social and material environment that is more graded than the ritual and domestic dichotomy. Harvey describes Maori living in a relational universe where conceptual pairs are related collaboratively rather than oppositionally (2005a, pp. 50–65). Concepts that are seen as dualities in the West, such as human and animal, object and subject, sacred and profane, are instead understood as intertwining associative complements, inseparably coupled. The ever-changing interpenetration of such pairs engenders life and gives rise to all the manifold possibilities of creation (Harvey, 2005a, p. 52).

It has already been described in Chapter 2 in what ways the apparent polarity in contemporary academia between materiality and religion is a product of many strands of religious, philosophic and academic history. It can be argued that the sacred and profane dichotomy, as well as its correlates such as the ritual and domestic, are also contingent on Western history and that when they have been imposed on to the past it has resulted in subtle and deeply layered interpretative dilemmas (Bruck, 1999, pp. 313–14). The isolation of the ritualistic, or sacred, actions from the domestic, or profane, may be based upon structures of thought and practice peculiar to Western post-Enlightenment rationalism and modernity. Namely, the Cartesian model of the world in which perceived reality is split into a number of paired opposites, such as mind and body, culture and nature, subject and object, sacred and profane. Such opposites are also hierarchically ranked, so that mind may be privileged over body, subject over object, and so on (Foucault, 1965). In such a scheme, factual knowledge and functionality are privileged while ritual may be relegated to a secondary role (Bruck, 1999, pp. 317–8; Bell, 2005). Where there is no distinction, however, between the sacred and profane then ritual action may not necessarily be distinguished from domestic or mundane actions. In such a case, ritual can best be understood as an integrated part of daily life.

Ritual may not always be best thought of as a drastically differing type of action, but instead as a form of communication that is inherent within much daily action and social practice (see Asad, 1983; Harvey, 2005b; Bell, 1992). This perspective, seeing ritual as a type of communication that is potentially present within all action, largely breaks down the sacred and profane dichotomy. For Sperber (1975) any object could be treated as symbolic, or used as a ritual item. For Edmund Leach, ritual is not a distinct type of action or behaviour but is, rather, the symbolic, communicative and expressive aspect of human behaviour in general. Many objects and activities have practical and technical as well as expressive and aesthetic aspects. Ritual is where the aesthetic, communicative component is prominent (Leach, 1982). Mary Douglas gives the example of the Dinka herdsman, who, in a rush to get home in the evening in time for a meal, knots a bundle of grass in a material sign of delay. Douglas describes how the herdsman then redoubles his effort to hasten home once his mind has been sharpened and his attention focused by the performance of the ritualistic rite. It is not a magical or 'sacred' act which then allows the herdsman to take his time, it has no practical effective power, but rather is a personal performance of an action that creates a desired mental state (Douglas, 1966, pp. 78–80). This ritualistic rite of the knotting of the grass as a materialized sign of delay can be understood as being one material discourse within a wider religious framework that transcends the mere human and contingent. It is a practice that has as its goal the production of a proper world that is in conformity with the Dinka assumptions about that world. This fits with the definition of religion given in Chapter 1.

Some archaeologists have also attempted to treat ritual not as a unique kind of action, but rather as one communicative aspect that is potentially inherent within all action, and that is displayed within much daily practice (Lane, 1986; Barrett, 1991; Bruck, 1999). For Harding, ritual and religion are best seen, not as a particular *thing*, but as an *aspect* of things. Instead of terming some environments 'ritual landscapes', he advocates that all prehistoric landscapes can best be considered as examples of sacred geography. Although Harding still adopts the term sacred, without fully considering its implications, he does present a view of the material past that is amenable to the embedded nature of religion, in which religion, economy and environment are all very closely related parts of normal everyday life (Harding, 1991; see also Lane, 1986).

However, this very notion of embedded religion is highly problematic. For instance, Timothy Insoll in his *Archaeology of Islam* (1999, p. 8) attempted to illustrate how all aspects of past life could be structured by religion. Insoll exerted considerable effort to stress that this was not a recapitulation of Eliade's ideal and normative traditional world of *homo religiosus*, in which a total immersion in sacred time is contrasted with the secular, modern present, yet, his notions of how such a view differed, or could be translated into an archaeology of religion, were ill-defined. Although Insoll's years of fieldwork in Islamic Africa granted him the ability hold a generous and 'ethnographically engaged' notion of the place held by religion and ritual in traditional daily life, this 'embeddedness' is, ultimately, indefinable. Insoll's later work attempted to identify elements of sacred belief in the material residue of past actions, but his notions of religion as 'the key building block of identity' and a 'holistic package possibly structuring all aspects of life' were difficult to transfer into material correlates (2004a, pp. 17–18, 150). His generalized archaeology of religion, perhaps inevitably, becomes a sort of general reminder, or 'rule of thumb', for the archaeologist to consider religion as a holistic cultural superstructure. So, in the case of ritual, determining where exactly, if anywhere, expressive, communicational action becomes necessarily ritualistic is difficult. If all human actions have a ritual component, then eventually almost all spheres of life become, in some way, religious (for the argument against such a loosely defined and all-embracing 'non-definition' of ritual, see Goody, 1977). In addition, the entire landscape, and every aspect of the material world, would be considered religious as well – depending on an individual's point of view.

Debates such as these quickly encompass issues of perception and meaning, specifically issues of objective versus subjective perceptions of landscape. For processual and environmental archaeologists, landscapes are best perceived as fully objective, a set of neutral resources and material objects 'out there'. For some phenomenologists, however, landscapes are instead thought of as fully subjective, as always-already enculturated 'horizons of intelligibility'. However if, as we have seen, these 'horizons of intelligibility' are conceptualized as cosmological worldviews with transcendent, or at least transhuman referents (such as ancestors, divinities, non-human subjects, etc.), if they are basically 'religious' landscapes, then it is debatable whether terms such as 'sacred' and 'ritual' retain useful explanatory value at all.

The debate within landscape archaeology during the late 1990s between Derks and Oosten on the nature of cosmological landscapes illustrates these issues well. For Derks, landscapes were experienced dually. They were 'double faced' and consisted of 'a foreground actuality of every-day existence and a background potentiality of an imagined timeless ideal'. These two views of landscape, the phenomenal and the imagined, were alternately perceived and became inextricably intertwined in the minds of subjects because 'people continuously seek to realise in ordinary life the ideals of an imaginary existence'. So, the appearance and organization of a landscape inevitably reflects the dominant associations of a culture; it will be secular, capitalistic and neutral in the West while being religious, cosmological and significant in 'other societies' (Derks, 1997, p. 126). For Derks, there was a dichotomy between two ways of perceiving. A person's vision constantly flickers between the objective and the subjective, and the physical reality supplies the foundation for the imaginary or constructed. For, 'hidden behind the observable landscape lies the imaginary one, referring to a permanent cosmological order of ancestors, spirits and gods' (Derks, 1997, p. 126).

In replying to Derks, Oosten advocated instead a singular vision of how landscapes were perceived, claiming that any landscape is a cosmology from the first, and that 'a landscape is never objectively given, it is a social construction' (1997, pp. 152–4). Influenced by Heidegger's conviction that meaningful perception is a process that precedes analytical neutral observation, Oosten claimed that all 'new' landscapes will be invariably interpreted in accordance with culturally determined precedents. 'New land is organized in old categories [and] the phenomenal landscape can only be described in terms of an imaginary landscape; the landscape is named, interpreted, categorized etc., in terms of a cosmological order' (Oosten, 1997, pp. 152–4). Hence any perceived landscape is a cosmology from the first. Cosmological orders are not only 'reflections of a landscape but instruments to organise it' (Oosten, 1997, p. 154). Hence, ritualized and meaningful landscapes are not imagined entities but rather modes of experiencing and ordering the world, of categorizing it from the first.

This is similar to Merleau-Ponty's concept that reality can only be understood through an 'actual experience which is prior to the objective world' (1945, p. 57). Human beings never escape their own 'phenomenological field', which patterns the material world according to previously experienced routines, actions and perceptions. Interestingly, for Merleau-Ponty, this phenomenological field structures both the interaction between human beings, as well as between human bodies and material bodies. Related is Heidegger's notion of 'being' and 'dwelling', in which humans negotiate skilfully and make sense of their material surroundings, without having to think about them analytically for much of the time (1962, p. 79). Perception and interpretation are coextensive, and the material world is never accessed in its 'raw' neutral state. Material things are not seen primarily or first to the human eye as 'blank' and 'meaningless', as a neutral objective stratum upon which humans then subsequently inscribe cosmological value and meaning. Rather, this notion of a precognized blank and neutral materiality is a characteristic of the modern condition of *gestell* or 'enframing' in which observers reduce the world and its contents down to objects of instrumental reason.

Within archaeologies of landscape that have been influenced by these concerns the desirability of imposing notions of sacred and profane or ritual and domestic onto elements of material culture appears to be inappropriate. This has important implications for how one can conceptualize the relationships between materiality and religion. If there is no prediscursive materiality, if people are instead always-already within a context of meaning which refers to cosmological and religious referents, then the great sum of subjective relationships with the material world would all partake, to some degree or another, in what we would call the religious. Accordingly, people can be understood to experience the material world, live in it, move through it, and discover it religiously, from the first and at all times. In such a case, archaeological landscapes should be regarded as being neither ritual nor domestic but rather as infused religious geographies that play a vital part in an overarching worldview in which religion and material culture are inseparable. From ethnographic examples taken from Australian Aboriginal, Saami, Pacific Northwest and Neolithic cultures, Thomas states that 'at the risk of oversimplifying this material, each example appears to present the landscape as in some sense animated, and involved in a link of reciprocity with human beings' (2001, pp. 173–5).

This notion of landscapes as intersubjective fields of significance is reminiscent of the worldviews of some animist cultures, where much of the material world is perceived to consist of 'other-than-human persons' (Harvey, 2005a, pp. 109–13 esp.), entities which although perhaps material, must be interacted through sophisticated codes of social etiquette. Religions then are the etiquette by which human beings interact with other persons, some of which may be non-human. Religion does not need to have reference to 'divine' beings, but rather it can be the grounded interaction with many aspects of the concrete and imagined landscape, from other humans to stones and trees. Much of religion then becomes 'relational', that is, the relationships of practice between a world of persons, many of which are non-human and some of which may be embodied materially as things or objects. Harvey's use of the term 'animism' in this context may be somewhat unhelpful, however, as it does imply that everything in the world believed to be 'ensouled', which may not be the case, but it does have the major benefit to describe a material world that is 'animate', that is made up of material objects and things that are active social 'persons' – whether considered 'alive' or not. Basically, this is another way of saying that a culture's worldview is based upon cosmological referents and is embedded in aspects of their social and material world. Or that religion is a general ordering structure that encompassed a great many aspects of past life, notwithstanding the material.

At the close of this wide-ranging discussion, it must be concluded that both the sacred and profane as well as the ritual and domestic dichotomies are artificial and misleading structures to impose on to people's relationships with the material world in the past, or for that matter in the present. Ethnographic examples from non-modern societies reveal other, more diverse, more relational and more intersubjective ways in which people can interact with their social and material landscapes (for excellent examples from Mesoamerica, see Astor-Aguilera, 2010). Attempts to see ritual as an aspect of all action and religious cosmological meaning as a precondition for phenomenological experience of the world open up examinations of landscape and materiality to notions of the 'embededdness' of religion within all aspects of daily life. These approaches, however, have been considered largely problematic by archaeologists, as they appear to erase the religious as a special sphere of life from the past, rather than aiding to recover it. Yet, these views do allow for a far more mutually reflexive, active and dynamic understanding of the relationship between material culture and religiosity. All material things can be seen as potentially religious and potent, active and engaged in social reproduction, and it is to the further elaboration of this theme that we shall now turn.

Reflexive religious landscapes

So far the argument has been made from a number of differing perspectives that there is a need for both archaeology and studies in religion to acknowledge the existence of a more mutually recursive relationship between material culture and human religiosity. In this chapter it has been shown how the phenomenology of landscape has been an exceedingly productive site for archaeological explorations of just such a relationship. Although archaeologists have rarely used the term 'religion' in these studies, the questions that have been raised about the relationship between people's cosmological perceptions of the world and their material environments have encouraged understandings of the materiality of the past as being fundamentally religiously active and potent. In this section, the nature of material culture as an active agent in religious life is explored, especially in relation to the ideas of supposed 'sacred' continuity and change at archaeological sites that were outlined above.

Pierre Bourdieu was no friend of religion, but his theory of habitus has been used by many landscape archaeologists to understand how everyday ritual action may have reconstituted society over generational time and left material traces in the archaeological record. Bourdieu himself rarely considered religion, and when he did it was as an example par excellence of the subtle and repressive process of symbolic violence: the naturalization of arbitrary power relationships and systems of meaning so that they are perceived by social actors as eternal, immutable and objective facts of nature. As a classic 'Master of Suspicion', in the intellectual tradition of Marx, Durkheim and Foucault, Bourdieu's work effected to imply that religion was a form of particularly sinister symbolic violence, one that effectively masks arbitrary human whim as immutable divine law, and which establishes, legitimizes and reproduces social inequality and unjust political systems. 'God is never anything other than society' Bourdieu was fond to stating (Rey, 2007, p. 80), and for him and those of his post-structuralist ilk, society is rarely anything other than repressive.

In a similar way to concepts of honour or duty, religion was analysed by Bourdieu as a socially sanctioned lie that allows us to accept the injustices of the world. Yet, surprisingly, from this unpromising set of hoary modernist assumptions, Bourdieu's theoretical concepts have been used by archaeologists to examine some of the materialized and embodied expressions of religiosity and how these contribute to the social reproduction of religious life.

For instance, habitus has been a major influence on postprocessual archaeologies of landscape. First coined by Marcel Mauss to refer to habitual bodily interactions with the environment, Bourdieu (1977) used habitus to denote the process whereby people interact non-discursively with their surroundings through subtly transmitted habits, routines and cultural norms. For Bourdieu, habitus included strategies of practical habitual logic and bodily technique, embedded in day-to-day activity, which were used to negotiate the social and material world. It was prediscursive, unconscious and unable to be reduced to an objective understanding. This was because Bourdieu considered it to be the result of preconceptual habits that serve to make social life regular and predictable, rather than abstract rarefied rules, which are after-the-fact intellectualizations. So, for the most part, habitus is passed down the generations, not through discursive communication, but through unconscious enculturation, practice and emulation. This focus on the primacy of actions and practices in transmitting knowledge and understanding, rather than words or script, is illustrated by a member of the Daribi tribe in New Guinea telling a curious anthropologist to 'eat our pandanus fruit, smoke our tobacco, and you will know our language' (Tilley, 1999, p. 262).

For landscape archaeologists such as Tilley and Thomas, this concept of habitus reinforces Heidegger's conviction of the primary nature of being, and Merleau-Ponty's idea (also expressed as 'habitus') that people for the most part interact with their landscape through preconceptual movement and habit. It is posited that in the past, people did not commonly examine or 'think' about their surroundings, but unconsciously interacted with their environments through repetitive modes of action and practice: through habitus. As with Oosten's always-already cosmological landscape, the material environment becomes less the subject of people's discursive or analytical thoughts, their symbolic schemes, but rather it is understood as a largely unregarded force that structures the very fabric of their experience and existence, and does so in accordance with cosmological referents, mythic stories, ancestral precedents, and so on. Poetically, it could be said that the religious landscape is 'breathed' in.

As we have already touched upon, this notion that a landscape provides the medium of social action, shapes that action and also embodies the outcome of that action, has been linked with Antony Giddens' theory of structuration, in which there is a reflexive relationship between individuals and the social structures they create. For Giddens, these structures, conceived generally as intangible social institutions rather than material things, are both the 'medium and outcome of action' (1979, pp. 72–3; 1984). Social reproduction occurs through the constant reconstitution of society as it is repetitively enacted and practised. Cultures are in a process of constant recreation, as are individual biographies (Tilley, 2004; 2006). Cultural change is a constant because meaning is constantly worked out through an ongoing and fluid process of negotiation with past structures. Continuity occurs when past structures, memories and institutions reproduce themselves in similar fashions through successful re-enactments. So this approach envisions a dialectical relationship between the past and the present, in which present society is constantly being reshaped through the appropriation and reinterpretation of pre-existing social structures remembered from the immediate past.

As the material context for both a society and an individual, the landscape structures social life through exerting an influence on its inhabitant's thoughts, expectations and physical movements. It does this in at least two distinct ways: as a fundamental material constraint on somatic bodily action, and as an embodiment of a mental framework that patterns daily life through the association of memories. In the first method, the landscape exerts cultural meaning as a physical parameter determining the context for all actions and experiences open to an individual and society. Many forms of meaning can be enculturated through the constraint of bodily movement, including the religious. In archaeological studies concerned with bodily somatic movement, there has been an interest in the ways in which material structures and locations may have influenced individual's thoughts and actions in the past by determining the potential avenues of movement and sight that were available to populations (Thomas, 1990, pp. 167–8; 1991; Tilley, 1994; 1996b).

The second way in which landscape exerts cultural meaning is as a heuristic device recording and transmitting precedent and norm through the medium of memory. An example is the seemingly ubiquitous human custom of superimposing mythic stories, legends and values on to any visible geography in a landscape. A slightly less overt example is the use of language metaphors, idioms and stories. For instance, the culture and language of the Western Apache in Arizona is enriched with large numbers of landscape metaphors. The landscape 'is said to "stalk people with stories" and because of this they know how to "live right"' (Tilley, 1999, p. 181; see also Basso, 1996). To act rightly is expressed by the idiom 'the straight valleys', and to lie to one's relatives or close kin is to 'cross into the red earth'. More concretely, an area of jagged and uplifted stones in the central Nevada desert is taught to be the place where many adulterers have petrified to stone. To wander in or near this area is to break kinship taboos (Tilley, 1999, p. 181).

Landscapes can also be constructed and their meanings 'rewritten' through their material embellishment and modification. Rowlands (1994) has described two different ways in which memory can be enshrined in the landscape. One is through the commemoration of events, people, occurrences, and so on, in the special construction of monuments. These are intended to make concrete a memory, to formalize and control it through the use of material culture. But this material culture may then be reinterpreted and reused as time goes on.

For instance, monuments can embody authority within a landscape – sometimes drawing that authority from a landscape itself and at other times stamping their own authority on to a certain place. Hence monuments can *confer* meaning on to a place and as such they can be moved around the landscape in order to transform and even revolutionize its pre-existent religious and political associations. One example is the *lat* pillars that have monumentalized the landscapes of North India from Mauryan times onwards. They were originally transported over 1,000 kilometres from their quarry sites and later many were moved from their original positions to various urban environments (Irwin, 1987). For instance, a pillar was moved by Islamic sultan Feroz Shah from Khizrabad to Delhi in the fourteenth century and re-erected at his palace, presumably to embellish his authority through the conferring of historical legitimacy and brute power. Such a practice is reminiscent of young Western nation-states appropriating and re-erecting ancient Egyptian obelisks in prominent public spaces, such as the Cleopatra's Needles in London and Paris. A more continuous and impressive example would be the Vatican Obelisk originally transported from Heliopolis to the new Roman Forum in Alexandria during Classical Antiquity, and then to Rome itself, and eventually erected in the centre of St Peter's Square during the late Renaissance – a stone memorial that signified three religions and conferred authority on three polities over a space of over 4,000 years. Such monuments are places of cultural memory in the landscape. Like the sites of exceptional 'sacred' continuity uncovered in Britain and elsewhere, mentioned above, monuments may have no fixed meaning, but rather a string of meanings through time, utilized by differing groups (Irwin, 1987).

The other way of creating memories is through acts that leave no lasting obvious trace behind them, for instance, acts such as the deposition of valuables or the destruction of monuments. Such acts leave few physical traces in which the memories can be embodied consciously, or from which they can be latter recalled. In this case, the meaning and memory of the place may be transmitted through oral traditions (stories, songs, the naming of places) or perhaps through repeated rituals of some type (the placing of votive deposits, the occurrence of ceremonies, pilgrimage). The second type is more fluid than the first type, and hence religious change may be more apparent in the first.

Concepts of habitus and structuration, when applied to the material landscape, reveal the process through which a material world can project religious and cosmological schemes of meaning down through time in a fashion that is seemingly unconscious or 'natural' to its inhabitants. Also, while such structures are passed down through time, the landscape is itself structured and restructured by their transmission, through repetitive actions and practices. Hence both continuity and change are incorporated in such a theory. The landscape can be seen as in a state of fluid interaction between its inhabitants, their thoughts, actions and the material results of these actions.

Change occurs because the landscape is negotiated through practice, or praxis: a set of often habitual bodily movements, routines, repetitive actions and preunderstood techniques of action. These practices can modify material things, leave marks and remain materialized long after their initial act has passed. The moving of monumental pillars around the landscape, for example, is an example of durable praxis, albeit of an elitist, exceedingly dramatic and state-sponsored kind. For Bourdieu, the landscape was lived not read, and any meanings that were given to places and the spatial order were not fixed or invariant givens but must be invoked in the context of practice and recurrent usage. Meanings adhere to a spatial frame only through the medium of human agency. For Heidegger, the relationship between landscape and praxis was embodied in the idea that 'space is practice' (for examples, see Parker-Pearson and Richards, 1994, p. 5). He posited that it is only through a person's dealings with the objects within the material world that they are immersed perpetually within that these objects come to have ontological significance. This means that knowledge of the material world resides in a person's actions, how they use and interact with things. Things are significant according to how they participate and are used in everyday activities.

For example, the stone idol that represents a deity, found in the inner sanctum of a South Indian temple, such as the Meenakshi temple at Madurai, has a number of mythological associations attached to it, or better still attached to that which it represents. Yet, its religious significance is also mediated through recurrent and familiar usage of its material form and its surrounding material environment that adheres to certain socially understood rules. The statue can only be handled by priests of a certain caste, only after a number of ritual purifications are performed, and while ritual sounds are uttered, and only at a certain time of the day. The statue may be carried to the outer boundaries of the temple enclosure and carried in a procession that circumnavigates the temple precincts. In this procession, the idol is accompanied by many other material objects (standards, a throne, sceptres, trumpets, etc.), all of which act as mediators in the social relationships between the people who accompany the idol. These forms of recurrent usage communicate a host of social and religious rules, between the priests and the onlookers, but also between the priests, onlookers and the divine. Rules and norms about the access to sacrality, purity, caste, boundaries and the temporal order of the day, and by extension also the year and even the cosmic eon, are all expressed through the habitual use of this material idol and how it participates and co-creates the human–material dynamics of the ritual procession. This is an example of how a material object can be significant according to how it participates and is used in everyday activities. This human–material dynamic as it relates to religion and the archaeological record is further illustrated in the following chapter.

This is the difference between Heidegger's *Zuhandenheit*, 'readiness-to-hand', in which the objects of the world are known through their physical proximity with our selves and bodies, and their usability, and *Vorhandenheit*, 'presence-at-hand', where objects are seen as individual 'things in themselves', with their own discrete properties and identities (1962, p. 101). For Heidegger's phenomenology of being, 'presence-at-hand' is a secondary and derivative mode of knowing the world, characteristic not of living and acting in it, but of thinking about it while standing removed from it. As this secondary thinking about the world is supported by the prior intuition of the world as ready-to-hand, as practised and engaged with, any thoughts or theories of the world are also first and foremost 'thought' through embodied engagement and praxis.

Therefore, it is partially the practical actions of the human agent, in broad conformity with the habitus of a society, which transmit and reconstitute society through the re-enactments of social forms. But just as the social structures are constituted, to some degree, by the subjective powers of human agency, so these very powers of agency are constituted in some way by the objective social structures. Hence, individual human praxis plays a role in the structuration of society, but the wider landscape that embeds social structure within its form plays an equally important role in the structuration of individual praxis. There is a recursive relationship between the two.

One form of praxis that may play a part in the continual structuration of society is ritual. For Bourdieu, ritual was an important, prescriptive form of habitus that was used for sustaining relations of domination in societies lacking objectified institutions (1977, p. 2). Such relations could only be maintained in a masked form, under the veil of an enhanced, perhaps divine, relationship, lest by revealing itself domination provoked violent dissent from its 'victims'. This is what Bourdieu termed 'symbolic violence' (1977, p. 192). In a manner reminiscent of the Marxist influenced archaeologists examined in the previous chapter, unspeakable social truths were thought to be reproduced, reiterated, conserved and protected through ritual, itself given authority through close connection with the supernatural. That ritual can play a role in the structuration of social forms is also suggested by interpretations of ritual as practice. For Sperber (1975), in most societies rituals and symbols had no specific meaning, or many differing and conflicting meanings. Similarly, for Lewis (1980), rituals can and do exist without exegesis. Rituals may be explicit and prescribed in regard to the bodily actions of the performers and material interactions that are played out, while any interpretation of an interior meaning hidden behind this exterior performance may not be given, may be fluid, may be forgotten or may never have existed at all. In the manner of Mervyn Peake's fictional *Gormenghast* (1950), the importance inherent within a ritual may be whether it is performed properly and hallowed by tradition, not any obscure underlying symbol or meaning. In this way, it may be that in many traditional contexts social reproduction was partially effected through habitual ritual performance, and these ritual contexts may have been the primary locales for the creation of social order and social change (Bloch, 1977). This is an opposite position to the processualists, who along with Durkheim, saw religion as an abstracted collection of beliefs and practices that symbolized social facts and as a whole provided a representation of the social order. Instead, ritual is the means of both social stability and change, ritual action can provide a society with homeostasis, but it is also a field of discourse, as suggested by Barrett.

Archaeologists such as Edmonds have taken these concepts a step further and suggested that ritual was not only practice, but was everyday mundane practice; what archaeologists have usually termed 'the domestic'. For Giddens, it was the practices of daily life that were the most common context within which social reproduction occurred. For Bourdieu, both ritual and domestic activities drew from the same cosmological worldviews of a society in order to give them symbolic meaning, but this did not make them identical. For Edmonds, rituals were woven into the cycles of everyday routine existence, and his reconstructions of Neolithic Britain present an image of religious and cosmological belief-systems being passed down over the generations through simple acts such as knapping flint, collectively felling an oak or going on a seasonal trading expedition. According to this picturesque vision, daily practice was the link between the cosmologically infused paradigmatic past and the social present: '[P]eople's sense of who they were and what was expected of them would shape and be shaped by their participation in the everyday rituals going on around them' (Edmonds, 1999, pp. 49–50 esp.). These ethnographies of the Neolithic are important attempts to break down the sacred and profane/ritual and domestic dichotomies in the manner described in the previous section. However, such images of ritual and daily life being fused into a timeless past tend to suffer from the drawback that they present a seemingly unchanging and somewhat folksy prehistory, one that appears to be almost idealized into a Neolithic version of preindustrial Britain.

In terms of the interaction between material culture and religion, however, the concept that the structuration of social life occurs through practices constrained by an enculturated landscape raises the possibility for the beginnings of a theory of the materiality of religion. If an individual's actions are constricted and informed by their material environment, but at the same time these actions leave durable traces on that material environment, then one of the structures that is transmitted and modified down through time through repetitive practice is the material environment itself. In this way, the religious landscape is in a constant state of social interaction with individuals, it is an agent and a subject.

Also, if materiality is one of the mediums and results of social action, its very durability and seeming permanence would allow the material structures of social life to change at a slower rate than other, intangible social institutions. This has implications for sites where there are long sequences of material continuity but set against a background of dramatic social and religious change. Rather than perceiving such sites of material continuity as the transmission of 'the sacred', or a 'tradition', it would be more appropriate to see them as locales where materiality and human action have been in a long reflexive relationship with one another in the context of renegotiated cosmological worldviews. What is interesting is that the very materiality of the site appears to have an element of agency that is independent of the specific cosmological frame of reference within which it is interpreted. This can be seen in the very common case of material structures or features that are reappropriated by differing religious traditions, either sequentially or simultaneously.

Giddens was interested primarily in the mutually interdependent relationship between subjective social agents (individuals) and constraining social structures (institutions such as the law or kinship) rather than material structures like the landscape. He did not explore in any detail the implications of his theory of structuration for material culture (Barrett, 1994; Bradley, 2000).

For Bourdieu, however, the physical locale of habitus, its very materiality, may be one of the primary embodiments of habitus. He explored how the same material world, holding within its built form an entire array of cosmological, ethical, moral, practical and religious frames of meaning, could be perceived differently by different social groups – such as men and women in a North African Berber house (Bourdieu, 1970). However, neither Giddens nor Bourdieu considered the very materiality of material things as a major factor in the formation of social life, and certainly not in religious life.

Furthermore, the idea that material things may be one of the primary locations of religious meaning creation is an implication raised by the adoption of Giddens' and Bourdieu's theories by archaeologists, but it has not been widely applied outside of an archaeological frame, if at all. In terms of landscape, if people's subjective experience and sense of identity was in part embodied within, and drawn from, the material matrix they inhabited, then their religious experiences and frames of meaning had an ingrained material component and were not merely subjectively superimposed upon the world. If this is in fact the case then it must be acknowledged that a good part of religion dwells within material culture, and that the 'spiritual' and the 'material' are in fact not opposed at all.

A good non-landscape example of the material structuration of social life that includes the religious is the basket weaving of the Yekuana tribes of the Orinoco River of southern Venezuela. According to an ethnography by Gus (1989), all social communication occurs in unison with the simultaneous practice of weaving; the process of making baskets orchestrates dialogue 'conversation simply did not occur without someone making a basket' (Guss, quoted in Tilley, 1999, p. 68). For the Yekuana, to tell a story is to weave a basket, and vice versa. Baskets also provide a material prism through which the Yekuana universe is reflected, cast in a metaphor of endless dualities. The symbols and structure of the baskets refer to the oppositions between chaos and order, visible and invisible, and this cosmological scheme of concentric circles and mandala-like patterns, is repeated in many spatial and social structures, including houses, gardens and the village territory. This cosmology is not taught to the younger generations primarily through verbal communication, however. Instead, the meanings of the baskets is internalized through their repetitive use and creation and patterning and this does not require verbalization: 'Meaning and making are thus linked and through them culture is reproduced' (Guss, quoted in Tilley, 1999, p. 69). So in this case, material culture is not merely the context in which religious and social life is played out, but rather it is the arena and medium through which social relationships and structures are created and recreated, and simultaneously it is the area in which the cosmological and religious world is explained, produced and actualized.

It has been shown that landscape archaeologists have applied a range of social theories to the material record in order to engage with past landscapes in a broadly phenomenological manner. Through doing this, they have raised a number of interesting implications for the materiality of religion, although explaining processual change, rather than investigating the interaction between material culture and religion have been their primary concern. All aspects of society, including by implication the religious, are transmitted through a process of structuration. For interpretative landscape archaeologists, this process of social reproduction occurs through the mediums of a negotiated and dwelt landscape. Especially important, because archaeologically visible, is the creation and destruction of material culture, and the actions of people (praxis) as they negotiate and interact within these constraints. Material culture, especially in the form of monuments or significant natural places, embodies cosmological structures and exerts its influence through the attachment of coded meaning, memory, authority, and these are realized through the medium of praxis. Forms of religious authority and power are enshrined, encapsulated and manipulated through the material form of the landscape. However, the religious agency exerted by some material locales appears to have an element of autonomy, as is seen in the cases where many different religious cosmologies congregate at one place, either at once or over long periods of time. This autonomy is a function of the continuing agency that is exerted by the material structures, perhaps termed material 'beings', present at these sites. The relationship between supposedly autonomous agency and material sites of long continuity is the theme explored further in the next chapter.

* * *

We can now see how landscape archaeology, and especially the phenomenology of landscape, has radically broadened the possibilities for the archaeological examination of religion in the past. Landscape archaeology has utilized a more reflexive and active conception of material culture, a conception that has opened the way for an examination of the materiality of religion. Although the sacred and profane dichotomy and essentialist concepts of numinous 'power' have hampered much landscape archaeology and taken it down a series of wrong turns towards an essentialized and static understanding of religion, it has been shown that other ways of looking at the past, in which ritual and religion are embedded in daily life, can and have also been applied to the material record with some success.

The theoretical concept of religion as an 'embedded' aspect of past life, one which infuses all aspects of social and individual existence and that is expressed through habitual ritual and practice, has wide implications. As we have seen, in some ways the removal of the category of the sacred from the past has been problematic, as it has removed any criteria for looking for religion as a discrete and identifiable thing. Yet, the understanding of a religiously infused material landscape, one that structures and is structured by ongoing human–material interaction, is attractive. This view replaces the ahistoricism of the sacred and profane dichotomy and allows for multiple forms of meaning and agency to be expressed by material things, and it allows for the polarity between the 'material' and 'spiritual' to begin to be finally deconstructed away.

The phenomenologies of Heidegger and Merleau-Ponty, as well as the practice theories of Giddens and Bourdieu, have all been essential in the reconceptualizing of a religious past without the monolithic sacred. What we have been able to gather from the theories of Heidegger and Merleau-Ponty is a phenomenological perspective that situates human being in the material world prior to any considerations of thought, reflection and objectivity. This perspective counters the tendency to think of the material world as a product of human thought as is often the case, and instead it can be seen as a co-producer of human thought and understanding. This allows an understanding of religion, in the form of a cosmology, as able to be expressed through the primary and non-discursive interaction with the material world: a religion that is in fact inseparable from the material world.

The theories of Giddens and Bourdieu have also allowed us to attempt to understand how this relationship with materiality may begin to convey, transmit and co-produce religious institutions through time. According to theory of structuration through habitus following Giddens/Bourdieu, social structures are continuously created and perpetuated through the actions and thoughts – the daily lives – of individuals: in other words their agency. Yet, this subjective agency is itself shaped simultaneously by pre-existing objective social structures that unconsciously mould human thought and action. The two are in a reflexive relationship in which each shapes and determines the other. When the realm of material culture (in the form of the all-encompassing landscape) is added to this equation then material culture can be perceived as forming an important, and at times the most important, medium through which this reflexive interaction between individual agency and mass social systems occurs. It can be posited that when cultural experience, meaning and value are recreated in the human mind as time goes on, they are transmitted imperfectly from one generation to the next not merely through social discourse but through the subtle mediums of material culture and landscape as well. There is a second discourse occurring at the same time, one between people and things.

That this discourse is intimately connected with the religious life of individuals and societies is amply demonstrated by the examples of apparently long periods of material and religious continuity at locales, often in the midst of dramatic cultural change. Whole religious cosmologies can change, from say pre-Christian to Christian, but the materiality of the site appears to continue to exert some form of religious agency. It is to an exploration of how material culture can be thought to interact and co-produce the religious world that we shall now turn.

5

Archaeology and the Materiality of Religion

In this final chapter we continue our examination into the materiality of religion, but widen our perspective from the purely archaeological to consider some of the ways in which material culture from the archaeological record structures religious life in the present. This is done through reconsidering the argument so far and adding to it. The previous chapters are revisited in reverse order and the conclusions reached in each are coupled with further approaches to the materiality of religion that have not originated from within the discipline of archaeology. In this way, the ideas of structuration and habitus critiqued in Chapter 4 are coupled with a more active and dynamic understanding of material agency, taken from the work of the art historian Alfred Gell. The problematic understanding of material culture as primarily a form of symbolic communication, explored in the context of Marxist and Durkheimian 'symbolist' understandings of materiality in Chapter 3, is resolved through the adoption of the ideas of index and abduction, also taken from Alfred Gell. The exploration in Chapter 2 of the perceived dichotomy between religion and materiality, and its origins in the thought patterns of modernity, is furthered through a consideration of Bruno Latour's notion of non-modern hybridized networks of human and non-human agents forming the basis of social life. These thinkers from outside of the fields of archaeology and studies in religion bring differing perspectives on how material culture can interact with society and be a vital agent in the creation of religious life, both in the past and in the present.

In this way, a discussion of the relationships between material culture and religion is initiated which goes beyond the purely archaeological, although archaeological evidence is still used to facilitate the argument. Also, characteristics of any materiality of religion that have already been touched on are further examined and speculated upon, but from differing perspectives. These include notions of animism as one of the primary forms of religious engagement with the material world; the role of material culture in the structuration of society; the existence of an indwelt numinous 'power' seeming to independently arise out from parts of the material world; and the nature of sites of long-standing religious significance continuing to exist in the face of continuous cultural and religious change.

* * *

In Chapter 4 it was argued that landscape archaeology, and especially the phenomenology of landscape, has radically broadened the possibilities for the archaeological examination of religion in the past. It was also suggested that landscape archaeology has utilized a more reflexive and assertive conception of material culture, a conception that has opened the way for an examination of the materiality of religion. The work of Heidegger and Merleau-Ponty certainly has provided a phenomenological perspective that situates the human being within the material world prior to the world of thought, reflection and objectivity. This perspective counters the tendency to think of the material world as solely a product of human thought, and instead to see it as a co-producer of human thought, understanding and identity. So, in this way, human thoughts, understandings and identities can be perceived as in symbiotic co-production with their material (as well as non-material) surroundings.

The theories of Giddens and Bourdieu have allowed archaeologists to attempt to understand how this relationship with materiality may begin to convey, transmit and co-produce social institutions through time. According to the theory of structuration through habitus following Giddens/Bourdieu, societies are created and perpetuated continuously through the reflexive relationships between individuals and greater social structures. Material culture can be perceived as forming an important medium through which this reflexive interaction between individual agency and mass social systems occurs. When cultural social practice, ritual and religious custom, narrative and meaning are recreated in the human mind over time they are transmitted with variation from one generation to the next, not only through social discourse but also through the mediums of material culture and landscape as well.

This has allowed postprocessualist archaeologists in general, and landscape archaeologist in particular, to talk about and examine the levels of agency that material things may exert within this continuous reflexive social discourse.

The diverse and seemingly limitless realm of our material environment constitutes the context within which all life is played out. Materiality may remain a passive environmental backdrop to human action, one virtually unnoticed and of minimal (but never completely absent) influence on cultural understandings about the world. Materiality may be engaged with directly by individuals as distinct objects which may be taken up as tools which extend human instrumentality, and in so doing enhance an individual's subjectivity and personal agency. However, of primary interest to this examination of the potential interaction between materiality and religion, are objects that may take on the role of active subjects within society. They may exert agency themselves and take part in intersubjective social relationships with people. In short, they may become dynamic social agents, appearing to exert an autonomous and self-generated 'power'.

In the previous chapter it has been shown that material agency means more than just the reflection of information in a symbolic or non-verbal way. Agency goes further than structuralist or symbolist concepts of indwelling syntax or ideological meaning being patterned within the built material world. For instance, decoration and religious iconography on objects can act as a syntax that may reflect religious forms of information, even highly subtle and complex ones. This decoration can also interact with the very material form of the object onto which it is applied to create yet more subtle levels of symbolic meaning. Jamal Elias' (2005) study of the decoration of Pakistani trucks has revealed polarities in the forms of decoration used at the front and back, top and bottom of the vehicles that reflect the religious identities of the drivers. By reflecting religious information, the truck also plays an active role in the projection and creation of religious life by displaying and disseminating iconographical expressions across the landscape, sometimes new and revolutionary ones such as of missionary Islamic movements like the *Tablighi Jama'at*. However, although the trucks, in this case, are acting as social agents, through disseminating religious information, they have little autonomous agency. The materiality of the truck is a canvas on to which messages or subtle syntaxes are displayed. It is less an object thought to have its own indwelling religious power or agency, but it is instead predominantly an extension of the religious worldview and agency of its creators, owners and drivers. However, the reality is not quite as straightforwardly reflective as this example might suggest, and Elias does show how the religious syntax and material form of the trucks unconsciously structures the positions, stances and movements of people in relationship with the truck when it is parked at a pit stop (2005, p. 54). The agency of the material does appear to effect individuals in a way that goes beyond the mere symbolic and reflective expression of 'ideology'; the trucks are participating autonomously in social life, directing how people move and stand and interact, even if those individuals are unaware of it.

Agency means having the power to do or to act in some way. It can be expended with seeming autonomy or on the behalf of another, as in the case of the Pakistani trucks, where human agency has been transferred to a material thing in the form of elaborate decoration. In this case, material objects can be seen to have merged with human society in order to extend, and somewhat modify, the agency of people, their power to act in the world. But as we have seen in the previous chapter, in such cases the material world does not just simply 'reflect' culture but also takes on an active role in producing it. Agency gives objects power and potency, and at times they seem to act independently of their human creators or modifiers.

Archaeologists have explored similar ideas of material agency since at least Hodder's *Symbols in Action* (1982), which was one of the first examples of an increasingly sophisticated material culture theory being developed within the discipline. For Hodder, material culture was 'meaningfully constituted' in the sense that its symbolism was not simply a passive reflection of the actions and motivations of past people. Instead, material objects once formed will 'act back' upon the individuals within society in an apparently autonomous fashion; they are social agents (Hodder and Hutson, 2003, chapter 1).

However, for Hodder, and following him for postprocessualist archaeologists in general, material culture has not been theorized as having any primary agency. Instead, somebody must use the material in some way to engineer an effect, and so it has secondary or instrumental agency. Hodder and Hutson give the example of spears in Kenya being used by human agents to negotiate social life. Such spears do not simply reflect or symbolize social and religious boundaries as signs of prestige, kin and class but they are used by young men to actively frustrate and change the power of older men through public displays, ostentatious processions and other highly visible public performances (Hodder and Hutson, 2003, chapter 1). Once produced, these material things can then act back on society, they have a force and a power the can be used in various ways. This is the rational that underpins the concept of the landscape structuring society that we examined in the last chapter. However, in this example the spears' ability to act back on society is achieved through their conscious use and manipulation by ambitious and agitated young men. They are a material field of negotiation, a material resource and also a social resource, that can be utilized by different human agents in a variety of ways. The material objects can be said to have widespread and flexible social instrumentality.

However, when thinking about religion and materiality, the more unusual, dynamic and interesting form of agency that is sometimes projected by material things is the apparently autonomous type, as seen in the examples of sites of long-lasting religious power and material continuity in religious landscapes. At such sites, where some form of religious continuity and appropriation has been ongoing, often in the face of profound change in religious beliefs and cosmologies, the very materiality of the locale appears to be exerting a religious presence independent of any human will or intention. For an understanding of how such seemingly autonomous agency may be projected from the material world, and to begin to think about what type of agency it may be and what it may mean for the materiality of religion, we can leave for a moment the discipline of archaeology and look instead at the anthropology and art theory of the late Alfred Gell.

Gell's examinations of art focused on art as a technology, rather than as a subject of aesthetics, and especially on the social roles that art plays. In particular, Gell considered how art is utilized in order to enchant, to beguile, dazzle, and also to project power and agency on individuals. He was interested largely in the agency of art as a material object, and his understandings of the origins and forms of expression that agency could take are useful outside of art theoretical circles as an example of a larger theory concerned with the agency of material culture in general. For Gell, objects are persons, they are social agents in the full sense of the term and so the 'anthropology of art . . . is just anthropology itself, except that it deals with those situations in which there is an "index of agency" which is normally some kind of artefact' (1998, p. 66).

For Gell, material things are persons because they take part in social relationships (see also Hoskins, 2006). Social agency can be applied to either living or non-living things because its definition is relational. 'It does not matter, in ascribing "social agent" status, what a thing (or a person) "is" in itself; what matters is where it stands in a network of social relations' (Gell, 1998, p. 123). The interesting thing about material agents is the role that they play in mediating wider networks of social relationships, between other material things and between people. Gell did not 'read' art as if it was a symbolic text, but rather he considered art as a series of material objects that act as mediators in social life. For material things to take on these social roles, all that had to happen is for them to be in the vicinity of human people. To be in the vicinity of stones, trees, tables and landscapes is to interact with a whole network of social agents, of non-human persons; it is almost a form of 'new animism' (Harvey, 2005a).

However for Gell, as well as for Hodder, although such objects may appear to project independent power in society they do so as the mediators of what is ultimately some kind of distanced human agency. Gell theorized that primary agents (human persons), distribute their own agency through a network of secondary agents, which may include material things. These things then render the agency of the primary agents effective. Material objects do not have intentionality themselves, but they do have causal efficacy. For instance, in a similar way to the practice theorists mentioned in the last chapter, Gell posited that ritual actions by people are a primary way in which human agency is spread and infused throughout the habitus of a society (Gell, 1998, p. 127). For Gell, ritual was nothing but action which modern secular people found unexplainable, but it was a type of action that was particularly efficient at externalizing mind and agency into the material world. According to Gell's general theory of idolatry (1998, pp. 116–6), repeated ritual engagement with objects such as icons, idols, statues and fetishes results in the perpetual mediation of human social life by these objects. Idols, because of their behavioural ineffectuality, cannot be considered primary agents in the full sense. But they are social others in that they conform to the roles given to them in society. They mediate social practice and confer divine agency into the social realm. For example, a Hindu priest holds and upkeeps that role in society partly because he regularly interacts in prescribed ways with material idols, religious spaces and architectures, which confer sanctity onto him.

This view that material things have the ability to act back on society through the medium of their use, or the instrumentality to which they are put, and that they mediate social relationships through their agency, is little different to the notions of structuration that we looked at in the last chapter, or the 'meaningfully constituted' nature of material culture as advocated by Hodder and others. According to this view, primary agents (humans) simply communicate to one another through the medium of material objects, and through so doing our externalized 'statements' are in some ways modified by the materiality of the medium. To see how Gell's understandings of material agency go beyond that of postprocessual archaeologists, and are of interest for any materiality of religion, we have instead to look at the *types* of agency which material objects can project and to look at how these forms of agency differ from that of verbal, textual, discursive or symbolic communication.

In Chapter 3 it was explained how Marxist and Durkheimian functionalist assumptions have been the major influences determining how archaeologists have treated both material culture and religion during the course of the twentieth century. An emphasis on functionalism, where religion was seen as a symptom of larger social processes that acted to provide a 'hidden' social function, and Marxism, where religion was seen as an intrinsically false manifestation of social consciousness, a mostly unimportant by-product of larger social truths, both effectively prevented archaeologists from examining religion in its own terms. But such attitudes also had influential and long-lasting implications for how the materiality of religion was perceived.

For processual archaeologists, considerations of religion were mostly removed from the archaeological record. When religion was included in theoretical approaches, such as systems theory, it was seen as a secondary and reflective subsystem that was used to regulate the behaviour of members of a society in relation to their environment in order to effect homeostasis. Material culture was seen to be reflective of this process, that is, it could tell members of a society what each other should be doing, and it could tell archaeologists what long-dead people had been doing. For cognitive archaeologists, material culture could tell what people had been thinking; it was symbolic and communicative. For postprocessualist archaeologists both religion and material culture were predominantly read as symbolic and reflective of ideological statements made by those who monopolized power relations. This position neither allowed for considerations of dynamic religious diversity, change nor creative forms of religious experience in the archaeological past. Furthermore, material culture was capable of expressing religious information, but it did so only as a reflection of a premeditated ideology. Materiality and religion had no roles other than passive and communicative reflections of deeper social truths.

So, in both processual and postprocessual systems, religion, and by extension the materiality of religion as well, was conceived as serving purely to further a larger social function that was basically communicative. For processual archaeologists religion and material culture, in the final analysis, communicated and regulated economic relationships between a culture and its environment, for postprocessual archaeologists they symbolically masked power relations between individuals within a culture. For some later postprocessualists ritual and material culture could be 'read' like a text and could act as a field of negotiation of social relations. For cognitive and postprocessual archaeologists, as well as many processualists, material culture was always, in the final analysis, a medium of symbolic or sign-based communication between either individuals within a society, or a way of regulating their understandings of the external environment.

Such a position has also been influential outside purely archaeological circles. Schiffer, in attempting to develop a theory to account for the relationship between human beings and their material environment, worked on the premise that all human behaviour was, by definition, communicative (1999, p. 4). Material objects, from personal adornments to dwellings, facilitated human social communication through enhancing people's potential field of expression. In a similar way to Shanks' and Tilley's interpretation of the materiality of Neolithic burials as the transmission of ideological information, this view limits the ways in which people are thought to be able to perceive material things. Other possible perceptions of the material world that are not based upon it being seen as a sign or symbol are not considered. For instance, the emotional, aesthetic or non-discursive appreciation of things, unmediated by language or thought is left untouched. Nor is there even any easy way to express how non-discursive interactions with things could be characterized or described within an academic framework.

This difficult distinction between material culture as communicating through a syntax or symbolic frame, and it doing so through some other form of perception is widened dramatically when the analogy between materiality and text has been made. Material things, places, landscapes and so on, can all provoke different modes of experience rather than simple reading, they can 'mean in ways that texts do not' (Plate et al., 2005, p. 6). 'Reading' and 'text' may in fact be metaphors that particularly appeal to academics because they are some of the primary ways in which they are trained to experience, evaluate and express the world, but this does not necessarily mean that material culture is best understood as communicating in a textual fashion. Macdonald, for instance, has made this point in regard to the active and emotive raw power of the monumental architecture of Berlin erected during the period of National Socialism. At the time of its creation, this grandiose monumentality was sometimes described as 'words in stone' (*Worte aus Stein*), but these 'words' were understood as being perceived in a direct and para-cognitive fashion which bypassed reasoning (Macdonald, 2006). Certainly, religious objects, icons, idols, relics, monuments, holy places, numinous sites, significant locals and so on – the list is long – can elicit strong emotional and bodily responses that do not appear to be based upon textual or even linguistic frames of reference.

This is another way of saying that material things have multiple forms of agency, some of which are non-discursive. Material things have latent powers and abilities to project agency that can do more than communicate information (even unconsciously) between one person and another. Objects have the ability to enchant, cause wonderment, terrify, overawe, produce the sense of the sublime or uncanny, and, in the case of some religious items of perceived apotropaic power, to heal and modify mental and bodily states. Material items can also play roles in the mediation of human relationships that are nowhere consciously realized as being a form of communication between the participants involved (for examples, see Hill, 2007). An amulet or religious icon can be gifted, bequeathed, lost, found and pass through a number of social transformations, and still project various types of potent non-discursive agency.

Again, in this respect Alfred Gell's view of the power of art objects is illuminating. For Gell, art, and hence all material culture, is 'action-centred'. It is not about meaning and communication, as usually understood, but about doing and agency. It is not intrinsically communicative, semiotic or symbolic (although it can be used as such), but rather it is a system of action, intended to change the world, and act on the world, rather than encode symbolic propositions about the world (Gell, 1998, pp. 5–6). Gell termed this form of perception 'abduction', to refer to inferential schemes that have nothing to do with discursive language, grammar, conscious symbolism, text or linguistic communication.

For Gell, the emotive-intuitive abduction of an object's agency could be seen as an 'index', in that it pointed to a power outside of itself from which its agency originated. For example, the index of a Kenyan spear may be the warrior who made it, the prowess that is involved in its use or the strength and cunningness of the animal that it may have dispatched. However, the forms of agency that an object such as the spear projects may be less discursive and closer to Gell's idea of abduction; they may be raw and emotive rather than thought out and explicitly meaning-laden.

A Catholic Bible, for example, may be used as a dense distillation of the agency and law of God and His Church, built up over thousands of years; but at the same time it may predominantly function, in an everyday sense, as a way of mediating the intersubjective relationships between a priest who wields the book and the subordinate audience who do not. It may be a symbol of authority, an object of power, a vital participant in the creation and performance of effective ritual and more.

So an index can objectify a whole series of relations in its form. The relationships are not symbolically represented in the object, rather the object is the 'visible known which ties together an invisible skein of relations' (Gell, 1998, p. 62). These relations have produced and are produced by an external object. In the case of the Bible these relationships include those between God, the Catholic Church, various supernatural agents such as Angels and the like, priests and parishioners, and the book now contains and projects all of these various types of power or agency into the world.

However, one of the crucial elements of Gell's theory of agency is that this objectified power may then go on to be attributed to a very different index from the one it originally derived its effectiveness from. For instance, an expertly made and beguiling artefact may enchant by pointing to the sublime primary agency of its maker who was an expert craftsperson. As a text, a Bible may contain within the words recorded in its pages the agency of dozens or even hundreds of writers, editors and compilers working over thousands of years; in its creation and illumination a medieval Bible will also hold within its bound material form the work of dozens of monks, craftspeople and others, it will congeal within itself the scriptural, political and economic power of the Church and its sheer ability to mobilize its production, distribution and use; but, all of this human agency will be indexed upwards towards the divine, to God. The index may be displaced from the human to the other-than-human, and then all the abductions contained 'within' the object, artefact or place are considered in some regard 'transcendent'.

Certainly, if the creator of the object is unknown then its non-discursive agency may be thought to point instead to an index that is very different from the human. Malinowski's (1922) examinations of the exchange of *Kula* shell-based valuables between 18 communities spread across the Massim archipelago in southwest Papua New Guinea, provide an example of a case in which the original maker of the objects has been forgotten, and instead a whole network of social relations becomes materialized into the very fabric of the shells. In Mauss's (1923) examination of the gift he identified how elements of human agency are invested in objects of exchange. Not only do such objects symbolize things such as social status and wealth, but they are also concrete objects which mediate the ties of reciprocity between humans. In such a way, gift objects have an element of social agency, in that they are a large factor in regulating and sustaining social relationships. They do not just symbolize or represent social relationships (as Mauss stressed), but they are also crucial and indispensable players in those relationships. Their agency has become a free-floating form of power, utilized by individuals to negotiate their own social worlds and by the society as a whole to mediate the relations of its members.

In such an example, the agency that a material object embodies works as an 'index', referring, or 'pointing', back to its human origins while at the same time being apparently remote from them. This is the crucial characteristic which materiality brings to the religious world, its *apparent* immutability, durability and potential for externalizing abductions of non-discursive agency. Material things, from icons to cathedrals can point to a transcendent referent while projecting the non-discursive agency and power of a collective social group; 'Even if God is the ultimate author of his resemblance in the forms of magnificent structures and works of art, it remains the case that . . . human agency is essential' (Gell, 1998, p. 114). For instance, prehistoric monuments that are visible in the landscape often attract local names ascribing them to the work of giants, supernatural beings, ancestors and so on (Scarre, 2000). As people try to understand and verbalize the agency that such places appear to exude, a series of differing stories and mythologies accrete around them, in a similar way that increasing layers of physical embellishment and materiality will often do as well.

In this way, 'divine', transhuman agency may be externalized into material things. As with the examples in Chapter 4, landscapes, and especially the monuments erected by religious cultures within those landscapes, are very often thought to be the material manifestations of a superhuman agency and potency, even though they are the remains of human labour. For example:

> The great monuments that we have erected to God, the great basilicas and cathedrals are indexes from which we abduct God's agency over the world, and over his mortal subjects who have striven and laboured to please him, and have left these massive shells (or skins) in their wake. (Gell, 1998, p. 114)

These buildings, ruined or still functioning, are ultimately examples of the agency of human beings. Yet, the narratives and actions of individuals and groups that are played out in their vicinity are in response to a perceived non-human agency, perhaps that of a deity, ancestor or other powerful no-human source.

These responses could refer to the agency of a real–historical 'divine' figure that has become distributed through objects, the effective power coming in part from the collective memory of that figure's life. In India, for instance, the ashes and remains of some Hindu gurus or yogis are buried in the ground as their bones are powerful and the places where the remains rest are special places of healing. This is an example of an apparent desire to preserve 'divine' agency in the material realm, even though the revering of human remains, and their preservation through burial or transformation into relics, goes against most orthoprax Hindu and general South Asian purity norms that usually ensure the ritual burning of 'impure' corpses. The religious subculture of Tantric ritual, which influences Hindu, Jain, Buddhist and even some Islamic religious groups, gains much of its perceived religious power and transformative agency through the self-conscious utilization of impure material things (*bali*), one of the most important of which is the remains of the dead human body. For instance, the use of the skullcaps of powerful or inspired individuals in religious rites is particularly prevalent in left-hand (*nastika*) Aghora Hindu Tantrism as well as forms of *Mahamudra* Vajrayana Buddhism (Gold, 1986, p. 234).

A similar example writ large, and of enormous importance in the creation of early imperial systems in South Asia, is the power of the Siddhartha the Buddha's relics deposited across the landscapes of North India within monumental stupas after his *parinirvana* (extinction/final death). These stupas were indexes of both the Buddha's own popularly celebrated 'divinity' (although this term is inexact in a pre-Mahayana context), as well as the stately power of those who funded and managed their construction (see Coningham, 2001, p. 82). The relics contained within these monuments were later redistributed many times by differing rulers, always capitalizing on the spiritual agency of the dead, as well as the actual power relations which they actively mediated (between the state which commissioned the monument and the craftsmen who built it, their families who took pride in it, those who visited it, made pilgrimage to it, worshipped and donated at it, to name a few). By mediating the social relations of people within the landscape a process of structuration occurred which dramatically changed the roles the monuments played in social life. Today, original Buddhist monuments such as the Asokan column capital from Sarnath have become material representations of the modern Indian nation-state. They have been completely removed from their original cosmological context, while still capitalizing on the agency of the original Buddha, the work of craftspeople, the power projection of kings, as well as the historical prestige of the early states. Many other narratives including references to the reappropriation of these great monoliths by Islamic rulers or their later rediscovery by colonial rulers play a part in their significant mediating role today.

However, such explications of the materiality of religion do not differ substantially from ideas such as Barrett's cultural objects that act as 'text-like' fields of negotiation unless we understand that the type of agency being projected from such material things can be neither discursive nor conscious. Instead, more basic emotions may be felt, or deeds enacted. Gell noted that the overwhelming and awe-inspiring captivation of a cathedral or pyramid may invoke an overpowering abduction of awe of a thing, an emotive experience that is attributed not to the humans who built it, but to the divine source that inspired it (1998, p. 114). In such ways the agency of gods is literally distributed through the material things of the world.

It could be argued that this process is comparable with Durkheim's theory that religion and ritual are expressed through the externalization of group affiliation into external social structures. For those influenced by Durkheim, religion is the reified and externalized aspirations of the social group, made significant through the perception of the 'sacred'. Yet, the process described above is different in at least three important respects. First, material objects that act as social agents are not symbolic reflections of a reified society but rather are active participants involved in co-creation and continuation of that society. Second, these material objects or places are not necessarily experienced emotively as 'the sacred', although they may perhaps be in certain cultural contexts, but are also the basis for a wider range of emotive, intellectual or action-based abductions. Onto these experiences a range of non-Western epistemologies, cosmologies and religions that do not adopt the concept of the 'sacred' may be built. Third, such objects are of course material, and so their very quality of 'being', of durability and of externalization, is dramatically different from that of projected abstracted social institutions such as 'the law' or even Durkheim's concept of social organized 'religion', that are insubstantial and formed and maintained through collective interior belief and external ritual. Instead, through abduction, the transhuman and the transcendent are literally infused into the material world. They become materialized social agents, and can perhaps best be thought of as non-human external and apparently autonomous 'persons', active beings that take part in the religious and social life of the community.

An example would be the striking situations where there is an 'imputation that there is inherent agency in the material index' itself (Gell, 1998, p. 32). This perception of 'self-made' material indexes is a common theme from the history of religions. A good illustration of ubiquity and importance of sites of apparently self-made agency are the self-manifested idols, objects and religious sites in the Hindu context. Found across the subcontinent, these self-manifested objects and places include the *pithas*, or seats of chthonic power (*sakti*), of the goddess Devi, and the *jotirlingams*, or self-created ithyphallic *linga* of the god Siva. In both cases, the sites are spread across the geography of the Indian subcontinent and are thought to be self-made, either appearing at the beginning of creation (as with the *linga*) or as a result of the actions of a particular god in an earlier era. For instance, the *Sakti pithas* are commonly held to be places where parts of the body of the goddess Sati, as well as her clothing and jewellery, fell to the earth after her self-immolation and sacrifice. It often appears to be the perceived indwelling 'power' of such object and places, their very removal from the realm of the human but uncanny sense of their significance nonetheless, that is respected, venerated or worshipped. This is different from Eliade's or Otto's concept of the experience of the sacred arising *through* the material world. Instead, the material world itself can be thought to project various forms of agency; and objects and places can be thought of as social agents.

This is a perspective somewhat similar to Graeme Harvey's (2005a) concept of 'new animism', where the non-human world, including material culture, is thought of as made up of communities of active, relational and social beings. All of these beings are active participants in society, but that does not necessarily mean that they are thought of as being 'ensouled' or 'alive'. By definition, animist cultures conceive of many elements of the material world as being social agents. They are so, not necessarily because they channel human or 'divine' agency (although they may), but rather because they are social agents in their own right, in need of respectful and etiquette-based forms of interaction in and of themselves (Harvey, 2005a). This relational perspective is not the result of a prescientific 'category error' as conceived by some nineteenth-century commentators such as Tylor or de Brosses, but an acknowledgement of the status that things and places in the material world can have as active subjects. It is an acknowledgement of their 'active centred' role in influencing social life and in structuring social relationships.

Furthermore, the material objects, structures or locales that are acknowledged as exerting some form of non-human and transcendent agency within a religious cosmology may in fact be the remains of human-modified material culture; they can often be, in contemporary parlance, archaeological. This has been shown is the case in regard to structures dating from the British Neolithic (Bradley, 1998), and the local veneration and acknowledgement of power residing in archaeological remains is common across South Asia as well (Chakrabarti, 2001; Lahiri, 1996). For instance, in South Asia slag refuse from the tops of old village ruins is interpreted as being the bones of superhuman *naga* (snake) spirits and to have curative powers. However, the village identification of the curative agency of archaeological refuse as that of *naga* spirits is done through reference back to the *Mahabharata* and other epic stories, usually transmitted orally (Lahiri, 1996). In such a case the material of the deep past has transferred its effective agency from what may be a site of very old cultural associations to the supernatural *naga* spirits, and it has done this through references to textual traditions.

In these cases it may be forgotten that a thing, monument or place was originally human-made, modified or used, but nevertheless it may still project social agency (abduction) on the people who reside in its vicinity through long periods of enculturated interaction. These sites can be understood as examples of the index of agency being transferred away from the human to the other-than-human and transcendent. Alternatively, such apparently self-made indexes may imitate or emulate the shape, structure and form of human monuments or artefacts, but in fact be perfectly natural, or they may be associated with strikingly enchanting and captivating situations of natural beauty, in which case any ability to project the agency of captivation is truly chthonic.

Certainly it appears likely that the materiality of religion can adopt roles in social relationships far beyond that of mere communication, and the forms of agency that can be expressed go beyond conscious or unconscious projections of power by primary agents. Although the ultimate frame of reference for the origins and meaning of any agency that a material thing projects will always be the human, the powers and social roles that material things adopt allow them to effectively escape such boundaries and act on their own. Not only do they appear to be acting autonomously, but they actually do act autonomously, they create/mediate/prolong and 'contain' networks of active interaction with humans. Exactly where the human ends and the non-human begins becomes increasingly difficult to determine in these cases, a consideration to which we will now turn.

In Chapter 2, we explored the assumed polarity between material culture and religion from the perspectives of both the discipline of studies in religion and archaeology. It was shown how a disjunction between religiosity and material culture was common to the intellectual climate within which both disciplines emerged, and how it has been one of the influential post-Cartesian principles of modernity. In terms of the early study of religion in anthropology and archaeology, the dual ambivalent nature of material culture, where it was used as a diagnostic tool in ascertaining the cultural and religious progression of differing peoples while at the same time being a sign of their spiritual backwardness, was noted. The views of some of the nineteenth-century commentators on religion, such as de Brosses on Fetishism and of Tylor and Lubbock on animism, were seen to systematize this ambivalent attitude to materiality with evolutionary ideas of progress. In addition, privileged visions of religion as interiority, belief and sacred experience were identified as having played a role in furthering this polarity, where 'true' religion was seen as being an elevated state of mind/spirit/soul emancipated from the material world. Overall it was argued that this state of affairs had arisen from a unique historical context and that it did not reflect the actual nature of religion or materiality either in the past or today.

In light of the previous discussion on forms of religious agency which may be expressed by the things of the material world, it is useful to introduce the work of French social philosopher Bruno Latour at this point, as it explicitly critiques the notion of the human/non-human split at the basis of modern thought and instead advocates the existence of hybrid 'networks' of interacting human and non-human subjects. This framework is useful for conceptualizing how material objects not only exert their own agency within a society, but how they can co-produce all social life, including the religious.

For Latour, knowledge is created through the constant and varying interactions of assemblages/networks consisting of human and non-human elements. It is the constant and fluctuating small-scale relationships between people and things that constantly create and recreate human individual identities, social institutions, knowledge and experience. Like Giddens' structuration, Latour's theory suggests that things (material as well as non-material) are not simply reflective of social life in a Durkheimian sense, but are contributing agents to social life: 'if religion, arts or styles are necessary to "reflect," "reify," "materialise," "embody" society – to use some of the social theorists' favourite verbs – then are objects not, in the end, its co-producers?' (1993, p. 54). The resulting socio-technological networks are hybrids of real material (and non-material) things, and invented socio-cultural narratives. The natural and human are united in a proliferation of such networks within which the natural world can never be seen as an independent thing in itself because it is constructed socially, and the social world is never independent either because it is constantly sustained by things. Rather than looking at things in themselves as a scientist might, or at humans among themselves as a social scientist may, or even at discourse between the two (semiotics, language and text) as many in the human sciences certainly do, Latour sees the networks as 'simultaneously real, like nature, narrated, like discourse, and collective, like society' (1993, p. 6). They hold facts, power and discourse within themselves simultaneously. For Latour, these networks prove the lie to modernist claims for the separation between the human and natural sciences, and that is why, for him, 'we have never been modern'.

According to this concept of 'networks', a monument in the landscape, such as a temple, is at once a real solid material thing, a social agent, a support for ideology and a contested site of varying narratives of mythology, to name but a few possibilities; it is an assemblage of differing forms of social agency. Although Latour does not focus on materiality especially (nor religion), material things are important elements in the creation of his networks of social, factual, moral and religious knowledges.

The example he uses is the creation of the air pump in seventeenth-century Europe, which became the material hub of a network of new concepts about experimentation, science, politics, morals, religion and so on. He drew on the work of Shapin and Schaffer (1985) who looked at the advances made in science and political theory by two influential seventeenth-century thinkers, Thomas Hobbes and Robert Boyle. The invention of the air pump, its material existence, facilitated the division of political theory and science into two different knowledge domains, by demanding the separation of Hobbes' attempts at non-empirical science from Boyle's, and Boyle's concerns about the nature of kingship from Hobbes. This was because Hobbes' views on science were based upon non-empirical ideals, while Boyle's political theory was grounded in materialistic empiricism, and it was the invention of the air pump that revealed the distinction. For Latour, it was the new technology of the air pump, its instrumentality, which demonstrated the proof of this split by acting as an active statement that science was empirical rather than social and that political theory was grounded in human ideals rather than material facts. Once the new technology of the air pump was activated then 'all ideas pertaining to God, the

King, Matter, Miracles and Morality are translated, transcribed, and forced to pass through the practice of making an instrument work' (Latour, 1993, p. 20). As such, it became the central material hub of an ever-expanding network of social and epistemological consequences. The multiplication of the air pump, its spread throughout the laboratories of Europe and its further technological modifications further extended this spreading network of social, material, political and natural knowledges.

So although Latour's work is not concerned with material culture theory, archaeology or religion, it has important bearings on all, and certainly on any notion of the materiality of religion. For instance, by adopting his notion of the network and applying it to the previous example of the Buddhist monuments erected around the landscape of North India at the time of the Mauryan Empire in the third and fourth centuries BCE, one can begin to conceptualize the effects of the expanding network of ethical, political, economic (temples often managed new forms of land use) and religious knowledges about the world, and ways of acting in the world, which it created. This is a more nuanced approach to understanding the mechanisms of the project of 'nation building' carried out by the Mauryan kings, an approach that sees the use of the materiality of the Buddha's death and its enshrinement in visible monuments in the landscape as of equal importance as the use of the more commonly cited bilingual rock and pillar inscriptions. Furthermore, the concept of 'network' allows the conscious political use of these monuments of power and meaning by ancient state elites to be framed within a wider historical trajectory, one that admits of pre-established radiations of changing ethical, political, economic and overly religious knowledges becoming established around the existing materiality of the landscapes of northern and central India in the fourth to third centuries BCE.

To bring this conception of the materiality of religion into a contemporary context, one could contrast such a network of differing forms of agency with those created by the proliferation of statues (contemporary idols) of the Buddha that are distributed throughout the gardens and homes of the middle classes in the contemporary West. Generally taken out of their original religious context, these fragments of the 'distributed person' (for this concept, see Gell, 1998, pp. 96–152) of the Buddha may disseminate abductions of aesthetics, authenticity, identity, non-modernity, spirituality or secularism; and they may also be material nodes in a hybridized material–social network – a subculture sharing similar political–ideological attitudes and forms of shared identity. It is the materiality of religion, however, that allows the agency of Siddhartha to continue to exert itself in numerous and ever-changing ways.

This raises the issue of the various discourses, textual and oral, that may be wrapped around materiality in order to explicate religious meanings. The abduction of materiality (Gell) and the existence of self-functioning networks of people and things (Latour) are both primary ways that materiality adopts primary roles in social life. However, there is also a narrative dimension as well, especially in terms of explicated religious meaning, although it is secondary to the primary agency that the materiality projects. A good example of archaeological materiality acting as a multivocal field of negotiation expressed through religious discourse can be found in Lahiri's (1996) examination of the landscape of Ballabgarh district in North India. In her study, she looked at how material culture at a village level acted as sites of negotiation between two levels of culture; high-textual-world religion, that is, Brahmanical Hinduism, and low-oral-folk religion, village Hinduism. High culture is represented by the epic texts and created through a nodal structure of temples and holy places. Temples have a wealth of symbolic associations (*Vastushastras Manasara*), working as syntax, and their meanings are textually constituted. Local communities, however, impose their own meaning on these nodal structures. For folk cultures the meanings of various temples are varied but are not based on doctrinal texts and are mostly commemorative, not being associated with a deity, but rather with the remembered exploits and powers of a hero or an ancestor. Village 'folk' cultures also appropriate many elements of the landscape that are not acknowledged by orthodox texts. However, both of these competing narratives can be seen as responses to a single resource; they are both making claims to the archaeological materiality of religion.

Latour contrasts the sentiments of modernity with those of pre- or non-modernity, claiming that the major strength of modern thought is also its primary weakness; that it does not acknowledge the existence of these hybrids of material things and social worlds, that it guarantees a false impression of a complete separation between the worlds of nature and culture. The 'representation of nonhumans belongs to science, but science is not allowed to appeal to politics; the representation of citizens belongs to politics, but politics is not allowed to have any relation to the nonhumans produced and mobilized by science and technology' (Latour, 1993, p. 28). In such a way modernity is able to completely dominate either realm on an individual basis, but is however absolutely unable to contend with the numerous invisible hybridized networks structuring the world. Certainly, if we adopt the notion that religions are always hybrids of material and social agents, networks of relationship that do not fit neatly into many pre-established categories, then Latour's critique of modernity fits with the demonstrated unwillingness of archaeologists to approach religion within the material record, and those who study religion to avoid addressing materiality.

Latour contrasts the modern position that dismisses such hybrids of nature and culture with traditional cultures where such hybridized creations are acknowledged, controlled and warded against. In non-modern societies without the same post-Cartesian perceptions, the realms of nature, culture, morals and religions are instead interlinked (not, one would assume, in an undifferentiated mass, but according to other non-Cartesian schemes, such as the Maori 'spiral' noted in Chapter 4). For Latour, non-modern societies obsess about the creation of these resulting hybrids and how they will affect them. He suggests that such non-modern cultures would not have accepted the air pump with all its inherent baggage, practical and social dangers, but instead would have 'conjured away its dangers at once' (Latour, 1993, p. 42), although he does not explain how.

This has direct bearing on the notions of materiality and religion, and the concept of the social nature of material agents explored above. Latour (1993, p. 42) claims that:

> Moderns were always struck by the diffuse aspect of active or spiritual forces in other so-called premodern cultures. Nowhere were pure matter, pure mechanical force, put into play. Spirits and agents, gods and ancestors, were blended in at every point. In contrast, from the moderns' viewpoint the modern world appeared disenchanted, drained of its mysteries, dominated by the sleek forces of pure immanence on which we humans alone imposed some symbolic dimension and beyond which there existed, perhaps, the transcendence of . . . God. Now if there is no immanence, if there are only networks, agents, actants, we cannot be disenchanted. Humans are not the ones who arbitrarily add the 'symbolic dimension' to pure material forces. These forces are as transcendent, active, agitated, spiritual, as we are.

As with Gell's suggestions about the social and active nature of things, Latour's hybridized networks of nature and culture infuse the material world with active power, and leave people existing within a society of numerous agents, both material and non-material, human and non-human.

One way that religion is embodied materially then is through the constant interaction between human–material subjects and non-human material subjects. Again, at this point Graham Harvey's concept of 'new animism' (2005a) is revealing. For Harvey, animism is not some form of prescientific category error performed by childlike savages, but is instead the acknowledgement of a world in which people interact with many other 'persons', many of whom are non-human. Aspects of the material environment, such as rocks, houses, trees and everyday objects are more often that non-seen as persons or subjects and are interacted with according to an ethical and respectful body of etiquette. This intersubjective relationship is not necessarily based upon peaceful and cooperative structures; things can still be used, exploited, eaten and so on, but it is based upon some integrative and relational form of reciprocity. In this context, much of what we call religion becomes relational, that is, the body of habitual practices, or praxis, occurring within a world of persons, many of which are non-human and may be materially embodied.

'New animism' is an appealing theoretical mode through which to think about the role and conceptualization of material agents in religious life, including from the archaeological past. However it is important to remember that the idea of material agents as being independently active is not necessarily one that can or should be transposed onto all cultures, living or past. Astor-Aguilera, for example, points out that for the Maya active objects are 'not literally considered animate since it is the invisible nonhuman persons in and surrounding the material vessel that are sentient' (2009, p. 176; 2010), and suggests the use of the term 'ecological' cosmologies, rather than either animistic or supernatural.

Yet, notwithstanding the terminology used, the use of non-Western ingenious cosmologies in order to think about the active role that material agents play in much religious life remains useful. In part, religion becomes the ordered series of relationships that exist between people and their material world (that includes other people such as animals, vegetation, natural features, artefacts and celestial objects to name just a few of the possibilities). In a similar way to the forms of landscape archaeology influenced by Heidegger's being and

Bourdieu's habitus, there is an automatic, reflexive and often non-discursive relationship between the material world and the cultural world as, in fact, they are not separated but actually form the same *religious* world. From such a perspective, animism can be seen as an acknowledgement of the active role that non-human subjects take in structuring culture, as well as the tendency of many aspects of the material world to act as apparently autonomous social agents.

When Gell's concepts of abduction and index are included in this discussion, then material artefacts and locales within the landscape can be seen as having a powerfully ambiguous nature. They have the ability to embody non-material intentionality, to act as indexes to other apparently non-human and transcendent forms of power and agency, but to remain within the sensual experienced material realm. Materiality, then, is integral to religiosity, rather than its opposite; it situates the agency of the non-human subject within the realm of the human. The detritus and refuse from the past, places that we might today term 'archaeological', have the ability to confer non-human agency onto human life – through various abductions such as those of blessing, power, protection, healing, danger, 'awe, the sublime, the uncanny, to name a few'.

This fits well with the definition of religion given in Chapter 1: '*Religion can be thought of as a discourse*', yes – which sometimes occurs in collaboration with the material world, '*whose concerns transcend the human*', yes – but not always the social, '*and contingent*', yes – when material things are seen as reflecting some type of permanence and as representative of cosmological order, '*and that claims for itself a similarly transcendent status*', – yes, '*that includes a set of practices whose goal is to produce a proper world*', – yes, especially when occurring within an enculturated religious landscape, '*as defined by a religious discourse*' – sometimes a discourse with the material world, '*and that can be engaged in by either an individual, a community or formalized into an institution*' – yes.

This final section lists some of the tentative conclusions that can be made about the nature of the materiality of religion, especially as it applies to archaeological artefacts. What follows is a series of general points that have been suggested in the discussions above. Each reveals one perspective from which to examine the interactions between material culture and religiosity, especially as it relates to material culture from the archaeological record. As such, all provide potentially fruitful areas of future study.

* * *

The solid nature of material culture and displaced agency

In looking for a materiality of religion the first and most essential quality to distinguish is the solid nature of much material culture, and its ability to allow forms of power, agency and social networks to become externalized within itself. This is the most basic quality of material culture, but also the most important, defining, and perhaps the only unique affordance that it brings to religious life. As we have seen, material culture because of its durability can have a lasting influence over time. Numerous discourses and forms of meaning, only some of which are conceptual, may come to be layered into its form, projecting their influence on a culture for exceedingly long stretches of time and only changing very gradually. In such cases the agency that a material object embodies operates as an 'index' referring back to its human origins while at the same time being apparently remote from them. The object or site can become something akin to a 'free-floating' social agent. This is the crucial characteristic which materiality brings to the religious world, its immutability, durability and potential for externalizing abductions of non-discursive agency.

Material culture as the context for individual and social life: Landscapes especially, in providing the phenomenological context within which all aspects of being are disclosed to an individual and to a society, can embody and perpetuate systems of cosmological order in material form. Because the landscape is imbibed, lived, dwelt within and generally taken for granted by most people, the abductions that it contains can appear as part of the objective, immutable and changeless world. Thus the landscape can also form a physical embodiment of an eternal and imperishable social/cosmological order. This quality of the landscape can be insidious in cases where unequal power relations are projected through time. In this way the abductions of agency that they embody also become part of that imperishable order, and may change very slowly.

Durability and changelessness: This form of distanciation, where a material thing can project and embody power while being removed from its ultimate source allows manipulations of religious power across space, from one context to the next. The durability of material things, their ability to last over generational timeframes allows them to project religious power over time as well. However, although these qualities could perhaps be expected to promote religious continuity and changelessness, this is not their only effect. Various media are available to be used by humans to communicate with one another, some of the most durable being physical artefacts and architectural forms. It is precisely because of this durability that material culture is so amenable to the task of conveying meaning across generations. However, this stable, durable and temporal aspect of materiality does not necessarily cause it to be a support for religious continuity. As we have seen, the power or agency of the material world, especially fixed structures or locales, may remain potent over exceedingly long periods of time, but the specific discourses that are overlaid on to that power, and enacted in relation to that power, will change. The solid and seemingly eternal nature of material culture when infused and pregnant with potency appears to encourage multiple and numerous manipulations of that externalized agency. The material world is a rich religious resource.

The archaeological past is a primary resource

Across the globe, elements of the landscape that are often adopted as playing central roles in the religious life often consist of archaeological remains such as tells, ruins and fragments of art. These archaeological sites may appear to distil perceptions of religious significance and power for those who live in their vicinity and interact with them. Although a number of competing oral and textual discourses may build up around these sites or objects, each revealing a differing religious meaning expressed in story, fable, myth, historical account and so on, these discourses exist in parallel to a primary interaction between people and their material world. These sites may appear to express a continuity of religious perception within a landscape, but this is not based upon any phenomenology of the sacred experience or division of the world into the sacred and the profane. Any religious continuity that such objects or locales afford may instead be based up their active role as material agents acting back on social life. These material things become 'crystallizations' of human agency cut loose from their original source. This potency that they still exude can then be ascribed to other non-human causes, for example the divine, transcendent or the dead, and it can then be used as a resource by the living in order to create new and ever-changing religious narratives and power systems in the present.

Bibliography

Allen, M. and Gardiner, J. (2002), 'A Sense of Time: Cultural Markers in the Mesolithic of Southern England?', in B. David and M. Wilson (eds), *Inscribed Landscapes: Marking and Making Place*. Honolulu: University of Hawaii Press, pp. 139–53.

Althusser, L. (1971), *Lenin and Philosophy and Other Essays*. London: New Left Books.

— (1990), *Philosophy and the Spontaneous Philosophy of the Scientist*. London: Verso.

Arnold, B. (2006), 'Pseudoarchaeology and Nationalism: Essentializing Difference', in B. Fagan (ed.), *Archaeological Fantasies: How Pseudoarchaeology Misrepresents the Past and Misleads the Public*. New York: Routledge, pp. 154–79.

Arweck, E. and Keenan, W. (2006), *Materializing Religion: Expression, Performance and Ritual*. Aldershot: Ashgate.

Asad, T. (1979), 'Anthropology and the Analysis of Ideology'. *Man*, 14, 607–27.

— (1983), 'Anthropological Conceptions of Religion'. *Man*, 18, 237–59.

— (1993), *Genealogies of Religion*. Baltimore: John Hopkins Press.

— (2001), 'Reading a Modern Classic: W. C. Smith's *The Meaning and End of Religion*'. *History of Religions*, 40, (3), 205–22.

Astor-Aguilera, M. (2009), 'Mesoamerican Communicating Objects: Maya Worldviews Before, During, and After Spanish Contact', in L. Cecil and T. Pugh (eds), *Maya Worldviews at Conquest*. University Press of Colorado, pp. 159–182.

— (2010), *The Maya World of Communicating Objects*. Albuquerque: University of New Mexico Press.

Bachelard, G. (1964), *The Poetics of Space*. New York: Orion.

Bacus, E. and Lahiri, N. (2004), 'Exploring the Archaeology of Hinduism'. *World Archaeology*, 36, (3), 313–25.

Barnes, G. (1999), 'Buddhist Landscapes of East Asia', in W. Ashmore and B. Knapp (eds), *Archaeologies of Landscape*. Oxford: Blackwell, pp. 101–23.

Barrett, J. (1989), 'Time and Tradition: The Rituals of Everyday Life', in H. Nordstrom and A. Knapp (eds), *Bronze Age Studies*. Stockholm: Statens Historika Museum, pp. 113–26.

— (1990), 'The Monumentality of Death: The Character of Early Bronze Age Mortuary Mounds in Southern Britain'. *World Archaeology*, 22, 245–78.

— (1991), 'Towards an Archaeology of Ritual', in P. Garwood, D. Jennings, R. Skeates and J. Toms (eds), *Sacred and Profane: Proceedings of a Conference on Archaeology, Ritual and Religion*. Oxford: Oxbow Books, pp. 1–9.

— (1994), *Fragments from Antiquity: An Archaeology of Social Life in Britain, 2900–1200 BC*. Oxford: Blackwell Publishers.

Basso, K. (1996), *Wisdom Sits in Places: Landscape and Language Among the Western Apache*. Albuquerque: University of New Mexico Press.

Bataille, G. (1989), *Theory of Religion*. Translated by R. Hurley. New York: Zone Books.

Bell, C. (1992), *Ritual Theory, Ritual Practice*. New York: Oxford University Press.

— (2005), 'Ritual Reification', in P. Harvey (ed.), *Ritual and Religious Belief: A Reader*. London: Equinox, pp. 265–85.

Bender, B. (1992), 'Theorising Landscapes and the Prehistoric Landscapes of Stonehenge'. *Man*, 27, (4), 735–55.

— (1993), 'Stonehenge: Contested Landscapes', in B. Bender (ed.), *Landscape: Politics and Perspectives*. Oxford: Berg.

— (1998), *Stonehenge: Making Space*. New York: Oxford.

Bennett, J. (2001), *The Enchantment of Modern Life: Attachments, Crossings and Ethics*. Princeton: Princeton University Press.

Berger, J. (1972), *Ways of Seeing*. Harmondsworth: Penguin.

Berger, P. (1999), *The Desecularization of the World: Resurgent Religion and World Politics*. Washington: Ethics and Public Policy Center.

Besancon, A. (2000), *The Forbidden Image: An Intellectual History of Iconoclasm*. Translated by J. Todd. Chicago: University of Chicago Press.

Bhan, P. (1989), *Bluff Your Way in Archaeology*. Horsham: Ravetta Books.

Binford, L. (1964), 'A Consideration of Archaeological Research Design'. *American Antiquity*, 29, 425–41.

— (1965), 'Archaeological Systematics and the Study of Culture Process'. *American Antiquity*, 31, 203–10.

— (1967), 'Smudge Pits and Hide Smoking: The Use of Analogy in Archaeological Reasoning'. *American Antiquity*, 32, (1), 1–12.

— (1971), 'Mortuary Practices: Their Study and Potential', in J. Brown (ed.), *Approaches to the Social Dimensions of Mortuary Practices*. Washington: Society for American Archaeology, pp. 6–29.

— (1972a), *An Archaeological Perspective*. New York: Seminar Press.

— (1972b), 'Archaeology as Anthropology'. *American Antiquity*, 28, 217–25.

— (1981), 'Behavioural Archaeology and the "Pompeii Premise"'. *Journal of Anthropological Research*, 37, 195–208.

— (1983), *In Pursuit of the Past: Decoding the Archaeological Record*. London: Thames and Hudson.

Bintliff, J. (1991), 'The Contribution of an Annaliste/Structural History Approach to Archaeology', in J. Bintliff (ed.), *The Annales School and Archaeology*. London: Leicester University Press.

Blain, J. and Wallis, R. (2007), *Sacred Sites, Contested Rites/Rights: Contemporary Pagan Engagements with the Past*. Discussion document and report of current research. London: Sussex Academic Press.

Bloch, M. (1977), 'The Past in the Present in the Present'. *Man*, 12, 278–92.

Bloch, M. and Parry, J. (1982), 'Introduction: Death and the Regeneration of Life', in M. Bloch and J. Parry (eds), *Death and the Regeneration of Life*. Cambridge: Cambridge University Press, pp. 1–44.

Bourdieu, P. (1970), 'The Berber House or the World Reversed'. *Social Science Information*, 9, 151–70.

— (1977), *Outline of a Theory of Practice*. Cambridge: Cambridge University Press.

Bowden, M. (1991), *Pitt Rivers*. Cambridge: Cambridge University Press.

Bradley, R. (1984), *The Social Foundations of Prehistoric Britain: Themes and Variations on the Archaeology of Power*. London: Longman.

— (1987), 'Time Regained: The Creation of Continuity'. *Journal of the British Archaeology Association*, 140, 1–17.

— (1991), 'Monuments and Places', in P. Garwood, D. Jennings, R. Skeates and J. Toms (eds), *Sacred and Profane: Proceedings of a Conference on Archaeology, Ritual and Religion*. Oxford: Oxbow Books, pp. 15–44.

— (1998), 'Ruined Buildings, Ruined Stones: Enclosures, Tombs and Natural Places in the Neolithic South-West of England'. *World Archaeology*, 30, (1), 14–22.

— (2000), *An Archaeology of Natural Places*. London: Routledge.

— (2005), *Ritual and Domestic Life in Prehistoric Europe*. London: Routledge.

Brady, J. and Ashmore, W. (1999), 'Mountains, Caves, Water: Ideational Landscapes of the Ancient Maya', in W. Ashmore and B. Knapp (eds), *Archaeologies of Landscape*. Oxford: Blackwell, pp. 124–48.

Braudel, F. (1981), *The Structures of Everyday Life: The Limits of the Possible*. Translated by M. Kochan. London: Collins.

Brown, P. (1988), *The Body and Society: Men, Women, and Sexual Renunciation in Early Christianity*. New York: Columbia University Press.

Bruck, J. (1999), 'Ritual and Rationality: Some Problems of Interpretation in European Archaeology'. *European Journal of Archaeology*, 2, 313–44.

Carmichael, D., Hubert, J., Reeves, B. and Schanche, A. (1994), 'Introduction', in D. Carmichael, J. Hubert, B. Reeves and A. Schanche (eds), *Sacred Sites, Sacred Places*. London: Routledge, pp. 3–21.

Chakrabarti, D. (1995), 'Buddhist Sites Across South Asia as Influenced by Political and Economic Forces'. *World Archaeology*, 27, (2), 185–202.

— (2001), 'The Archaeology of Hinduism', in T. Insoll (ed.), *Archaeology and World Religion*. London: Routledge, pp. 33–60.

Childe, G. (1925), *The Dawn of European Civilization*. London: Alfred A. Knopf.

— (1937), *Man Makes Himself*. London: Watts.

— (1942), *What Happened in History*. London: Max Parrish.

— (1945), *Progress and Archaeology*. London: Watts.

— (1947), *History*. London: Corbett Press.

Clarke, D. (1968), *Analytical Archaeology*. London: Methuen.

Clarke, J. (1997), *Oriental Enlightenment: The Encounter Between Asian and Western Thought*. London: Routledge.

Coleman, S. and Collins, P. (2006), 'The Shape of Faith or the Architectural Forms of the Religious Life', in E. Arweck and W. Keenan (eds), *Materializing Religion: Expression, Performance and Ritual*. Aldershot: Ashgate.

Coningham, R. (2001), 'The Archaeology of Buddhism', in T. Insoll (ed.), *Archaeology and World Religion*. London: Routledge, pp. 61–95.

Conrad, G. and Demarest, A. (1984), *Religion and Empire: The Dynamics of Aztec and Inca Expansionism*. Cambridge: Cambridge University Press.

Crosby, A. (1997), *The Measure of Reality: Quantification and Western Society, 1250–1600*. Cambridge: Cambridge University Press.

Cunningham, R. and Lewer, N. (2000), 'A General Introduction'. *Antiquity*, 74, (258), 664–7.

Daniel, G. and Renfrew, C. (1988), *The Idea of Prehistory*. New York: Edinburgh University Press.

Dant, T. (2005), *Materiality and Society*. New York: Open University Press.

Darwin, C. (1972) [1859], *The Origin of Species*. London: Dent.

David, B. and Wilson, M. (2002), 'Introduction', in B. David and M. Wilson, *Inscribed Landscapes: Marking and Making Place*. Honolulu: University of Hawaii Press, pp. 1–9.

Davis, T. (2004), *Shifting Sands: The Rise and Fall of Biblical Archaeology*. Oxford: Oxford University Press.

Deetz, J. (1977), *In Small Things Forgotten: The Archaeology of Early American Life*. New York: Anchor Press.

Demarest, A. (1987), 'Archaeology and Religion', in M. Eliade (ed.), *The Encyclopaedia of Religion*. London: Macmillan, pp. 372–9.

Derks, T. (1997), 'The Transformation of Landscape and Religious Representations in Roman Gaul'. *Archaeological Dialogues*, 4, (2), 126–48.

Descola, P. and Pálsson, G. (1996), *Nature and Society: Anthropological Perspectives*. London: Routledge.

Dillon, M. (2003), 'The Sociology of Religion in Late Modernity', in M. Dillon (ed.), *Handbook of the Sociology of Religion*. Cambridge: Cambridge University Press, pp. 3–16.

Douglas, M. (1966), *Purity and Danger*. London: Routledge and Kegan Paul.

— (1972), 'Symbolic Orders in the Use of Domestic Space', in P. Ucko, R. Tringham and G. Dimbleby (eds), *Man, Settlement and Urbanization*. London: Routledge, pp. 513–21.

Drennan, R. (1976), 'Religion and Social Evolution in Formative Mesoamerica', in K. Flannery (ed.), *The Early Mesoamerican Village*. New York: Academic Press, pp. 245–68.

Dunnell, R. (1992), 'The Notion of Site', in J. Rossignol and L. Wandsnider (eds), *Space, Time and Archaeological Landscapes*. New York: Plenum Press, pp. 21–41.

Durkheim, E. (2001) [1926], *The Elementary Forms of Religious Life*. Translated by C. Cosman. Oxford: Oxford University Press.

Ebert, J. (1992), *Distributional Archaeology*. Albuquerque: University of New Mexico Press.

Eco, U. (1980), 'Function and Sign: The Semiotics of Architecture', in G. Broadbent, R. Bunt and C. Jencks (ed.), *Sings, Symbols and Architecture*. Wiley: Chichester, pp. 12–33.

Edmonds, M. (1999), *Ancestral Geographies of the Neolithic: Landscape, Monuments and Memory*. London: Routledge.

Eliade, M. (1954), *The Myth of the Eternal Return*. Translated by W. Trask. New York: Harcourt Brace.

— (1957), *The Sacred and the Profane*. Translated by W. Trask. New York: Harcourt Brace.

— (1969), 'Sacred Architecture and Symbolism', in D. Apostolos-Cappodona (ed.), *Symbolism, the Sacred and the Arts*. New York: Routledge, pp. 102–39.

— (1986), *Symbolism, the Sacred and the Arts*. New York: Crossroad Press.

Elias, J. (2005), 'Truck Decoration and Religious Identity: Material Culture and Social Function in Pakistan'. *Journal of Material Religion*, 1, (1), 48–71.

Elster, J. (1982), 'Belief, Bias and Ideology', in M. Hollis and S. Lukes (eds), *Rationality and Relativism*. Oxford: Blackwell, pp. 123–48.

— (1985), *Making Sense of Marx*. Cambridge: Cambridge University Press.

Evens, C. (1985), 'Tradition and the Cultural Landscape: An Archaeology of Place'. *Archaeological Review from Cambridge*, 4, (1), 80–94.

Fagan, B. (1988), *From Black Land to Fifth Sun*. Reading: Addison-Wesley.

Finegan, J. (1952), *The Archaeology of World Religion*. Princeton: Princeton University Press.

Foucault, M. (1965), *Madness and Civilisation: A History of Insanity in the Age of Reason*. New York: Vintage.

— (1977), *Discipline and Punish: The Birth of the Prison*. Translated by A. Sheridan. London: Allen Lane.

Forde, C. (1930), 'Early Cultures of Atlantic Europe'. *American Anthropologist*, 32, (1), 19–100.

Frend, W. (1996), *The Archaeology of Early Christianity: A History*. Minneapolis: Fortress Press, 1996.

Friedrich, P. (1989), 'Language, Ideology and Political Economy'. *American Anthropologist*, 91, 295–312.

Fritz, J. (1978), 'Palaeopsychology Today: Ideational Systems and Human Adaptation in Prehistory', in C. Redman (ed.), *Social Archaeology: Beyond Subsistence and Dating*. New York: Academic Press.

Gadamer, H. (1975), *Truth and Method*. London: Sheed and Ward.

Garwood, P. (1991), 'Ritual Tradition and the Reconstruction of Society', in P. Garwood, D. Jennings, R. Skeates and J. Toms (eds), *Sacred and Profane: Proceedings of a Conference on Archaeology, Ritual and Religion*. Oxford: Oxbow Books, pp. 38–51.

Garwood, P., Jennings, D., Skeates, R. and Toms, J. (1991a), 'Preface', in P. Garwood, D. Jennings, R. Skeates and J. Toms (eds), *Sacred and Profane: Proceedings of a Conference on Archaeology, Ritual and Religion*. Oxford: Oxbow Books, pp. v–x.

— (1991b), *Sacred and Profane: Proceedings of a Conference on Archaeology, Ritual and Religion*. Oxford: Oxbow Books.

Geertz, C. (1960), *The Religion of Java*. New York: Free Press.

— (1966), 'Religion a Cultural System', in M. Banton (ed.), *Anthropological Approaches to the Study of Religion*. London: Tavistock, pp. 1–46.

Gell, A. (1998), *Art and Agency: An Anthropological Theory*. New York: Oxford University Press.

Giddens, A. (1977), *Studies in Social and Political Theory*. London: Hutchinson.

— (1979), *Central Problems in Social Theory: Action, Structure and Contradiction in Social Analysis*. Cambridge: Polity.

— (1984), *The Constitution of Society*. Cambridge: Polity Press.

Gold, D. (1986), 'Guru's Body, Guru's Abode', in J. Law (ed.), *Religious Reflections on the Human Body*. Indianapolis: Indiana University Press, pp. 230–50.

Goody, J. (1962), *Death, Property and the Ancestors: A Study of the Mortuary Customs of the Lodagaa of West Africa*. Stanford: Stanford University Press.

— (1977), 'Against "Ritual": Loosely Structured Thoughts on a Loosely Defined Topic', in S. Moore and B. Mejerhalf (eds), *Secular Ritual*. Assen: Van Garcum, pp. 25–35.

Guss, D. (1989), *To Weave and Sing: Art, Symbol and Narrative in the South American Rain Forest*. Berkley: University of California Press.

Harding, J. (1991), 'Using the Unique as the Typical: Monuments and the Ritual Landscape', in P. Garwood, D. Jennings, R. Skeates and J. Toms (eds), *Sacred and Profane: Proceedings of a Conference on Archaeology, Ritual and Religion*. Oxford: Oxbow Books, pp. 141–51.

Harvey, G. (2005a), *Animism: Respecting the Living World*. Kent Town: Wakefield Press.

— (2005b), 'Introduction', in G. Harvey (ed.), *Ritual and Religious Belief: A Reader*. London: Equinox, pp. 1–17.

Hawkes, C. (1954), 'Archaeological Theory and Method: Some Suggestions from the Old World'. *American Anthropologist*, 56, 155–68.

Hawkings, G. (1970), *Stonehenge Decoded*. London: Fontana.

Heidegger, M. (1962), *Being and Time*. Translated by J. Macquarie. London: SCM Press.

— (1971), 'Building Dwelling Thinking', in M. Heideggar, *Poetry, Language, Thought*. New York: Harper & Row, pp. 143–62.

Hill, J. (2007), 'The Story of the Amulet: Locating the Enchantment of Collections'. *Journal of Material Culture*, 12, 65–87.

Hirsch, E. and O'Hanlon, M. (1995), 'Landscape: Between Place and Space', in E. Hirsch and M. O'Hanlon (eds), *The Anthropology of Landscape: Perspectives on Place and Space*. Oxford: Clarendon Press, pp. 1–19.

Hodder, I. (1982a), *The Present Past*. London: Batsford.

— (1982b), *Symbols in Action: Ethnoarchaeological Studies of Material Culture*. New York: Cambridge University Press, 1982.

— (1984), 'Burials, Houses, Women and Men in the European Neolithic', in D. Miller and C. Tilley (eds), *Ideology, Power and Prehistory*. Cambridge: Cambridge University Press, pp. 41–65.

— (1991), *Reading the Past*, 2nd edn. Cambridge: Cambridge University Press.

— (2006), *Catalhoyuk: The Leopard's Tale: Revealing the Mysteries of Turkey's Ancient 'Town'*. London: Thames and Hudson.

— (2010a), 'Probing Religion at Catalhoyuk: An Interdisciplinary Experiment', in I. Hodder (ed.), *Religion in the Emergence of Civilization: Catalhoyuk as a Case Study*. New York: Cambridge University Press, pp. 1–31.

— (2010b), *Religion in the Emergence of Civilization: Catalhoyuk as a Case Study*. New York: Cambridge University Press.

Hodder, I. and Hutson, S. (2003), *Reading the Past: Current Approaches to Interpretation in Archaeology*, 3rd edn. Cambridge: Cambridge University Press.

Hodder, I. and Meskell, L. (2010), 'The Symbolism of Catalhoyuk in Its Regional Context', in I. Hodder (ed.), *Religion in the Emergence of Civilization: Catalhoyuk as a Case Study*. New York: Cambridge University Press, pp. 32–72.

Holtorf, C. (1995), 'Megaliths, Monumentality and Memory'. *Archaeological Review from Cambridge*, 12, (2), 45–66.

Hoskins, J. (2006), 'Agency, Biography and Objects', in C. Tilley, W, Keane, S. Kuchler, M. Rowlands and P. Spyer (eds), *Handbook of Material Culture*. London: Sage, pp. 74–84.

Hubert, J. (1994), 'Sacred Beliefs and Beliefs of Sacredness', in D. Carmichael, J. Hubert, B. Reeves and A. Schanche (eds), *Sacred Sites, Sacred Places*. London: Routledge, pp. 9–18.

Hultkrantz, A. (1978), 'Ecological and Phenomenological Aspects of Shamanism', in V. Dioszegi and M. Hoppal (eds), *Shamanism in Siberia*. Budapest: Akademiai Kiado.

Insoll, T. (1999), *The Archaeology of Islam*. Oxford: Blackwell.

— (2001), 'Introduction: The Archaeology of World Religion', in T. Insoll (ed.), *Archaeology and World Religion*. London: Routledge, pp. 1–32.

— (2004a), *Archaeology, Ritual, Religion*. London: Routledge.

— (2004b), *Belief in the Past: The Proceedings of the 2002 Manchester Conference on Archaeology and Religion*. Oxford: Archaeopress.

Irwin, J. (1987), 'Asokan Pillars: The Mystery of Foundation and Collapse', in G. Pollet (ed.), *India and the Ancient World: History, Trade and Culture Before A.D. 650*. Leuven: Motilal Banarsidas, pp. 87–94.

James, W. (1902), *The Varieties of Religious Experience: A Study in Human Nature*. New York: Modern Library.

Jordan, P. (2006), 'Esoteric Egypt', in B. Fagan (ed.), *Archaeological Fantasies: How Pseudoarchaeology Misrepresents the Past and Misleads the Public*. New York: Routledge, pp. 109–28.

Kenoyer, M. (1991), 'The Indus Valley Tradition of Pakistan and Western India'. *Journal of World Prehistory*, 5, (4), 331–85.

— (1998), *Ancient Cities of the Indus Valley Civilization*. Oxford: Oxford University Press.

Khambatta, I. (1989), 'The Meaning of Residence in Traditional Hindu Society', in J. Bourdier and N. Alasayyad (eds), *Dwellings, Settlements and Traditions: Cross-cultural Perspectives*. Lanham: University Press of America, pp. 145–86.

Kieschnick, J. (2003), *The Impact of Buddhism on Chinese Material Culture*. Oxford: Princeton University Press.

Knapp, A. and Ashmore, W. (1999), 'Archaeological Landscapes: Constructed, Conceptualized, Ideational', in W. Ashmore and B. Knapp (eds), *Archaeologies of Landscape*. Oxford: Blackwell, pp. 1–32.

Kopytoff, I. (1986), 'The Cultural Biography of Things: Commoditization as Process', in A. Appadurai (ed.), *The Social Life of Things*. Cambridge: Cambridge University Press, pp. 64–91.

Kosambi, D. (1962), 'At the Crossroads: A Study of Mother Goddess Cult Sites', in D. Kosambi (ed.), *Myth and Reality*. New Delhi: Motilal Banarsidas, pp. 82–109.

Kunin, D. (2003), *Religion: The Modern Theories*. Edinburgh: Edinburgh University Press.

Lahiri, N. (1996), 'Archaeological Landscapes and Textual Images: A Study of the Sacred Geography of Late Medieval Ballabgarh'. *World Archaeology*, 28, (2), 244–64.

— (2000), 'Archaeology and Identity in Colonial India'. *Antiquity*, 74, 670–89.

Lal, B. (2002a), 'Historicity of the Mahabharata and the Ramayana: What has Archaeology to Say in the Matter?' in S. Settar and R. Korisettar (eds), *Indian Archaeology in Retrospect: Vol IV, Archaeology and Historiography*. New Delhi: Indian Council of Historical Research, pp. 30–56.

— (2002b), *The Saraswati Flows On: The Continuity of Indian Culture*. New Delhi: Aryan Books International.

Lane, P. (1986), 'Past Practices in the Ritual Present: Examples from the Welsh Bronze Age'. *Archaeological Review From Cambridge*, 5, (2), 181–92.

Larrain, J. (1979), *The Concept of Ideology*. London: Hutchinson.

Larson, F. (2007), 'Anthropology As Comparative Anatomy? Reflecting on the Study of Material Culture during the Late 1800s and the Late 1900s'. *Journal of Material Culture*, 12, (1), 89–112.

— (1995), *India's Agony Over Religion*. Albany: State University of New York Press.

Latour, B. (1993), *We Have Never Been Modern*. Translated by H. Wheatsheaf. Cambridge: Harvard University Press.

Lawrence, R. (1987), *Housing, Dwelling and Homes*. Chichester: Wiley.

Leach, E. (1966), 'Ritualization in Man in Relation to Conceptual and Social Development', in J. Huxley (ed.), *Ritualization of Behaviour in Man and Animals*. Philosophical Transactions of the Royal Society of London Series B 251, pp. 403–8.

— (1982), *Social Anthropology*. New York: Oxford University Press.

Lefkowitz, M. (2006), 'Archaeology and the Politics of Origins: The Search for Pyramids in Greece', in B. Fagan (ed.), *Archaeological Fantasies: How Pseudoarchaeology Misrepresents the Past and Misleads the Public*. New York: Routledge, pp. 180–202.

Lekson, S. (1996), 'Landscape With Ruins: Archaeological Approaches to Built and Unbuilt Environments'. *Current Anthropology*, 37, 886–92.

Leone, M. (1984), 'Interpreting Ideology in Historical Archaeology: Using the Rules of Perspective in the William Paca Garden in Annapolis, Maryland', in D. Miller and C. Tilley (eds), *Ideology, Power and Prehistory*. Cambridge: Cambridge University Press, pp. 21–49.

Leroi-Gourhan, A. (1968), *Art of Prehistoric Man in Western Europe*. London: Thames and Hudson.

Levi-Strauss, C. (1973), *Tristes Tropiques*. Translated by J. Russell. Harmondsworth: Penguin, 1973.

Lewis, G. (1980), *Day of Shining Red: An Essay on Understanding Ritual*. New York: Cambridge University Press.

Lincoln, B. (2003), *Holy Terrors: Thinking about Religion after September 11*. Chicago: University of Chicago Press.

Lohse, J. (2007), 'Commoner Ritual, Commoner Ideology: (Sub-) Alternative Views of Social Complexity in Prehispanic Mesoamerica', in N. Gonlin and J. Lohse (eds), *Commoner Ritual and Ideology in Ancient Mesoamerica*. Boulder: University Press of Colorado, pp. 1–32.

Lopex, D. (1998), 'Belief', in M. Taylor (ed.), *Critical Terms for Religions Studies*. Chicago: Chicago University Press, pp. 21–35.

Lowenthal, D. (1976), 'The Place of the Past in the American Landscape', in D. Lowenthal and M. Bowden (eds), *Geographies of the Mind: Essays in Historical Geography in Honour of John Kirtland Wright*. New York: Oxford University Press, pp. 122–54.

Lubbock, J. (1865), *Pre-Historic Times: As Illustrated by Ancient Remains and the Manner and Customs of Modern Savages*. London: Williams and Norgate.

Lyman, R., O'Brian, M. and Dunnell, R. (1997), *The Rise and Fall of Culture History*. New York: Plenum.

Maberg, C. (1977), 'Archaeology and Religion: What can we Know?' *Temenos*, 13, 54–66.

Macdonald, S. (2006), 'Words in Stone?: Agency and Identity in a Nazi Landscape'. *Journal of Material Culture*, 11, 105–26.

Maclean, R. (2001), 'Gender in the Archaeology of World Religions?' in T. Insoll (ed.), *Archaeology and World Religion*. London: Routledge, pp. 145–96.

Maffly-Kipp, L. (2005), 'Engaging Habits and Besotted Idolatry: Viewing Chinese Religions in the American West'. *Material Religion*, 1, (1), 72–97.

Malinowski, B. (1922). *Argonauts of the Western Pacific: An Account of Native Enterprise and Adventure in the Archipelagoes of Melanesian New Guinea*. London: Routledge and Kegan Paul.

Marshack, A. (1971), *The Roots of Civilization: The Cognitive Beginnings of Man's First Art, Symbol, and Notation*. New York: McGraw Hill.

Marx, K. (1994) [1844], 'Contribution to the Critique of Hegel's Philosophy of Right', in J. O'Malley and R. Davis (eds and trans.), *Marx: Early Political Writings*. New York: Cambridge University Press.

— (1973) [1935], 'Techniques of the Body'. *Economy and Society*, 2, (1), 70–88.

Mauss, M. (1970) [1923], *The Gift*. Translated by Ian Cunnison. London: Taylor and Francis.

Mellaart, J. (1967), *Catal Huyuk: A Neolithic Town in Anatolia*. London: Thames and Hudson.

Meltzer, D. (1979), 'Paradigm and the Nature of Change in American Archaeology'. *American Antiquity*, 44, 644–57.

— (1981), 'Ideology and Material Culture', in R. Gould and M. Schiffer (eds), *Modern Material Culture: The Archaeology of Us*. New York: Academic Press, pp. 113–25.

Merleau-Ponty, M. (1962) [1945], *Phenomenology of Perception*. London: Routledge.

Michaels, A. (1998), *Hinduism: Past and Present*. Translated by B. Harshav. Princeton: Princeton University Press.

Michel, J. (1982), *Megolomania*. New York: Routledge.

Miller, D. (1985), 'Ideology and the Harappan Civilisation'. *Journal of Anthropological Archaeology*, 4, 34–71.

Miller, D., Rowlands, M. and Tilley, C., (1989), 'Introduction', in D. Miller, M. Rowlands and C. Tilley (eds), *Domination and Resistance*. London: Unwin Hyman, pp. 1–26.

Mithen, S. (1996), *The Prehistory of the Mind: A Search for the Origins for Art, Religion and Science*. London: Thames and Hudson.

— (2001), 'Archaeological Theory and Cognitive Evolution', in I. Hodder (ed.), *Archaeological Theory Today*. Oxford: Blackwell, pp. 98–121.

— (2003), *After the Ice: A Global Human History, 20,000–5000 BC*. London: Weidenfeld and Nicolson.

Muller, F. (1897), *Contributions to the Science of Mythology*. London: Longmans Green.

Nash, R. (1997), 'Archetypal Landscapes and the Interpretation of Meaning'. *Cambridge Archaeological Journal*, 7, 57–69.

O'Kelly, M. (1983), *Newgrange, Co. Meath, Ireland: The Late Neolithic/Beaker Period Settlement*. Oxford: In House Publication.

Oosten, J. (1997), 'Landscape and Cosmology'. *Archaeological Dialogues*, 4, (2), 152–4.

Otto, R. (1924), *The Idea of the Holy*. London: Oxford University Press.

Parker-Pearson, M. (1982), 'Mortuary Practices, Society and Ideology: An Ethnoarchaeological Study', in I. Hodder (ed.), *Symbolic and Structural Archaeology*. Cambridge: Cambridge University Press, pp. 99–113.

— (1984), 'Economic and Ideological Change: Cyclical Growth in the Pre-State Societies of Jutland', in D. Miller and C. Tilley (eds), *Ideology, Power and Prehistory*. Cambridge: Cambridge University Press, pp. 69–92.

— (2001), 'Death, Being, and Time: The Historical Context of the World Religions', in T. Insoll (ed.), *Archaeology and World Religions*. London: Routledge, pp. 203–19.

Parker-Pearson, M. and Richards, C. (1994), 'Ordering the World: Perceptions of Architecture, Space and Time', in M. Parker-Pearson and C. Richards (eds), *Architecture and Order: Approaches to Social Space*. London: Routledge, pp. 1–37.

Patrik, L. (1985), 'Is There an Archaeological Record?' in M. Schiffer (ed.), *Advances in Archaeological Method and Theory*, vol. 8: New York: Academic Press, pp. 27–62.

Peake, M. (1950), *Gormenghast*. London: Eyre & Spottiswoode.

Peatfield, A. (1993), 'Cognitive Aspects of Religious Symbolism: An Archaeologist's Perspective', in A. Peatfield (ed.), *Cognitive Aspects of Religious Symbolism*. Cambridge: Cambridge University Press, pp. 4–47.

Piggott, S. (1968), *Ancient Europe*. Edinburgh: Edinburgh University Press.

— (1986), *Ancient Britons and the Antiquarian Imagination: Ideas from the Renaissance to the Regency*. London: Thames and Hudson.

Pitt-Rivers, A. (1906), *The Evolution of Culture and Other Essays*. Edited by J. Meyres. Oxford: Clarendon Press.

Plate, S., Meyer, B., Morgan, D. and Paine, C. (2005), 'Editorial Statement'. *Material Religion: The Journal of Objects, Art and Belief*, 1, (1), 4–9.

Possami, A. (2005), *In Search of New Age Spiritualities*. Burlington: Ashgate Publications.

Postel, M. and Cooper, A. (1999), 'Baster Folk Art: Shrines, Figurines and Memorial'. *Project for Indian Cultural Studies*, 8, 2–33.

Rappaport, R. (1968), 'Ritual Regulation of Environmental Relations among a New Guinea People', in A. Vayda (ed.), *Environment and Cultural Behaviour*. Austin: Texas University Press, pp. 181–201.

— (1971), 'Ritual, Sanctity and Cybernetics'. *American Anthropologist*, 73, 59–79.

— (1979), 'The Sacred in Human Evolution'. *Annual Review of Ecology and Systematics*, 2, 23–44.

Rathje, W., Hughes, W., Wilson, D., Tani, M., Archer, G., Hunt, R. and Jones, T. (1992), 'The Archaeology of Contemporary Landfills'. *American Antiquity*, 57, (3), 437–47.

Ray, H. (2004), 'The Archaeology of Sacred Space: Introduction', in H. Ray and C. Sinopoli (eds), *Archaeology as History in Early South Asia*. New Delhi: Aryan Books International, pp. 350–75.

Ray, H. and Sinopoli, C. (2004), 'Preamble', in H. Ray and C. Sinopoli (eds), *Archaeology as History in Early South Asia*. New Delhi: Aryan Books International.

Reinach, P. (1909), *Orpheus: A History of Religions*. Translated by F. Simmonds. London: Heinemann.

Relph, E. (1976), *Place and Placeness*. London: Pion.

Renfrew, C. (1973), *Before Civilisation: The Radiocarbon Revolution and Prehistoric Europe*. London: Penguin.

— (1985), *The Archaeology of Cult: The Sanctuary at Phylakopi*. London: British School of Archaeology at Athens.

— (1994a), 'The Archaeology of Religion', in C. Renfrew and E. Zubrow (eds), *The Ancient Mind: Elements of Cognitive Archaeology*. New York: Cambridge University Press, pp. 47–54.

— (1994b), 'Towards a Cognitive Archaeology', in C. Renfrew and E. Zubrow (eds), *The Ancient Mind: Elements of Cognitive Archaeology*. New York: Cambridge University Press, pp. 11–28.

Renfrew, C. and Bahn, P. (2000), *Archaeology: Theories Methods and Practice*, 3rd edn. London: Thames and Hudson.

Renfrew, C. and Zubrow, E. (1994), *The Ancient Mind: Elements of Cognitive Archaeology*. New York: Cambridge University Press.

Rennie, B. (1996), *Reconstructing Eliade: Making Sense of Religion*. Albany: State University of New York Press.

Rey, T. (2007), *Bourdieu on Religion: Imposing Faith and Legitimacy*. London: Equinox.

Richards, C. (1993), 'Monumental Choreography: Architecture and Spatial Representation in Late Neolithic Orkney', in C. Tilley (ed.), *Interpretive Archaeology*. London: Berg, pp. 143–78.

— (1996), 'Monuments as Landscape: Creating the Centre of the World in Late Neolithic Orkney'. *World Archaeology*, 28, (2), 190–208.

Richards, C. and Thomas, J. (1984), 'Ritual Activity and Structured Deposition in Late Neolithic Wessex', in R. Bradley and J. Gardiner (eds), *Neolithic Studies*. Oxford: British Archaeological Reports 133.

Richards, J. (1999), 'Conceptual Landscapes in the Egyptian Nile Valley', in W. Ashmore and B. Knapp (eds), *Archaeologies of Landscape*. Oxford: Blackwell, pp. 83–101.

Rountree, K. (2007), 'Archaeologists and Goddess Feminists at Çatalhöyük: An Experiment in Multivocality'. *The Journal of Feminist Studies in Religion*, 23, (2), 33–60.

— (2001), 'The Past Is a Foreigners' Country: Goddess Feminists, Archaeologists, and the Appropriation of Prehistory'. *Journal of Contemporary Religion*, 16, 5–27.

Rowlands, M. (1994), 'The Politics of Identity in Archaeology', in G. Bond and A. Gilliam (eds), *Social Constructions of the Past: Representations as Power*. New York: Routledge, pp. 128–43.

Santosh, C. (2004), *Religious Fundamentalism in the Contemporary World: Critical Social and Political Issues*. New York: Lexington Books.

Scarre, C. (2000), 'Forms and Landforms: The Designs and Setting of Neolithic Monuments in Western France', in A. Ritchie (ed.), *Neolithic Orkney in Its European Context*. Cambridge: Cambridge University Press, pp. 309–20.

Schama, S. (1995), *Landscape and Memory*. London: Harper Collins.

Schiffer, M. (1999), *The Material Life of Human Beings: Artefacts, Behaviour and Communication*. London: Routledge.

Schnapp, A. (1996), *The Discovery of the Past: The Origins of Archaeology*. London: British Museum Press

Schopen, G. (1997), *Bones, Stones and Buddhist Monks: Collected Papers on the Archaeology, Epigraphy and Texts of Monastic Buddhism in India*. Honolulu: University of Hawaii Press.

Segal, E. (1994), 'Archaeology and Cognitive Science', in C. Renfrew and E. Zubrow (eds), *The Ancient Mind: Elements of Cognitive Archaeology*. New York: Cambridge University Press, pp. 22–8.

Service, E. (1972), *Primitive Social Organization: An Evolutionary Perspective*. New York: Random House.

Shanks, M. and Tilley, C. (1982), 'Ideology, Symbolic Power and Ritual Communication', in I. Hodder (ed.), *Symbolic and Structural Archaeology*. Cambridge: Cambridge University Press, pp. 129–54.

— (1987), *Social Theory and Archaeology*. Oxford: Polity Press.

— (1992), *Reconstructing Archaeology: Theory and Practice*. London: Routledge.

Shapin, S. and Schaffer, S. (1985), *Leviathan and the Air-Pump: Hobbes, Boyle and the Experimental Life*. Princeton: Princeton University Press.

Sharpe, E. (1986), *Comparative Religion: A History*, 2nd edn. Chicago: Open Court Press.

Shults, L. (2010), 'Spiritual Entanglement: Transforming Religious Symbols at Catalhoyuk', in I. Hodder (ed.), *Religion in the Emergence of Civilization: Catalhoyuk as a Case Study*. New York: Cambridge University Press, pp. 73–98.

Sidky, H. (2008), *Haunted by the Archaic Shaman: Himalayan Jhakris and the Discourse on Shamanism*. New York: Lexington Books.

— (2010), 'Perspectives on Differentiating Shamans from Other Ritual Intercessors'. *Asian Ethnology*, 69, (2), 213–40.

Smart, N. (1969), *The Religious Experience of Mankind*. New York: Collins.

Smith, H. (1992), *Forgotten Truth: The Common Vision of the World's Religions*. San Francisco: Harper.

Smith, R. (1887), *Lectures on the Religion of the Semites*. Edinburgh: Black.

Smith, W. C. (1963), *The Meaning and End of Religion*. New York: Collins.

Sperber, D. (1975), *Rethinking Symbolism*. Translated by A. Morton. Cambridge: Cambridge University Press.

Starbuck, E. (1899), *The Psychology of Religion: An Empirical Study of the Growth of Religious Consciousness*. London: W. Scott.

Steward, J. (1955), *Theory of Cultural Change: The Methodology of Multilinear Evolution*. Chicago: University of Illinois Press.

Tacon, P. (1999), 'Identifying Ancient Sacred Landscapes in Australia: From Physical to Social', in W. Ashmore and A. Knapp (eds), *Archaeologies of Landscape: Contemporary Perspectives*. Oxford: Blackwell, pp. 33–57.

— (1990), 'The Power of Place: Cross-Cultural Responses to Natural and Cultural Landscapes of Stone and Earth', in J. Vastokas (ed.), *Perspectives of the Canadian Landscape: Native Traditions*. North York: York University, pp. 11–43.

Taylor, W. (1948), *A Study of Archaeology*. Memoirs of the American Anthropological Association, no 69.

Thomas, J. (1990), 'Monuments from the Inside: The Case of Irish Megalithic Tombs'. *World Archaeology*, 22, 168–78.

— (1991), *Rethinking the Neolithic*. Cambridge: Cambridge University Press.

— (2000), 'Introduction', in J. Thomas (ed.), *Interpretive Archaeology: A Reader*. London: Leicester University Press, pp. 1–18.

— (2001), 'Archaeologies of Place and Landscape', in I. Hodder (ed.), *Archaeological Theory Today*. Cambridge: Polity, pp. 165–86.

— (2004), *Archaeology and Modernity*. London: Routledge.

Thomas, S. (2004), *The Global Resurgence of Religion and the Transformation of International Relations: The Struggle for the Soul of the Twenty-First Century*. New York: Palgrave Macmillan.

Thomsen, C. (1848), *A Guide to Northern Antiquities*. Copenhagen: National Museum of Copenhagen.

Tiele, C. (1877), *Outlines of the History of Religion*. Translated by J. Carpenter. London: Publisher Unknown.

Tilley, C. (1991), *Material Culture and Text: The Art of Ambiguity*. London: Routledge.

— (1994), *A Phenomenology of Landscape: Places, Paths and Monuments*. Oxford: Berg.

— (1996a), *An Ethnography of the Neolithic*. Cambridge: Cambridge University Press.

— (1996b), 'The Power of Rocks: Topography and Monument Construction on Bodmin Moor'. *World Archaeology*, 28, (2), 161–76.

— (1999), *Metaphor and Material Culture*. Oxford: Blackwell.

— (2004), *The Materiality of Stone: Explorations in Landscape Phenomenology*. Oxford: Berg.

— (2006), 'Introduction: Identity, Place, Landscape and Heritage'. *Journal of Material Culture*, 11, (1/2), 7–13.

Trompf, G. (1978), *Friedrich Max Mueller: As a Theorist of Comparative Religion*. Bombay: Shakuntala Publishing House.

— (2005), *In Search of Origins: The Beginnings of Religion in Western Theory and Archaeological Practice*, 2nd edn. Elgin: New Dawn Press.

Tuan, Y. (1974), *Topophilia: A Study of Environmental Perception, Attitudes, and Values*. Englewood: Prentice-Hall.

— (1977), *Space and Place: The Perspective of Experience*. London: Edward Arnold.

— (1978), 'Sacred Space: Explorations of an Idea', in K. Butzer (ed.), *Dimensions of Human Geography*. Chicago: University of Chicago Press.

Tylor, E. (1871), *Primitive Culture* (2 volumes). London: John Murray.

Ucko, P. (1969), 'Ethnography and Archaeological Interpretation of Funerary Remains', *World Archaeology*, 1, 262–80.

Underhill, E. (1911), *Mysticism: A Study in the Nature and Development of Man's Spiritual Consciousness*. London: Methuen.

Van der Leeuw, G. (1963) [1933], *Religion in Essence and Manifestation*. Translated by J. Turner. Gloucester: Peter Smith.

Van Huyssteen, J. (2010), 'Coding the Nonvisible: Epistemic Limitations and Understanding Symbolic Behavior at Catalhoyuk', in I. Hodder (ed.), *Religion in the Emergence of Civilization: Catalhoyuk as a Case Study*. New York: Cambridge University Press, pp. 99–121.

Veblen, T. (1925), *The Theory of the Leisure Class: An Economic Study of Institutions*. London: Allen and Unwin.

Von Bertalanffy, L. (1968), *General System Theory: Foundations, Development, Applications*. New York: George Braziller.

Von Daniken, E. (1969), *Chariots of the Gods? Was God an Astronaut?* London: Souvenir Press.

Wallis, R. (2002), 'Waking the Ancestors: Neo-Shamanism and Archaeology', in G. Harvey (ed.), *Shamanism: A Reader*. London: Routledge, pp. 402–23.

— (2003), *Shamans/Neo-Shamans: Ecstasy, Alternative Archaeologies and Contemporary Pagans*. London: Routledge.

Wasserstrom, S. (1999), *Religion after Religion: Gershom Scholem, Mircea Eliade, Henry Corbin at Eranos*. Princeton University Press.

Watson, P., LeBlanc, S. and Redman, C. (1984), *Archaeological Explanation: The Scientific Method in Archaeology*. New York: Columbia.

Webster, D. (2006), 'The Mystique of the Ancient Maya', in B. Fagan (ed.), *Archaeological Fantasies: How Pseudoarchaeology Misrepresents the Past and Misleads the Public*. New York: Routledge, pp. 129–53.

Wheatley, L. (1971), *The Pivot of the Four Quarters: A Preliminary Enquiry into the Origins and Character of the Ancient Chinese City*. Edinburgh: Edinburgh University Press.

White, L. (1949), *The Science of Culture: A Study of Man and Civilization*. New York: Farrar.

Wiener, M. (1995), *Visible and Invisible Realms: Power, Magic and Colonial Conquest in Bali*. Chicago: University of Chicago Press.

Wittfogel, K. (1957), *Oriental Despotism: A Comparative Study of Total Power*. London: Yale University Press.

Witzel, M. (2006), 'Rama's Realm', in B. Fagan (ed.), *Archaeological Fantasies: How Pseudoarchaeology Misrepresents the Past and Misleads the Public*. New York: Routledge, pp. 203–32.

Woodroffe, J. (1919), *The Serpent Power*. London: Publisher Unknown.

Index